Pacific Northwest

John Doerper
Photography by Greg Vaughn

D1468822

COMPASS AMERICAN GUIDES
An Imprint of Fodor's Travel Publications, Inc.

Pacific Northwest
First Edition

Copyright © 1997 Fodor's Travel Publications, Inc.
Maps Copyright © 1997 Fodor's Travel Publications, Inc.
First Edition

LIBRARY OF CONGRESS CATALOGING-IN-PUBLICATION-DATA
Doerper, John
  Pacific Northwest; John Doerper, photography by Greg Vaughn —1st ed.
  p. cm. —(Compass American guides)
  Includes bibliographical references (p.) and index.
  ISBN 1-878-86785-7 : $18.95
  1. Pacific Northwest—Guidebooks. I. Vaughn, Greg II. Title.
  III. Series: Compass American guides (Series)
F852.3.D64 1997   97-7006
917.9504'43—dc21   CIP

Editors: John Doerper, Kit Duane   Creative Director: Christopher Burt
Managing Editor: Kit Duane   Designers: Christopher Burt, David Hurst
Production Editor: Deborah Dunn   Map Design: Mark Stroud, Moon Cartography

Compass American Guides, Inc., 5332 College Ave., Suite 201, Oakland, CA 94618, USA
10 9 8 7 6 5 4 3 2 1
Production House: Twin Age Ltd., Hong Kong; Printed in China
Cover: Bandon Beach, Oregon

PUBLISHER'S ACKNOWLEDGMENTS
The publisher wishes to thank the following people and institutions for the use of illustrations: **American Museum of Natural History,** pp. 21, 106; **BC Archives and Records Service,** p. 89, neg. A-04656; **City of Vancouver Archives,** p. 41 neg BU.P. 403.N.387; p. 44 neg. DIST.P.76.N.6; p. 66, neg MI.P. 43.N.33; **Columbia River Maritime Museum,** p. 335; **Ken Straiton,** pp. 11, 42; **Museum of History and Industry,** pp. 173, 174, 175; **Royal BC Museum,** p. 16 neg 7376, p. 107 neg 4606; **Underwood Photo Archives,** p. 195; **University of Washington Libraries,** p. 26; **Vancouver Public Library,** p. 33 neg. 1091; **Washington State Historical Society, Tacoma,** pp. 185, 204. We also wish to thank **Nancy Falk** for proofreading and **Lesley Bonnet** for indexing.

To Victoria
who loves the Pacific Northwest more than her native California

AUTHOR'S ACKNOWLEDGMENTS

A book is more than a product of a single mind. I would therefore like to thank the many people who have made this guide possible: Christopher Burt, Kit Duane, Julia Dillon, and Debi Dunn of Compass American Guides for asking me to write this book, and for making me feel like I could do it, and for welcoming me so graciously when I drop by the office. I would especially like to thank Kit Duane for her truly inspired editorial guidance. I must also show my appreciation for the splendid Thai meals Ben Burt has created for our get-togethers. Special thanks go to Deborah Wakefield of Portland and Irene Hoadley of Salem, Oregon, to Louis Richmond of Seattle, and to Eileen Mintz and Norma Rosenthal of Mercer Island, Washington, and to the Eclipse Bookstore and Village Books in Bellingham for the splendid variety of books on the Northwest they carry. I would also like to thank Rising Sun Motors in Bellingham for keeping my car going as I burned up the miles.

C O N T E N T S

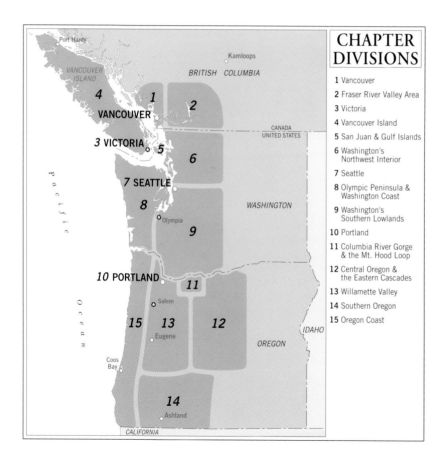

CHAPTER DIVISIONS

1 Vancouver
2 Fraser River Valley Area
3 Victoria
4 Vancouver Island
5 San Juan & Gulf Islands
6 Washington's Northwest Interior
7 Seattle
8 Olympic Peninsula & Washington Coast
9 Washington's Southern Lowlands
10 Portland
11 Columbia River Gorge & the Mt. Hood Loop
12 Central Oregon & the Eastern Cascades
13 Willamette Valley
14 Southern Oregon
15 Oregon Coast

Food Tours

Maps

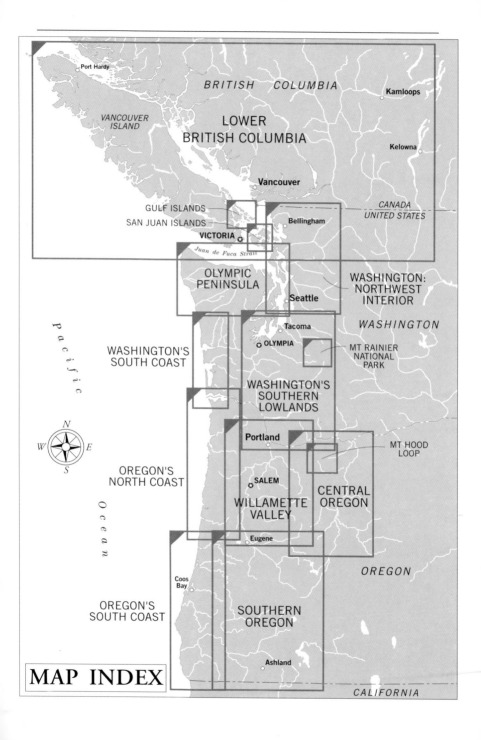

MAP INDEX

THE PACIFIC NORTHWEST

O V E R V I E W

THE PACIFIC NORTHWEST'S coastline is one of quiet river estuaries,
sand dunes, and rock-walled fjords.
Dense forests border the shore and
tall alpine peaks rise above the horizon. The beauty of the landscape
and the quality of the cuisine in sophisticated Vancouver, Seattle, and
Portland attract an ever greater
number of visitors. But the spaces
are so vast, no one feels crowded.

1 VANCOUVER
2 FRASER RIVER VALLEY

Bordered by saltwater fjords, towered over by alpine peaks, Vancouver truly is one
of the most beautiful cities in the world. Here you can sail in the morning and ski
in the afternoon. But the city has other attractions as well: excellent accommodations, theaters, art galleries, museums, sports arenas, and restaurants, including
some of the best Chinese restaurants this side of Hong Kong.

KEN STRAITON

The Fraser rises in the Rocky Mountains and cuts a swath across the wilds
of central British Columbia before it
descends to tidewater in a deep, rocky
gorge. Before reaching salt water, it
flows through a beautiful pastoral valley bounded by tall mountain ranges
to the north, east, and southeast.

3 VICTORIA
4 VANCOUVER ISLAND, B.C.

Enjoy Victoria's lovely English colonial architecture and views of its beautiful harbor. Sip afternoon tea in the lobby of the Empress Hotel or in the tropical lushness of the Crystal Garden. And relax. Victoria is a very laid-back city, just made for taking it easy.

Beyond the city lies the misty west coast of Vancouver Island, a wonderland of deep fjords, rocky islands, and remote sandy beaches where the only noise you hear is the roar of the surf, the lonely croak of a raven, or the splash of a gray whale. There are few towns here and even fewer roads, making this a great region to explore by kayak or canoe. The rain-sheltered east coast of the island has coves and beaches warm enough for taking a summer swim.

5 THE ISLANDS

Incredibly beautiful and rugged, the San Juan and Gulf islands are but a short boat or plane ride from the major metropolitan cities of the Pacific Northwest. Rocky cliffs and sandy beaches alternate along the maze of tidal waterways that resemble white-water rivers at the change of the tide. Here mountains rise straight from the sea. In quiet bays, the flexible boughs of red cedar hang out over the water and catch eelgrass at low tide.

6 WASHINGTON'S NORTHWEST INTERIOR

With its jagged, razor-sharp peaks flanked by glaciers that glow with an inner blue-green light, the North Cascades are among the most beautiful mountains found anywhere. Secluded valleys and wildflower meadows beckon hikers; rivers and lakes attract fishermen.

7 SEATTLE

A vibrant, modern city, facing the blue waters of Puget Sound, Seattle has more restaurants and museums than any other Washington city. To see the city at its best, take a harbor tour, which will also take you into the ship canal and through the locks connecting Lake Washington to Elliott Bay, or grab a window table in a waterfront restaurant just at sunset.

8 OLYMPIC PENINSULA AND WASHINGTON COAST

The lichen-, moss-, and fern-bedecked trees of the Olympic rainforest are about as close as a temperate forest can come to being a true jungle. Elk and black bear amble through these forests, and eagles fly overhead. On lonely beaches tall sea

stacks rise from the surf, and there are windswept headlands, whitewater rivers, cranberry bogs, and alpine peaks covered with summer wildflowers.

Along the southern coast, oysters thrive in estuaries. Taste them fresh from the shell or smoked; or stop at a local restaurant for barbecued, fried, or stewed oysters.

9 WASHINGTON'S SOUTHERN LOWLANDS

On hazy days, when the sun hits them just right, the tall volcanic peaks rising above the low, rolling southern Washington Cascades seem to float in the air, separated from the earth by their

own shadows. They can be seen from the cities of southern Puget Sound, or visited. Observe the devastation caused by the recent eruption of Mount St. Helens, or stroll through a wildflower meadow on the flanks of Mount Rainier.

10 PORTLAND, OREGON

The City of Roses is a beautiful, compact river city with many parks and a casual, cosmopolitan air. Enjoy the amenities of some of the region's finest hotels, sample the exquisite meals prepared by local chefs, watch a play, visit a museum, cruise on the river, enjoy the music scene, or just take a long walk.

11 COLUMBIA GORGE AND THE MOUNT HOOD LOOP

A beautiful snow-capped peak towering over a picture-perfect river gorge—what more can you ask for? The region has hiking trails through rugged canyons, quiet forests, and wildflower meadows by tall waterfalls. If you want to learn about the recreation possibilities, look at the cars: many carry both sailboards and skis on their roof-top racks. You might, on the other hand, just sit quietly and watch the river flow by or dangle your feet in the pool below a waterfall.

12 CENTRAL OREGON AND THE EASTERN CASCADES

This sunny country of open woods of tall ponderosa pines, of rock-bound white-water rivers running through lush meadows, of sagebrush flats and volcanic flows is a prime vacation destination. Hike across lava flows, visit the Warm Springs Indian Reservation, or sip a microbrew at a Bend pub. If you hear Indian drums and chanting on your car radio, you're not hallucinating. The Warm Springs radio station has a program called "Drums and Talk."

13 WILLAMETTE VALLEY

Forests of tall oaks alternate with a quilted pattern of fields, orchards, and vineyards in this beautifully pastoral valley, which was among the first in the West to be settled. The Willamette River runs through it, and tall volcanic peaks rise to the east; the forest-clad ridges of the Coast Range protect the valley from the chilly drizzle of the Pacific Coast. Visit wineries and covered bridges, stock up on berries at fruit stands, or hang out with the locals in a sidewalk cafe.

14 SOUTHERN OREGON
15 OREGON COAST

The lovely small town of Ashland and its Shakespeare Festival attract most visitors

to this region, but there are many more attractions to explore, including whitewater rivers and Crater Lake. To the west lies the wild Oregon coast, its headlands sculpted by wind and surf. Most of the towns along this coast are quiet but have excellent restaurants and interesting shops.

*A classic portrait of a Kwakiutl Indian taken by photographer Edward Curtis in 1914.
(Royal B.C. Museum)*

H I S T O R Y

LANDSCAPE AND CLIMATE ARE THE KEYS to the natural and human history of the Northwest Coast. On clear days, the mountains seem close enough to touch; on foggy or drizzly days you can't see them at all. Even east of the Cascades, where the weather is generally dry, storm clouds, dust storms, or the bright glare of the sun can obscure the landscape: near trees seem far away, and distant mountains appear close. This explains why early navigators often missed prominent landmarks obscured by fogs or mists, and why overland travelers became disoriented in the wide open spaces.

■ INDIAN CULTURES

During the perhaps 25,000 years that migrations of hunting peoples from Asia crossed into North America, tribes with very different origins and traditions washed back and forth across the face of the Pacific Northwest. We assume this because the tribes living in this area spoke languages deriving from all of America's major native language groups. The history of the ebb and flow of these tribes, their chiefs, battles, and traditions, has been for the most part lost, but we have some remains and artifacts that help us piece the story together. Sandals woven from sagebrush 13,000 years ago have been discovered in a cave near Fort Rock in Central Oregon. And 4,000-year-old settlements have been uncovered on Vancouver Island. The oldest house foundations from Ozette Village on the Olympic Coast of Washington state date back some 3,100 years.

When Europeans arrived in the area about 200 years ago, they found two distinct native ways of life had evolved in the Pacific Northwest, based on its natural geographic divisions. Those people living along the Pacific Coast and on the wooded western side of the Cascade Mountains developed a culture geared to the sea and the forest; those living in the high dry plains of the plateaus to the east lived as horsemen and traders.

■ PEOPLE OF THE COAST

The original inhabitants of the coast lived off the bounty of the sea, mostly on salmon, and on any other marine creature they could catch, dig up, or gather.

They carved sleek canoes from single logs of giant cedar, and they traveled far and wide hunting seals, sea lions, and even the mighty whale.

Native houses were windowless longhouses, huge dwellings some 60 feet wide and 100 feet long, their frames constructed from beams $2^{1}/_{2}$ to $3^{1}/_{2}$ feet in diameter and covered with thick cedar planks. Entrance was through a small hole at one end, which made the house more defensible during attack. From central Vancouver Island north, this hole might be carved into the lower end of a totem pole which rose high above the gable and proclaimed the owner of the house and his status through the animals carved on the face of the pole. More "crest" designs, as well as depictions of family myths or honors, might be painted on the face of the house.

In 1803, after visiting a plank house near the falls of the Columbia, American explorers Lewis and Clark noted that these structures were "the first wooden buildings we have seen since leaving the Illinois country."

The insides of these houses might be decorated with painted screens and painted or carved house posts. Several related families would live together, their living quarters partitioned off by screens. In the early 19th century, after raids on native Puget Sound villages by Tlinkit, Haida, and Kwakiutl warriors increased, houses were protected by tall palisades of cedar planks. Villages on Whidbey Island were unfortified when British navigator George Vancouver visited the region in 1792, but were enclosed by 30-foot-high palisades when the Wilkes Expedition visited the island in 1841.

Warfare among tribes was brutal. As Chief Martin Sampson wrote in his history of the Skagit tribe, "Heads were taken as trophies, villages were burned, and captives became slaves of the victors." In his mid-19th-century essay *Almost Out of the World*, schoolteacher James Swan describes one such raid that happened when he worked on the Makah Reservation:

> *I*magine yourself in the centre of a circle of wild and excited savages, standing beside two trunkless heads—a most shocking and revolting spectacle of itself— and knowing that these very dancers are a portion of a band of miscreants whose name has henceforth been a terror on the Straits of Juan de Fuca . . .

Afterwards, the heads were taken to other villages, where the dances were repeated. They were finally "stuck on two poles and will remain till time or the crows knock them down."

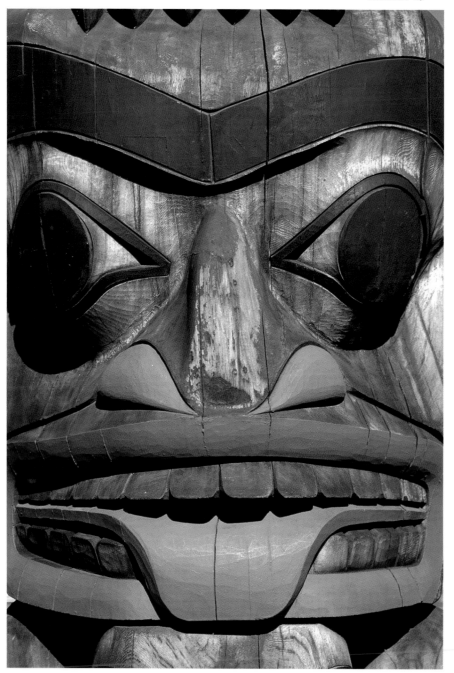

Detail of totem pole in Duncan on Vancouver Island.

■ COASTAL ART AND CULTURE

During the dark nights of winter, villages resounded with the telling of old stories, the singing of songs, and the performance of plays recounting the exploits of mythical beings.

Elaborately carved dance masks and totem poles, painted screens and house fronts, bowls, even spoons, are part of a Northwest Indian art—their forceful, symbolic abstractions of real and supernatural beings, drawn in fluid lines and cut in ovoid shapes. Each of the different peoples of the Northwest Coast—the Coast Salish, the Nootka, Kwakiutl, Tsimshian, Haida, and Tlinkit—shared a similar cultural, economic, and environmental background, as well as the basic forms of artistic expression. Yet there were tribal differences which are obvious to the expert eye. Nootka and Tsimshian used a more flexible, flowing line than the more formal Kwakiutl and Tlinkit. The Haida, perhaps the greatest artists on the Coast, combined the best elements of both in their highly expressive art works. The Coast Salish had their own unique, much more free-form abstract expression (though they have, in recent decades, adopted elements from the art of the northern tribes).

Contact with white fur traders gave the native tribes access to iron, and some of the most magnificent totem poles were carved after native artists of the coast began using iron tools. Carved totem poles found their highest (and tallest) expression among the Kwakiutl, Haida, and Tlinkit. The mythical beings depicted in masks, totem poles, screens, and house paintings were more than family crests: they were the actual *property* of families or powerful individuals. Owners had rights not only to the characters themselves, but to design features and the right to tell stories associated with these characters. These rights were jealously guarded, for their acquisition was a tedious—and expensive—process. It was possible to inherit them, but the prospective heir had to validate his inheritance by giving a potlatch, a very expensive proposition at best.

■ POTLATCH

A potlatch was an elaborate affair, requiring long preparation, formal invitations, observation of a strict ritual, and the giving away of valuable property by the host (a man of high caste in a strictly stratified society). Gifts eventually had to be returned in kind, with exorbitant interest. If this "gift" was not repaid within a reasonable time, the recipient would lose status, which is why the potlatch has also been referred to as "fighting with property." These notions of giving pervaded the everyday lives of the natives of the Northwest Coast—the reason why Lewis and Clark quickly decided not to accept gifts from native chiefs.

Before the arrival of white traders and their goods, the objects given away included canoes, hand-woven blankets, or valuable shield-like sheets of scarce copper. To show off his wealth, the host might break a sheet of copper or kill slaves along the beach where visiting canoes pulled up. As the Indians of the Coast began to work as commercial fishermen or sealers, they acquired—and gave away—many of the new consumer goods introduced by white traders.

Kwakiutls prepare for a potlatch at Fort Rupert in 1898. Photographs of potlatches are rare since the practice was banned by the government. (American Museum of Natural History)

GIVE-AWAY PARTY

One celebrated potlatch was held in 1922 by Kwakiutl chief Dan Cranmer on Village Island, off the northern coast of Vancouver Island. "I started giving out the property," he recalled. "First the canoes," twenty-four of them, "some big ones." He gave pool tables to two chiefs. Such large gifts cast high honor upon Cranmer and incurred a deep obligation upon the recipients to match the gesture in the future. "It really hurt them," commented Cranmer. "They said it was the same as breaking a copper," another display of unsparing wealth. Assu received a gas boat and $50 cash. Three more gas boats were given away and another pool table. Dresses, shawls, and bracelets went to the women, sweaters and shirts to the young people. For the children, small change: "I threw it away for the kids to get," Cranmer remembered. Then came blankets, gas lights, violins, guitars, basins, glasses, washtubs, teapots, boxes, three hundred oak trunks, sewing machines, gramaphone, bedsteads, bureaus and more cash. Finally, on Christmas Day, the fifth and last day of the ceremony, came the sacks of flour . . . Cranmer recalled a thousand bought for three dollars each.

Potlatches were accompanied by dances and feasts. Chief Charles Jones of the Pacheenaht (Nootka) tribe recalled a cooking vessel used at a Potlatch in the early 1900s:

> One day . . . a large steel buoy was found ashore. My father and other members of the tribe tried to cut the buoy in half. Axes and sledge hammers were used to cut through the half-inch steel and nine of the axes were worn out. A lot of tools were ruined but the men managed to split it in half. It was then decided to use it as a cooking pot. At one potlatch, we cooked an elk and 31 harbour seals in the pot—it was so big.

Potlatches might deteriorate from peaceful "fighting with property" to actual warfare, especially since war and raids on other villages were also a means of acquiring property, slaves, and status. The vessels of war were giant canoes carved from a single cedar log. They might be more than 50 feet long and up to eight feet wide—the size of a small Viking ship—and carry a considerable number of warriors. According to ethnographer Philip Drucker, the elegantly shaped canoes of the Nootka "inspired the New England designers of that queen of the seas, the American clipper ship, whose racy bow lines were nearly identical."

■ HORSEMEN OF THE COLUMBIA PLATEAU

Tribes living east of the Cascade Mountains on the high and dry plateaus were traders, desert wanderers, and by the early 19th century, when some tribes acquired horses from the Utes of Utah, accomplished horsemen who followed game as it migrated from the lowlands to summer forage in the mountains. These people counted their wealth in horses and on them traveled through their hunting lands to the greenest pastures, digging camas and other bulbs as staple food, and gathering by the rivers in July when salmon (before the construction of dams) still ran hundreds of miles inland to spawn. The people brought with them teepees or built long lodges covered with rush mats or buffalo hides.

Confident and well traveled, these people braved dangerous warrior tribes to the east when they visited the Plains to hunt the buffalo that had become extinct west of the Rocky Mountains early in the 19th century. Thus, the Nez Percé, Cayuse, and the Yakama were only a little impressed by the pale-skinned newcomers who began first to visit, then to invade their territories. When too many whites poured in, they fought brave battles and lost because their weapons were inferior.

The Painted Hills of north-central Oregon are at the southern end of the Columbia Plateau—
once the domain of the Nez Percé, Cayuse, and Yakama tribal groups.

Eventually, they were moved to reservations—small remnants of the lands they originally held. Here, deprived of their hunting lands and dependent on government handouts to eat, they suffered, despaired, and tried to preserve their ancient customs and myths.

The tribes living between the warrior cultures of the coast and horse-herding tribes of the east were great traders. These middlemen lived along rivers: the Columbia, Fraser, Skeena, and Stikine, controlling both the catching of salmon at the rapids and the movement of goods from the coast to the plateaus and the trade routes of the interior to the sea.

■ EUROPEANS ARRIVE

Three great expansionist powers sent navigators along the north coast of the American continent in the 16th, 17th, and 18th centuries: those of England, Spain, and Russia. The nations themselves were seeking power, conquest, gold, and new trade routes. The men who manned their ships were a uniquely courageous and curious breed, taking small wooden ships through unchartered waters to fulfill visions of glory and adventure, or perhaps to satisfy an incurable wanderlust. The writing in the log books of these ships possesses a courtly formality and grace; their records indicate that encounters with other mariners were for the most part cordial.

These explorers were the first Europeans to encounter the native people of the Pacific. England's Captain Cook, a great admirer of both the Hawaiians and the Eskimos, recorded that he was nonplussed by the Indians of Nootka Sound, especially after these natives expected him to pay for the wood and water his crew took. Captain George Vancouver found the natives of Puget Sound a gentle and friendly group. Russian fur traders, who had pushed east across Siberia to the Bering Sea, made alliances with the Aleut people of the Aleutian Islands. Establishing Sitka early in the 19th century, Russians sent kayak flotillas of Aleut hunters south along the Northwest coast to northern California and hunted the sea otter until it was virtually extinct. Then, at the beginning of the 19th century, a new player entered the scene: the fledgling United States of America.

GRAY DISCOVERS THE COLUMBIA RIVER

*T*he year 1792 was now come, and it was a great year in the annals of Oregon, three hundred years from Columbus, two hundred from Juan de Fuca. The struggle between England and Spain over conflicting rights at Nootka, which at one time threatened war, had been settled with a measure of amicability. As a commissioner to represent Great Britain, Captain George Vancouver was sent out, while Bodega y Quadra was empowered to act in like capacity for Spain. Spaniards and Britons alike realised that, whatever the Nootka treaty may have been, possession was nine points of the law, and both redoubled their efforts to push discovery, and especially to make the first complete exploration of the Straits of Fuca and the supposed Great River.

Two days later the lookout reported a sail, and as the ships drew together, the newcomer was seen to be flying the Stars and Stripes. It was the *Columbia Rediviva,* Captain Robert Gray, of Boston. In response to Vancouver's rather patronizing queries, the Yankee skipper gave a summary of his log for some months past. Among other things he states that he had passed what seemed to be a powerful river in latitude 46 degrees 10 minutes, which for nine days he had tried in vain to enter, being repelled by the strength of the current. He now proposed returning to that point and renewing his efforts. Vancouver declined to reconsider his previous decision that there could be no large river, and passed on to make his very elaborate exploration of the Straits of Fuca and their connected waters, and to discover to his great chagrin, that the Spaniards had forestalled him in point of time.

The vessels parted. Gray sailed south and on May 10, 1792, paused abreast of the same reflex of water where before for nine days he had tried vainly to enter. The morning of the 11th dawned clear and favourable, light wind, gentle sea, a broad, clear channel, plainly of sufficient depth. The time was now come. The man and the occasion met. Grey seems from the first to have been ready to take some chances for the sake of some great success. . . . So, as he laconically stated in his log-book, he ran in with all sail set, and at ten o'clock found himself in a large river of fresh water, at a point about twenty miles from the ocean.

—William Denison Lyman, *The Columbia River,* 1909

■ ONE REGION, TWO COUNTRIES

Less than 30 years after the American colonies fought the Revolutionary War with Britain, President Thomas Jefferson insured that his country, rather than any European power, would dominate North America when he acquired the Louisiana Territory from France. Knowing little of what these vast tracts of land encompassed, Jefferson sent explorers Meriwether Lewis and William Clark to chart a route to the Pacific and to open the area up for American trade and American settlers.

All of these people—explorers, navigators, adventurers, and merchants—unwittingly brought diseases to the Pacific Northwest that killed tribal people. But the greatest changes came after Russia and Spain pulled back from the Northern Pacific Coast, and American and British settlers began moving into the region.

In 1846, Britain and the United States divided their territories in the Pacific Northwest along the 49th parallel. British Columbia joined the Canadian Federation in 1871 and became a member of the British Commonwealth, a vast global

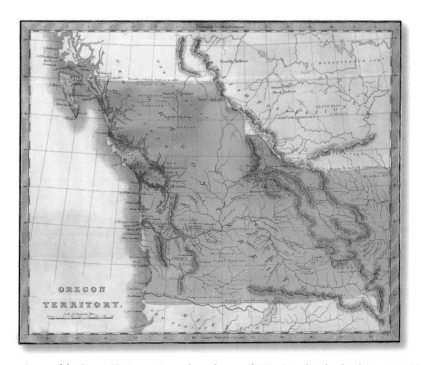

A map of the Oregon Territory prior to the settlement of U.S.–Canadian border claims in 1846. (University of Washington Libraries)

British Camp on San Juan Island was the site of occupation by British forces. The island was also inhabited by American citizens, and a dispute over the island's national status was not resolved until 1872, when San Juan became U.S. territory.

network of loyalties, traditions, and trade. The Americans of Washington and Oregon maintained a paradoxical attitude toward England. They spoke its language and its pioneers read the King James Bible and the plays of Shakespeare. But their American identity was infused with pride at having thrown off a great power and having established the first democracy in modern times. The Pacific Northwest was thus split, and yet its settlers maintained a civility which is still a pleasurable part of life in the Northwest.

■ PLUCK IN HARD TIMES

In 1893, the economy of the Pacific Northwest collapsed in the wake of the failure of banks back east. People had scarcely enough to eat. Tacoma pioneer Thomas Emerson Ripley wrote in *Green Timber*:

We quickly learned the trick of the clambake—the underlayer of dry wood, the seaweed, the clams, and then more seaweed. The long summer twilight was lighted up by the fires of the clambakers, and it was a heartening sight. What would have happened to the dwindling population of Tacoma without clams, I don't know.

The clams were immortalized by Congressman George Cushman in a speech before the House of Representatives. After telling his fellow lawmakers how hard the depression had hit the Puget Sound country, he concluded: "When the tide was out, our table was set. Our stomachs rose and fell with the tide."

This depression ended in 1897, when the steamer *Portland* arrived in Seattle carrying "a ton of gold" from the Klondike. The mayor was so excited, he jumped on a ship and went north himself. During the gold rush excitement, Seattle set itself up as the economic capital of Alaska—a distinction it still holds a hundred years later. Vancouver, Tacoma, and Portland also benefited. By the time the last miner had been outfitted, the economy had rebounded. The mainstays of the Pacific Northwest economy were its lumber harvests and its fishing.

■ MODERN TIMES

In the U.S. portion of the region, the great public works projects of Franklin Delano Roosevelt's administration—the Grand Coulee and Bonneville dams—opened up eastern Washington and Oregon to farming by providing water for irrigation. The dams made the Columbia River navigable, while they generated the cheap electric power that fueled the aluminum industry and large companies such as Boeing aircraft. At the same time, the salmon runs were destroyed, a loss which served as a warning of the potential dangers of unchecked timber harvest and fishing along the coast, and prodded locals and environmentalists to fight for regulation of logging and fishing. Controversy continues, but so do natural beauty, a fine lifestyle, clean cities, and new businesses—such as Washington's Microsoft and Oregon's Nike, which spurred economic growth in the 1980s and '90s. At the end of the 20th century, the province changing most dramatically is that of British Columbia which, true to its history as a member of the British Commonwealth, welcomed Hong Kong residents as the British pulled out and now finds itself booming with new business and a population 40 percent Chinese.

Gold fever strikes Seattle on July 17, 1897. The city's mayor resigned to join the exodus northward.

VANCOUVER, B.C.

■ HIGHLIGHTS

Stanley Park
Gastown
Chinatown
Granville Island
University Area
Museums and Botanical Gardens
Sunshine Coast
Whistler

■ OVERVIEW

YOU'RE DRIVING ALONG under a low overcast, past gray buildings brightened by colorful Chinese shop signs. Fallen petals of cherry blossoms swirl in the breeze and cling to curbs, sidewalks, and concrete walls, making you reflect on the brevity of spring. But, short as the floral splendor may be, you see how truly spectacular are the streets of Vancouver this spring afternoon. More than 40,000 flowering cherry trees line the streets of the city, and when they burst into full bloom, the pale pink blossoms are augmented by the deeper colors of 9,500 flowering plums, 4,500 flowering crabapple trees, 2,000 magnolias, and 2,000 dogwoods. As you admire the flowers, set off by the gray sky, the clouds part and the sun pours out, painting the waters of Burrard Inlet to the north a burnished gold. And there, right in front of you—looking close enough to touch—rise snow-covered peaks, straight from the water. Startled, you park your car and gaze at the scenery. Vancouver, you declare, is the most beautiful city on the West Coast.

The city sprawls at the very edge of the wild, over a peninsula delineated to the south by the north arm of the Fraser River, and to the north by Burrard Inlet, the southernmost of the deeply glaciated fjords which cut into the coast at frequent intervals from here all the way to southeast Alaska.

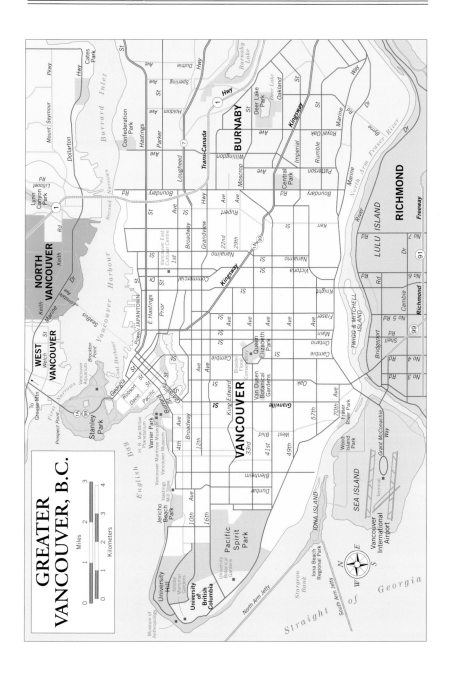

GREATER
VANCOUVER, B.C.

■ HISTORY

As a European settlement, Vancouver is a young city even for the Northwest, where most cities are less than a 150 years old. Spanish mariners were the first Europeans to visit the region, followed by British explorer George Vancouver in 1792. Vancouver, who had been exploring the coast in small boats, was heading south, back to his ships, when he spotted Spanish vessels and boarded that of Captain Dionisio Galiano. In June 1792, he reported in his journal that the captain spoke a little English. This eased communications considerably:

> Their conduct was replete with that politeness and friendship which characterizes the Spanish nation; every kind of useful information they cheerfully communicated. . . . having partaken with them of a very hearty breakfast, bad (sic) them farewell, not less pleased with their hospitality and attention, than astonished at the vessels in which they were employed.

The vessels in which the Spanish sailed were only some 15 meters (50 ft) long, hardly as long as the largest Indian canoes.

■ SETTLERS ARRIVE

The northern boundary of the present city of Vancouver experienced no great initial influx of settlers because its shores were covered by dense stands of tall timber, which made it unsuitable for agriculture. The less densely wooded banks of the Fraser River, to the south of Vancouver, were settled first, since the river offered the additional benefit of a water route up the Fraser Valley. But the pioneers soon learned that the river would freeze in severe winters, as it did in 1861-62, when it was covered with ice from the mountains to its mouth. That year, steamers ran into Burrard Inlet to deliver the mail, which was hauled by sleigh to New Westminster, the capital of the new province.

Clay for bricks and coal were discovered in the heart of present-day Vancouver in 1862, and a lumber mill began operating in 1867. A company store catered to the domestic needs of loggers and millworkers, but it didn't sell liquor. That deficiency was remedied by John "Gassy Jack" Deighton, who opened a saloon just west of the lumber mill's property line. The village springing up around Deighton's saloon became known as "Gastown." Gassy Jack is considered Vancouver's founding father. The city's street-numbering system starts from the site of his saloon, in the middle of the present five-way intersection in the Gastown quarter of the city.

■ VANCOUVER BOOMS

By the end of 1886, Gastown had been renamed Vancouver, and the town boasted a school, a hospital, an opera house, a bank, and a new two-story city hall, not to mention 14 office blocks, 23 hotels, 51 stores, nine saloons, two stables, a roller-skating rink, and a church. Over the next few years, as the new city's population grew from about 1,000 in mid-1886 to 13,000 by 1891, Vancouver acquired the

On May 23, 1887, the first transcontinental train pulled into Vancouver, thus joining the city with the rest of the country. (Vancouver Public Library)

small shops and terraced homes that gave its streets such a "European" look. As the population was swelled by immigration from Europe—between 1901 and 1911 Vancouver's population jumped from 27,000 to more than 100,000—multi-story office blocks, department stores, and hotels began to dominate the downtown business district.

This boom was fueled by the completion of the railway from eastern Canada. In May of 1887, the first transcontinental train steamed into the little wooden depot just west of Granville Street. Vancouver had joined the modern world. In June of that year the CPR steamer *Abyssinia* arrived from Yokohama, Japan, with a cargo of tea. The tea was shipped by rail via Montreal to New York, loaded aboard a fast steamship and unloaded in London 29 days after leaving Japan. The Vancouver route was two weeks quicker than the old route through the Suez Canal.

Vancouver became a major seaport almost overnight, strengthening the city's new ties to the Pacific as well as reinforcing the bonds tying it to eastern Canada and Britain. This new status encouraged Vancouverites to see themselves as a vital link of the Empire, and it separated B.C.'s consciousness from that of the Americans just south of the 49th parallel.

■ THE PACIFIC CONNECTION

Today the port of Vancouver is larger than ever and contributes a major share to the city's prosperity. EXPO 86, a world's fair, celebrated Vancouver's 100th birthday as well as the city's coming of age. It also brought a stream of visitors that has not yet abated.

Vancouver, right now, is a place of change—if you go away for a year, you may not recognize a once familiar neighborhood. That's because an influx of Hong Kong capital has led to major building projects in both commercial and residential sections of town. Some of these new buildings are attractive in a Postmodernist fashion; others reflect the waning powers of the International Style; yet others are simply large and cramped, designed to accommodate as many people as possible. This is especially true for some housing developments, where huge mansions are squeezed onto tiny lots. Yet most of the old residential neighborhoods, which helped give Vancouver its relaxed atmosphere of British prosperity, are untouched. While concrete and glass slowly replace clapboard houses and postage-stamp front lawns, Vancouver is still a city of gardens, where the scent of flowers mingles with the crispness of the sea breeze, and where on a warm day, you can smell the scent of conifers on nearby mountains.

Stanley Park on Vancouver's waterfront is a haven from the pressures of urban life.

■ CANADIAN IDENTITY

Canadian English is quite different from American English. In its intonation it is much closer to British English than, say, Australian is. The Canadian government, aware of the forces threatening to tear the country apart have made a conscious effort to promote "Canadian" things. You'll notice it when you switch on the TV set in your hotel room (there's even an all-Canadian country music channel—eat your heart out, Nashville), and you'll notice it in the absence of U.S. books and magazines in the shops. But this may be a temporary phenomenon.

Not all is well in paradise. British Columbians take every opportunity to stream south of the border, despite the disparity in the exchange rate (one Canadian dollar is worth about 70 U.S. cents), and they flock to events in Washington State in ever increasing numbers, ignoring the superior attractions of their largest city. That may change, as British Columbians and Vancouverites develop an ever stronger pan-Pacific, identity. In the meantime, they welcome visitors with open arms. Never, in the 20-plus years that I have visited Vancouver, have I found the natives as friendly and welcoming as they are now.

■ EXPLORING VANCOUVER

Vancouver is the largest and most important city of the Canadian west. Most of British Columbia's population lives in the city, its suburbs, and the lower Fraser River Valley. What sets Vancouver apart from other West Coast ports is the way the waterfront has changed in the last decade. No Pacific waterfront is as "user-friendly." Not only are there beaches for Vancouverites to frolic on, but there are bicycle paths and footpaths almost everywhere along the shores of Burrard Inlet and False Creek. A path even winds along the harbor front, past ship chandlers, boat-yards, restaurants, pubs, moored boats, and floatplane docks, which makes it not only visually stimulating but also interesting for curious minds.

Vancouver is divided into several distinct quarters and neighborhoods, each with its own character.

■ STANLEY PARK

Stanley Park has a shoreline promenade along the harbor, First Narrows, and English Bay shores, as well as hiking trails through the woods, totem poles, cricket grounds, a zoo, and the **Vancouver Aquarium.** This incredibly well-thought-out aquarium has it all: beluga whales, orcas, and sea otters, plus fish from local waters and exotic seas, a trek through a slice of Amazon jungle, and a wade in wetlands where a kid-sized "swamp-bubble" lets you enjoy a "frog's eye view" of a freshwater pond; (604) 268-9900.

Popular beaches line **English Bay** on the southern shore. A walk along the seawall to English Bay from Coal Harbour is 8 kilometers (5 mi) long and takes a minimum of two hours—if you're not distracted by bald eagles, nesting cormorants, or cruising sea lions. Near the Lumberman's Arch on the east shore is the site of Whoi-Whoi, one of the many native villages of the inlet.

The west end is an upscale residential area of high-rise condominiums and apartments, between Stanley Park and downtown, within walking distance of restaurants, shops, and beaches.

■ DOWNTOWN

Downtown, the commercial heart of the city, sprawls across a peninsula north of False Creek, a tidal inlet. Here are most of Vancouver's fancy hotels, restaurants, and shops, plus office buildings to support them. The heart of downtown is **the plaza,** which is located north of Robson Street, between Howe and Hornby and south of the **Vancouver Art Gallery.** The gallery is housed at 750 Hornby Street in the old courthouse designed by Francis Rattenbury, architect of Victoria's Empress Hotel and Parliament buildings. The new courthouse to the south looks more like a parking garage that wants to be a greenhouse. A sunken plaza in the square is filled with water during freezing weather and serves as a municipal skating rink. The grand old **Orpheum Theatre** at 601 Smithe Street rounds out the picture.

Howe Street north of Georgia is the city's financial heart, home to major banks and the Vancouver Stock Exchange, an institution known for arranging financing for mineral exploration and other risky investment schemes.

Granville Street downtown is a pedestrian mall, but there's also an underground mall underneath the street and the department stores between Granville and Howe. **Robson Street** is one of the city's main shopping districts. Instead of sidewalk tables, many of the restaurants have terraces on the roof where you can dine al fresco.

Canada Place, on the shore of Burrard Inlet, just west of Gastown, is a cruise ship pier with a hotel, restaurant, and convention center. You can't miss the place:

(following pages) False Creek Marina and the Vancouver skyline.

it's topped by huge, white, tent-like plastic sails. The best place for watching the cruise ship action is from the **Steamworks Brewing Co.** brewpub at The Landing, 375 Water Street.

The nearby marine building is the northernmost terminal for the **SkyTrain**, a high-tech commuter train that runs underground in the downtown area and on stilts to New Westminster and the southern suburbs. SeaBus is an efficient, fast people-mover ferry that runs north from here to the Lonsdale Quai in North Vancouver. You use the tickets you buy in a vending machine on either SeaBus or SkyTrain or both. A day pass is a great means of exploring other parts of town, as well as the North Shore.

DOWNTOWN VANCOUVER, B.C.

■ GASTOWN

Gastown, just to the east, is where Vancouver started, in the shacks built near "Gassy Jack's" saloon. In the 1960s, the old buildings and cobbled streets were resurrected to attract tourists, but the locals liked the area so much that restaurants, shops, and bookstores now cater mostly to residents. Which makes it even more of a fun place to visit. The oldest part of the city, with its pleasing late-Victorian buildings, stretches east from Canada Place to Maple Tree Square (which got its name from the tree that stood here and served as a municipal billboard). The Gastown Steam Clock at Water and Cambie sounds the time with the Westminster chimes on Big Ben on the Houses of Parliament in London.

■ CHINATOWN

Chinatown, south of Hastings and Main, and centered on Pender and Keefer, has some of the oldest buildings in Vancouver, and the most beautiful garden. It is the most exciting place in Vancouver. Long billed as North America's second largest Chinatown, it's rapidly on its way to becoming the largest, thanks to a great influx of immigrants from Hong Kong.

Hong Kong money is transforming Chinatown: the quarter is expanding beyond its borders; new shops and restaurants are springing up all over the place; the selection of artifacts and foods is greater and better than ever. Chinatown clothing stores sell some very fancy Chinese silk robes, porcelain, and art objects.

This pioneer family operated two of the city's first laundry services. Jennie Wah Chong (second from right) was the first Asian to attend public school in the city. (City of Vancouver Archives)

You will find many objects made from jade, since B.C. is the world's main supplier.

The **Dr. Sun Yat-Sen Classical Chinese Garden,** south of the Chinese Cultural Centre, is truly a unique place. The only complete Chinese garden outside China was completed by craftsmen from Suzhou, China's garden capital, in time for Vancouver's 100th anniversary. It is quite unlike any other garden most of us Westerners are familiar with. The walled garden consists of ponds, pavilions with curved roofs of blue tile, covered walkways, and terraces. These are set off by rocks, flowers and plants, and the water, which is kept deliberately murky to better reflect the buildings. A waterfall blocks out most of the city's noise. The garden changes with the seasons. It is as beautiful in spring, when a succession of blooms adds color, as it is in fall color, or on a snowy day in winter. The buildings are handcrafted in the traditional Suzhou style with exquisite carving and lacy screens of honey-colored ginkgo wood. The best place for contemplation is the Scholar's Study, which has its own enclosed courtyard. Tea is served daily in the main hall. A gift shop stocks art books, Chinese porcelains, and other objets d'art. Located at 578 Carrall Street; entrance fee; (604) 689-7133.

A pavilion in Dr. Sun Yat-Sen's Classical Garden. (Photo by Ken Straiton)

Dr. Sun Yat-Sen Park to the east shares the pond with the garden but is not as elaborate as the garden and is open to the public free of charge. Its grove of black bamboo and its island pavilion are a favorite lunchtime place for local office workers. Canada geese have been known to nest among the rocks, and a great blue heron likes to hang out at the pond's edge between the garden and the park.

■ YALETOWN AND THE THEATRE DISTRICT

Yaletown is a gentrified former warehouse district southeast of downtown, which now houses offices, movie and video produc-

This steam-powered clock is a landmark in Gastown.

ers, furniture showrooms, fancy shops, and restaurants where the young and fashionable gather. There's even a microbrewery, the **Yaletown Brewing Company** at 111 Mainland Street.

The loading ramps and loading docks leading to the former warehouses and the utilitarian brick building facades certainly give the district a unique atmosphere. The conversion of the warehouses began when EXPO 86 was held nearby. The district has been kept alive by highrise condominium construction in a neighboring area dubbed "Downtown South," and by the proximity of the theatre and stadium districts.

East of Yaletown is the **Stadium District** with the plastic-domed BC Place Stadium and the new GM Place, which also hosts concerts and other public events.

❖

Vancouver's theatre district is northeast of Yaletown, near the coliseum-shaped Vancouver Public Library. The **Queen Elizabeth Theatre** located on Hamilton at Georgia, (604) 280-4444, and the **Vancouver Playhouse** at 630 Hamilton Street, (604) 280-3311, have recently been joined by the grand new **Ford Centre for the Performing Arts.** One of the city's most popular theaters, the two-stage **Arts Club Theatre** is on Granville Island at 1585 Johnston Street; (604) 687-1644.

■ GRANVILLE ISLAND

Granville Island, in False Creek (below the Granville Street Bridge) can be reached by car from the south shore or by passenger ferry from downtown shore. The island was a sandbar until World War I, when the city dredged the inlet and used the dredged-up mud to create an island. After serving as a warehouse and industrial district for decades, the island is now mostly a collection of shops, restaurants, and a public market with fishmongers' and produce stalls that rivals Seattle's Pike Place Market. It is a great place to visit, especially since it has its own brewery which sells locally made unpasteurized lager beer. (The Granville Island Market is closed on Mondays.) Artists' studios, galleries, theaters, and shops occupy former warehouses. A modern hotel (with room service for visiting boats mooring out front) occupies the eastern tip; houseboats squeeze in along the north shore; and a cement company yard survives from the industrial era. Walks lead along much of the island shore as well as along the north shore of False Creek. Where condominiums rise now, once stood Snauq village of the local Salish tribe.

■ KITSILANO AND UNIVERSITY AREA ATTRACTIONS

Vancouver's Kitsilano district runs from Burrard and W. Fourth west to the **University of British Columbia** on Point Gray along the south side of False Creek. It has interesting shops, restaurants, and bookstores along Fourth and Broadway, and a small Greek district on Broadway. The university itself is one of the most beautiful campuses in the Northwest. This is an area of many fine museums and gardens, listed on the opposite page. They are also marked on the map of Vancouver on page 31.

■ GARDENS

Bloedel Floral Conservatory. 33rd Ave. and Cambie (in Queen Elizabeth Park); (604) 257-8570

The conservatory is in a triodetic dome with 1490 plexiglass bubbles protecting tropical plants from Vancouver's somewhat chilly weather. The conservatory has 500 species and varieties of plants native to different habitats from jungles to deserts. A creek-like pond holds koi, colorful macaws perch on snags, and small tropical birds freely flit through the enclosure. The conservatory is the perfect place to alleviate the gloominess of a drab Vancouver winter afternoon.

Nitobe Memorial Garden. 1903 West Mall, across from 6501 NW Marine Dr.; (604) 822-6038

Garden experts call this the most authentic Japanese garden outside Japan.

University of British Columbia Botanical Gardens. 6250 Stadium Rd., just north of 16th Ave. and Marine Dr.; (604) 822-6038.

First planted in 1916, this is Canada's oldest university botanical garden. It has an alpine garden, a garden for native plants, a Physick garden, a winter garden, and an Asian garden.

VanDusen Botanical Gardens. 37th Ave. and Oak St.; (604) 878-9274

Old golf courses don't die—this one was turned into a first-rate arboretum with one of the largest collections of ornamental plants in North America.

■ MUSEUMS

Hastings Mill Store. 1575 Alma St.; (604) 734-1212

This store once stood on the shore of Burrard Inlet just east of Gastown. It survived the 1886 fire and was moved to its present site in 1930. It is now a museum of Indian artifacts and early Vancouver relics.

Museum of Anthropology at the University of British Columbia. 6393 NW Marine Dr.; (604) 822-5087

This museum is truly impressive, with one of world's finest collections of Northwest Indian art.

Vancouver Maritime Museum. 1905 Ogden Ave. at Cypress St. (west of the planetarium); (604) 257-8300

This small but well-appointed museum traces the history of shipping on Canada's west coast, the British Columbia fishing industry, and much more. The ship models are a delight.

Vancouver Museum. 1100 Chestnut St.; (604) 736-4431

Canada's largest civic museum is a sort of urban folk museum, with a replica of a trading post, a Victorian parlor, an 1897 Canadian Pacific Railway car, and much more. There's the ubiquitous Indian cedar canoe, too.

■ PLANETARIUM

H. R. MacMillan Planetarium. 1100 Chestnut St. (near south end of Burrard Bridge); (604) 736-4431 or 738-7827

Voyage into outer space via shows beamed onto a 20-meter (66-ft) dome.

The shore west of Vanier Park has several popular beaches. South of Kitsilano, **Kerrisdale** is a genteel shopping and restaurant district at 41st Avenue and W. Boulevard.

The west side near the University of British Columbia and Point Gray is not to be confused with the West End or with West Vancouver. The area is popular for parks and beaches. **Wreck Beach** is the nudist beach—yes, it gets warm enough in summer to take your clothes off, and hardened locals do it at all times of the year.

■ VANCOUVER SOUTH AND EAST

On Main Street southeast of downtown and Queen Elizabeth Park is the East Indian shopping district known as the **Punjabi Market.** It is known for Indian silks, saris, and jewelry, as well as for shops selling uncommonly exotic foods.

The Vancouver East district along Commercial Drive has long been known as Little Italy, because it used to be an enclave of Italian shops, but since EXPO it has gone Latin-International and counter-cultural. **Vancouver East Cultural Centre,** one block away at 1895 Venables Street, often hosts ethnic performers; (604) 254-9578.

(above) Vancouver's varied ethnic makeup is reflected in the variety of food markets scattered throughout the city. (opposite) The lovely gardens in Queen Elizabeth Park.

If you don't want to park your car in the east—and occasionally dangerous—side of Vancouver, you can take the SkyTrain, which has a stop on Commercial Drive.

There is not much left of Vancouver's **Japantown** along Cordova and Powell east of Main, but you can still find a shop or two selling exquisite kimonos.

A word of caution about shopping: In Vancouver, as in Seattle, be careful when buying "genuine" American Indian artifacts or art objects—some of them are made in factory workshops employing no native workers.

An overview of Vancouver's ethnic groups would be incomplete without mentioning its large Scottish population. If you've been invited to a dress party but you forgot your tux, you can rent a kilt or buy the official British Columbia tartan at the **Scotch Shop** (you can also buy a bagpipe here, or a starter kit) at 674 Seymour; (604) 682-3929.

■ NORTH SHORE OF BURRARD INLET

The north shore of Burrard Inlet has become a very popular residential area in the last decade, as you can tell by the ranks of houses rising up the slopes of the foothills. There's a good reason for this. As one resident said, "I used to live in a west end condo. But now I have my own house and garden, with one of the best views in the world. I have the wilderness on one side, but I can also take SeaBus to the city and be in my office in half an hour."

The SeaBus passenger ferries run between Vancouver's Marine Building and the **Lonsdale Quai Public Market** in North Vancouver. At the market, you can sit in a pub overlooking the inlet and watch the ships come in. Just east of the quai is a **tugboat dock** and shipyard. If you're lucky, you can watch one of the tugs being hauled out, and you can see for yourself what stubby but powerful little machines these tugs are. More likely, you'll see tugs cast off their mooring lines and, with a "bone in their teeth" and a large wake, rush out into the channel to lead a ship to moorage. Since Vancouver is a very busy port, watching the ships come in is almost a spectator sport. (Before the market was built, I liked walking up the hill, to Pasparos Greek Taverna to watch the ships from the shade of the big fig tree in the courtyard out front.)

❖

North of town, Lillooet Road leads to the **Seymour Demonstration Forest**. Here the Capilano Suspension Bridge spans a steep-walled canyon above the tumbling waters of the Capilano River. At the top of Capilano Road, the **Grouse Mountain SkyRide** aerial tram rises 1,100 meters (3,700 ft) to a great view of Vancouver and Georgia Strait; the Peak Chairlift to the summit whisks you to an even better view.

Where the rushing waters of the Capilano River enter tidewater just east of the First Narrows, the Coast Salish village of Homulcheson once stood. A pleasant, tree-shaded path leads upstream to **Capilano Regional Park.** A gently swaying suspension bridge 140 meters (450 ft) across and 72 meters (230 ft) above the Capilano River has been attracting visitors for over a century—and it's still as popular as it was on the first day it opened. There is a trout stream fed by mountain springs, trails meandering through a forest of tall trees, a 62-meter (200-ft)-long cantilevered observation deck, and much more.

From the Upper Level Highway (TCH, Route 1, BC 99) in West Vancouver, Cypress Access Road leads uphill to **Cypress Provincial Park.** Like no other place, this mountain wilderness within easy driving distance of the city makes you aware of how young Vancouver is, and how recently the veneer of urban life spread out across the landscape.

An aerial tram transports visitors 1,100 meters (3,700 ft) up Grouse Mountain so they can enjoy a dramatic vista of the city. (Photo by Ken Straiton)

■ BURNABY

Burnaby adjoins Vancouver to the east, stretching from Burrard Inlet to the North Arm of the Fraser River. Though it is a major city, few visitors (or locals, for that matter) could tell where Vancouver ends and Burnaby begins, were it not for the conveniently named Boundary Road. Burnaby has an attractive green strip along the Fraser, with truck gardens where you can buy seasonal produce, and several very attractive parks. Near Burnaby Lake is the **Burnaby Heritage Village & Carousel** at 6501 Deer Lake Avenue. The village, in Deer Lake Park, consists of buildings from the 1890s through 1925. Guides dressed in historic costumes introduce visitors to the everyday life of that period through demonstrations, displays, and hands-on activities. The restored carousel dates from 1912 and has 36 wooden horses, a chariot, four metal horses, and space for a wheelchair.

At the north end of Burnaby, **Simon Fraser University** rises atop Burnaby Mountain. A park has totem poles and some great views west across Vancouver and north into Indian Arm, the wilderness fjord branching off Burrard Inlet. (Take Hastings Street east and follow signs to Simon Fraser University.)

■ SUNSHINE COAST EXCURSION

The Sunshine Coast is a very scenic stretch of land between the mountains and Georgia Strait north of Howe Sound. A narrow two-lane highway winds north between a rocky saltwater shore and the Coast Mountains (which here rise to heights of some 6,000 feet right from saltwater), past gnarled madrona trees, sandy beaches, and rocky headlands where wildflowers spill down to the water. The views of the strait, islands, and mountains are breathtaking. Trails lead to hidden lakes and river gorges east of the highway. There are numerous campgrounds and lodges.

The trip starts with a 45-minute ferry ride across **Howe Sound,** from Horseshoe Bay to Langdale. **Gibsons,** just west of the northern ferry terminal, is a quaint little town still living off the fame it gained in a popular TV series called "The Beachcombers." **Roberts Creek** is awiggle with painters and craftspeople; **Sechelt** is a rapidly growing retirement community.

Nearby **Skookumchuck Rapids** (also known as "Sechelt Rapids") are an awesome sight. They more than live up to their Indian name which means "strong waters." Rocks and islets restrict Sechelt Inlet near its junction with Jervis Inlet. In-flowing and out-flowing tidal waters turn the narrow channel into a churning white-water river. (The best viewing times are posted in local newspapers and at the beginning of the .4-kilometer [quarter-mile] trail.) The saltwater falls are highest on the incoming tide, an hour after slack water. The current, running at speeds of 10 to 12 knots, creates whirlpools powerful enough to suck down a 6.1-meter (20-ft) boat. On a three-meter (10-ft) tide, billions of gallons of water run through the shallow, 305-meter- (1,000-ft)-wide channel.

A 55-minute ferry ride takes you from Saltery Bay through Powell River to **Lund,** where the highway ends. North of here, no road reaches salt water until Bella Coola, and north of there the coast is roadless all the way to Prince Rupert. A ferry connects Powell River to Comox on Vancouver Island.

■ EXCURSION TO WHISTLER

Whistler, nestled in a beautiful alpine valley at the foot of two tall peaks in the British Columbia Coast Mountains, is considered to be North America's top ski resort. It is only 20 miles from salt water and a two-hour drive from Vancouver.

To get to Whistler, just follow Highway 99, the road that has brought you north from the U.S. border, or take the daily train from North Vancouver, or take a skiplane from Vancouver on Whistler Air. North of Horseshoe Bay, BC 99 winds about considerably, making the drive a bit adventuresome. But the scenery is grand. Don't rush. Turn out for the speed freaks on the highway and enjoy the views. The transition from maritime fjord to alpine creek is rather abrupt, and very spectacular in late spring and summer when the wildflowers are in bloom.

This resort fulfills all it promises. The setting is incredibly beautiful, the skiing is magnificent, the restaurants are excellent, the lodging is luxurious, the people are friendly. It's a perfect vacation spot in summer, too, with hiking trails leading to alpine meadows. Call (800) WHISTLER for detailed, up-to-date information.

■ TRAVEL AND CLIMATE

■ GETTING THERE AND GETTING AROUND

Located on the far southwestern shore of the Canadian mainland, Vancouver has high-speed road and rail connections to the other Canadian provinces to the east and to the U.S. to the south. Only a few winding roads lead into the rugged mountains to the north. Travel to the west, to Vancouver Island and the Gulf

*(following pages) Malaspina Strait and Texada Island
along the Sunshine Coast north of Vancouver.*

Islands, is by ferry or commuter plane. *(For general information on travel in British Columbia see page 354.)*

Vancouver is a city made for walking. Major hotels, restaurants, shops, museums, and theaters are close by downtown. You can travel by SkyTrain to more outlying districts, like Chinatown or Commercial Drive, and you can reach the north shore by SeaBus. **Regular buses** run to Stanley Park, the University of British Columbia, and other parts of town. Small **passenger ferries** cross False Creek from the downtown shore to Granville Island.

By Car

If you arrive in Vancouver by car from the south, you will be crossing the U.S. border at Blaine, Washington. *(For border, money, and passport information, see page 356.)* Watch for directional signs as you arrive in Vancouver via the BC 99 freeway. The freeway ends at the Vancouver city limits and BC 99 continues through town on a somewhat confusing maze of streets. Carefully look for signs directing you to downtown and to the north (directional signs in British Columbia tend to be small). North of the Fraser River Bridge, the freeway turns into Oak Street. Continue to 41st Street. Turn left (west), then right on Granville Street to down-

---

VANCOUVER WATER TRAVEL

Aquabus runs between the ArtsClub Theatre on Granville Island and the southern foot of Hornby St. Ferries run from 7 A.M. to 8 P.M. daily. For information call (604) 689-5858.

Granville Island Ferries stop at Bridges restaurant on Granville Island, at Stamps Landing, and at the Aquatic Centre at the northern foot of Burrard St. Bridge. On weekends, the ferries also cross to the Vancouver Maritime Museum. Call (604) 684-7781 for information. Wheelchair Accessible.

Paddlewheel Tours. The MPV *Constitution* takes visitors on a narrated 90-minute tour of the Port of Vancouver. In summer there's a nightly three-hour dinner cruise. Harbour Cruises, northern foot of Denman St.; (604) 688-7246.

SeaBus. Fast passenger-only catamarans run between Lonsdale Ave. in North Vancouver and the SkyTrain Waterfront Station downtown. For information, call (604) 521-0400. Partially wheelchair accessible.

town. North of the Granville Street Bridge over False Creek, take the off-ramp to Seymour Street (Granville turns into a pedestrian mall) and continue north to the heart of downtown. The Trans-Canada Highway (TCH) Route 1, skirts the eastern edge of town before crossing Burrard Inlet on the Second Narrows Bridge to North Vancouver. If you're coming in that way, turning west on Hastings Street will take you downtown.

By Bus

B.C. Transit buses run all over town. Deposit exact fare as you enter in front; free transfer slips on request for other buses, SeaBus, or SkyTrain. For information call (604) 521-0400. Partially wheelchair accessible.

Pacific Central Station, Main St. at Terminal, is Vancouver's long distance bus depot. Greyhound Lines, (604) 662-3222; Maverick Coach Lines, (604) 662-8051; Pacific Coach Lines, (604) 662-8074. Wheelchair accessible.

West Vancouver's Blue Buses connect downtown with the Horseshoe Bay ferry terminal. They leave from the corner of Homer and Georgia, next to the main post office. Allow an hour for the ride. Call (604) 985-7777 for schedule and fares.

By Train

B.C. Rail runs a daily train to Whistler, past the spectacular scenery of Howe Sound. B.C. Rail Station, 1311 West First St., North Vancouver; (604) 631-3500 or (800) 663-8238. Wheelchair accessible.

Royal Hudson, one of the few operational steam trains in Canada pulls excursion coaches along the scenic Howe Sound coastline from North Vancouver to the lumber town of Squamish at the head of the sound, a distance of 64 kilometers (40 mi). 1311 West First St., North Vancouver; (604) 68-TRAIN. Visitors can return by train or cruise one way on the MV *Britannia.* Call B.C. Rail for information at (800) 663-8238. The MV *Britannia* leaves from the northern foot of Denman St. For information call Harbour Cruises, (604) 687-9558.

SkyTrain is a nifty, fully computerized rapid transit train that runs from the Burrard Inlet waterfront downtown east to New Westminster and south to Surrey, with many stops en route. Downtown, the trains run underground, for the rest of the way on elevated tracks. On a clear day, the Fraser River crossing is spectacular. Wheelchair accessible.

■ CLIMATE

Winter comes late and does not linger. In some years no snow falls at all, but even if it does, it stays only a week or two before it is melted by warm sea breezes. Even at the height of the cold season, there are few days below 4.4 degrees centigrade (40°F), and even fewer below minus-1 (30°F). The warm rains, which melt the snow, also turn the land green in spring. Summer is usually warm and sunny, with an occasional shower to keep lawns and flowers refreshed, but temperatures rarely soar above 26 degrees (80°F). Fall is cool but sunny, with occasional rain or frost signaling the end of the balmy season. More often than not, a warm Indian summer keeps roses blooming till late November. The snow appearing on the peaks and on the higher hilltops provides a pretty contrast to the flowers which bloom from the earliest spring to the latest autumn.

■ ACCOMMODATIONS AND RESTAURANTS

☎   For chain lodgings see toll-free numbers on page 352.

$$ For room and restaurant price designations see page 352.

★   Means highly recommended.

CITY OF VANCOUVER

☎ **English Bay Inn.** 1968 Comox St.; (604) 683-8002
This small (5 rooms) and very romantic inn is utterly comfortable. It's just minutes by foot from Stanley Park and West End shops and restaurants. $$

☎ **Four Seasons.** 791 W Georgia St.; (604) 689-9333. In Canada (800) 268-6282; in the U.S. (800) 332-3442
It's huge and fancy and right next to the Stock Exchange; rooms are a bit on the small side. Service is excellent. $$$$

☎ **Granville Island Hotel.** 1253 Johnston St.; (604) 683-7373
This small hotel, partly old stucco and partly modern high tech, sits at the eastern tip of Granville Island next to a marina and within easy walking distance

of the island's theaters, restaurants, and galleries. $$$

☎ **Hotel Georgia.** 801 W Georgia St.; (604) 682-5566 or (800) 663-1111
This is a charming, old-fashioned hotel right in the heart of downtown. The hotel's two bars are very popular with locals. $$

☎ **Hotel Vancouver.** 900 W Georgia St.; (800) 441-1414
This grand old hotel, built by the Canadian Pacific in its trademark chateau-style is aging gracefully (it keeps having regular face-lifts). $$$

☎ **Hyatt Regency.** 655 Burrard St.; (604) 683-1234 or (800) 233-1234
A standard Hyatt hotel in the heart of Vancouver and within walking distance of many attractions (or at least close

enough for inexpensive taxi rides). **$$$**

☎ **Lonsdale Quay Hotel.**
123 Carrie Cates Court (at foot of Lonsdale Ave., atop the Lonsdale Quai Public Market), North Vancouver; (604) 986-6111 or (800) 836-6111
This modern hotel sits right on top of the Lonsdale Quai Public Market, and has some of the best views of the city across Burrard Inlet. The SeaBus terminal is right below, making it possible to reach Vancouver in 15 minutes. **$$$**

☎ **The Metropolitan.**
645 Howe St.; (800) 877-1133
This elegant hotel with great service is right in the heart of downtown. **$$$**

☎ **Pan Pacific Hotel.**
Suite 300–999 Canada Place; (604) 662-8111. In Canada (800) 663-1515; in the U.S. (800) 937-1515
You can't get much closer to the water than this hotel, which rises on a pier right over Vancouver's cruise ship terminal. The three-story lobby has a totem pole and waterfall; the restaurant and lounge have great harbor views. **$$$$**

☎ **Park Royal Hotel.** 540 Clyde Ave., West Vancouver; (604) 926-5511
This intimate Tudor-style hotel is about as good as lodging can get in the Vancouver area. It's on the north shore, on the bank of the Capilano River (with its great walking trails), and has a lovely dining room with outside dining in the garden if the weather's amenable, and a popular pub in the basement. **$$$**

☎ **Sutton Place** (formerly Le Meridien).
845 Burrard St.; (604) 682-5511 or (800) 961-7555
This sumptuous place in the heart of the

city is Vancouver's most elegant—and comfortable—hotel. Service is so good, it's spectacular. Best of all, Le Crocodile, arguably Vancouver's best restaurant, is right across the street. **$$$$**

☎ **Sylvia Hotel.**
1154 Gilford St.; (604) 681-9321
This is one of those places which some folks swear by yet which never satisfy others. The older rooms are tiny; newer ones are a bit unusual. **$$$**

☎ **Waterfront Centre Hotel.**
900 Canada Place Way; (604) 691-1991 or (800) 441-1414
This new, very comfortable hotel, across the street from Canada Place, may well be Vancouver's best waterfront hotel. **$$$**

☎ **Wedgewood Hotel.** 845 Hornby St.; (604) 689-7777 or (800) 663-0666
This utterly comfortable small luxury hotel is across the street from Robson Square and the Vancouver Gallery. **$$$**

☎ **Westin Bayshore.** 1601 W Georgia St.; (604) 682-3377 or (800) 228-3000
This comfortable chain hotel sits right at the entrance of Stanley Park. **$$$-$$$$**

✗ **Bianco Nero.** ✯
475 W. Georgia St.; (604) 682-6376
The bold black-and-white decor of this restaurant matches the bold flavors of the dishes, especially those made with lots of garlic and a little olive oil. The restaurant has one of the most comprehensive lists of Italian wines in Canada. **$$$**

✗ **Bishop's.** ✯
2183 W Fourth Ave.; (604) 738-2025
This is a great restaurant where consistently great food is served by greatly

accomplished waiters to the beautiful people who can afford it. $$$$

✕ **Caffe de Medici.**
1025 Robson St.; (604) 669-9322
This is the most pleasant restaurant of the Robson Street shopping district. The decor is tongue-in-cheek ducal Florentine; the food, especially pasta in its many incarnations, is great. The service is superb. $$$

✕ **Chartwell.** ✯
In the Four Seasons Hotel, 791 W Georgia St.; (604) 689-9333
Every city should have a clubby place like this. The food is consistently good (though chefs seem to be changing consistently often). $$$

✕ **Chez Thierry.**
1168 Hamilton; (604) 689-8425
This is one of the few restaurants anywhere still doing traditional French food—and the regulars love it. $$

✕ **Corsi Trattoria.** ✯ 1 Lonsdale Ave., North Vancouver; (604) 987-9910
This little trattoria run by the Corsi family is about as authentic as a simple Italian restaurant can get hereabouts. $$

✕ **Grand King Seafood Restaurant.** ✯
705 W Broadway; (604) 876-7855
Don't let the mundane setting in a run-of-the-mill Holiday Inn scare you off. Renowned Chinese chef Lam Kam Shing, who gave up a job at one of Hong Kong's top restaurants to move to Vancouver, reigns supreme in the kitchen. $$$

✕ **Imperial Chinese Seafood Restaurant.** ✯ 355 Burrard St.; (604) 688-8191
This place is elegant and also has a great view of Burrard Inlet and the alpine peaks rising above the North Shore. $$

✕ **Joe Fortes Seafood House.** ✯
777 Thurlow St.; (604) 669-1940
Joe Fortes was a black immigrant from Jamaica who became a lifeguard and one of Vancouver's most beloved characters. It's only fitting that a seafood restaurant was named after him. $$

✕ **Kirin Mandarin Restaurant.** 1166 Alberni St.; (604) 682-8833; and 201-555 W 12th Ave.; (604) 879-8038
The menu has items from several Chinese culinary regions (Canton, Sichuan, Shanghai, and Beijing), but the northern Chinese items are the best. $$$

✕ **Landmark Hot Pot House.** ✯
3338 Cambie St. (near Queen Elizabeth Park); (604) 872-2868
Hot pots once were dishes meant to keep the family warm during the cold winter nights of northern China. In Vancouver's cool maritime climate, they can be perfect every night of the year. $$

✕ **Le Crocodile.** ✯✯✯
100-909 Burrard, on Smith; (604) 669-4298
This is a truly great restaurant, arguably the best in Vancouver, if not in all of B.C. Folks who have eaten at both say it's even better than its namesake in Strasbourg, France. $$$

X **Le Gavroche.** *
1616 Alberni St.; (604) 685-3924
A romantic atmosphere, good French food, and a very good list of Burgundy and Bordeaux wines have long made this one of Vancouver's top French restaurants. $$$

X **Olympia Fish Market and Oyster Company.***
820 Thurlow off Robson St.; (604) 685-0716
This fish market serves great fish and chips. Unfortunately, the place serves neither beer nor wine. $

X **The Only Seafood Cafe.** *
20 E Hastings St.; (604) 681-6546
No alcohol, no credit cards, no checks, Spartan decor, and only two booths and a counter—yet the place is always packed. You won't find fresher fish or more competently fried fish anywhere. $

X **Phnom Penh Restaurant.** **
244 E Georgia St. near Main St. (Do *not* confuse East Georgia St. in Chinatown, a small back street, with the East Georgia St. Overpass just to the south); (604) 682-5777; and 955 E Broadway; (604) 734-8898
The preparation of dishes from various Southeast Asian cuisines is about as good here as you'll find anywhere. The service is knowledgeable and friendly. $

X **The Pink Pearl.** 1132 E Hastings (east of the railroad tracks); (604) 253-4316
This cavernous, often noisy restaurant is very popular with large families because it serves great seafood at reasonable prices. $$

X **Quattro on Fourth.** *
2611 W Fourth Ave.; (604) 734-4444
Antonio Corsi, of Corsi Trattoria has created one of Vancouver's most comfortable restaurants. $$

X **Raincity Grill.** **
1193 Denman St.; (604) 685-7337
This is a comfortable restaurant with a great view of English Bay and a chef who knows how to create great dishes with fresh, local ingredients. $$

X **Raintree.** **
375 Water St.; (604) 688-5570
Eating at the Raintree over a number of years has meant following the development of a unique cooking style based on the freshest of local ingredients. The wine list is well thought out and has some British Columbia bottlings unavailable anywhere else (and often sold out at the winery as well). $$$

X **Steamworks Brewing Company.**
The Landing, 375 Water St.; (604) 689-2739
This brew pub is very popular with the young professional crowd. The windows overlook the Canada Place cruise ship dock. $$

X **Tojo's.** ***
22777 W Broadway; (604) 872-8050
Tojo Hidesaku is an artist in the great Japanese tradition. His sashimi and sushi look almost too good to eat. Be sure to grab a seat at the 10-seat sushi bar (though the service and food are also excellent at the tables). This is a truly great restaurant, worth several special trips. $$$

X Vassili's Taverna.
2884 W Broadway; (604) 733-3231
The menu is traditional because most of
the customers are, but the preparation is
excellent. Best of all, the restaurant
exudes true Greek spirit and is just sim-
ply a fun place to visit. $$

X Villa del Lupo. *
869 Hamilton St.; (604) 688-7436
This is a very comfortable restaurant
serving generous portions of exquisitely
prepared dishes. The wine list is very
good; the service is professional but
friendly. It's a perfect place for a roman-
tic night out. $$$

X William Tell. *
765 Beatty St. (in the Georgian Court
Hotel); (604) 688-3504
Erwin Doebeli, the perfect host, brings a
touch of Swiss perfection to this su-
perbly elegant, continental restaurant.
The food is grand, and so is the wine
list—one of the best in Vancouver. $$$

SUNSHINE COAST: GIBSONS

⊞ Beach Gardens Resort Hotel. 7074
Westminster Ave. (half an hour north of
the Jervis Inlet ferry); (604) 485-6267
Plain but comfortable rooms and cabins,
a marina, tennis courts and an indoor
swimming pool. In summer, it's a hang-
out for scuba divers; in winter it's popu-
lar for conventions or retreats. $$

SUNSHINE COAST: ROBERTS CREEK

⊞ Country Cottage Bed and Breakfast.
1183 Roberts Creek Rd.; (604) 885-
7448
A cottage and a lodge on a small farm
make this a rustic delight. No credit
cards. $$

X The Creek House. 1041 Roberts Creek
Rd.; (604) 885-9321
Continental cooking in a garden setting.
$$

WHISTLER

⊞ Le Chamois. 4557 Blackcomb Way;
(604) 932-8700 or (800) 777-0185
Luxury lodging at the foot of the Blackcomb ski runs. Sit by your window with
a glass of wine and watch 'em tumble off
the slopes outside. $$$$

⊞ Chateau Whistler. 4599 Chateau Blvd.;
(604) 938-8000 or (800) 441-1414
The public rooms and restaurants make
this Whistler's grandest hotel; the guest
rooms are on the small side, however.
$$$$

⊞ Durlacher Hof. 7055 Nesters Rd.;
(604) 932-1924
This is a truly great and very homey
place, the place to stay in Whistler. Erika
and Peter Durlacher are the perfect
hosts, with their authentic spirit of Aus-
trian hospitality. Once you've stayed
here, you will not want to stay anywhere
else. Best of all the Durlachers know all
the ins and outs of Whistler—the best
restaurants, ski runs, cross-country

guides, et al. Erika's breakfasts are legendary. $$$

⊡ **Timberline Lodge.**
4122 Village Green (adjacent to Conference Centre in Whistler Village); (604) 932-5211 or (800) 777-0185
A comfortable place with simple, somewhat rustic rooms right in the center of the action. $$$

✕ **Le Deux Gros.**
1200 Alta Lake Rd.; (604) 932-4611
French country food in a romantic setting that includes a fire blazing away in a massive stone fireplace. Reservations advised. $$$

✕ **Rim Rock Cafe and Oyster Bar.**
2117 Whistler Rd. (Whistler Creek in the Highland Lodge); (604) 932-5565
Dinner only. This cozy cafe has been popular with an upscale local crowd for years. Visitors treat it like a secret they'll impart only to their best friends. The fresh seafood is just that, and cooked and sauced to perfection. $$$

✕ **La Rua.** ✩✩ (formerly Le Chamois)
4557 Blackcomb Way; (604) 932-5011
Eclectic cookery in a lovely restaurant with great service. Dinner and lunch in summer; dinner only the rest of the year; reservations advised. $$

✕ **Sushi Village.**
4272 Mountain Square (second floor of the Westbrook Hotel); (604) 932-3330
A refreshing retreat from an overload of continental cookery. Yes, the seafood is fresh. $$

✕ **Val d'Isere.** ✩✩✩
433 Sundial Place (upstairs in St. Andrew's House in Whistler Village); (604) 932-4666
Dinner only; reservations highly recommended. Whistler's top restaurant and one of the best restaurants in British Columbia, Val d'Isere turns out consistently great food. $$$

Blackcomb Mountain forms the backdrop to a lodge in the Whistler ski area, considered by many to provide the finest skiing in North America.

FRASER RIVER
AND LOWER MAINLAND

■ HIGHLIGHTS

Fraser River Canyon
Fraser River Delta
Harrison Lake
Richmond
Steveston
Westminster Abbey in Mission
White Rock

■ LANDSCAPE

THE LOWER FRASER VALLEY is unusually flat for a province where much of the landscape is vertical and where rivers always seem to be gushing over rocks. Once an arm of the sea, the Fraser Valley became flat as it was slowly filled by sand and silt carried downstream by the river and deposited here over a period of millions of years.

The Fraser River rises in the Rocky Mountains in Mount Robson Provincial Park near the Alberta border, not far from the sources of the Columbia, and flows at first in a northwesterly direction through the Rocky Mountain Trench towards the Yukon and Alaska. After leaving this deep narrow valley a few miles north of Prince George, the river turns sharply to the south. As it collects waters from tributaries—the Nechako, Chilcotin, and West Road—the volume of the river increases. Below Quesnel, the river cuts a steep-walled canyon through the mountains. The Thompson River, flowing in from the east, almost doubles the Fraser's volume of water. Between Lytton and Yale—the stretch known as the Fraser River Canyon—the river flows through a deep, beautiful gorge above which tower craggy peaks rising to almost 3,050 meters (10,000 ft) to the west and 2,135 meters (7,000 ft) to the east.

South of Yale, the mountains recede. At Yale, the river turns west through the flat lower Fraser Valley, which was once a glaciated fjord, but has been filled with alluvial debris the river carried from the mountains. To the north, the valley is hemmed in by steep, deeply cut mountains; to the south it stretches across the border into northwest Washington's Nooksack Plain.

After skirting the southern city limits of New Westminster, Burnaby, and Vancouver, the Fraser empties into the Strait of Georgia through the two main channels of a delta, after having traveled 1,368 kilometers (850 mi). The bottomlands along the lower river and the islands of the delta are protected from seasonal floods by tall dikes—which are open to the public and make for some great walks above the marshy edge of river and tidewater.

Deep-water freighters ascend the river as far as New Westminster. Fishing boats and other commercial vessels with shallow draft can go further upriver. Several species of salmon spawn in the Fraser and its tributaries, but stocks have been depleted in recent years, causing a virtual shutdown of the fishery. Because of the importance of these salmon runs, the Fraser has no dams for generating hydroelectric power and is thus the last major, free-flowing river of the Northwest. Upriver settlements of the river are dominated by logging and other forest industries; the lower Fraser Valley has highly productive dairies and farms.

■ HISTORY

The Fraser River is named for fur trader Simon Fraser, who explored much of it in 1808. The Hudson's Bay Company founded Fort Langley on the lower Fraser in 1827, anticipating a Fraser River route to the interior, but though that hope was dashed, the HBC kept the profitable fort. (Today it has been restored and is a popular visitor attraction.) In March of 1858 prospectors made a first big gold strike on the Fraser River, 10 miles north of Hope. Within weeks, gold seekers from adjacent Washington and from faraway California streamed into what was then the British territory of New Caledonia. The **Fraser River Gold Rush** was short but violent. In early summer of 1858, miners and Indians clashed at Spuzzum because the local Indians believed, quite reasonably, that any gold found in their river should belong to them. In retaliation, the miners destroyed an Indian village. The British Government quickly established the new colony of British Columbia on the mainland and passed laws to govern its inhabitants.

(following pages) The dramatic Fraser River Valley is one of British Columbia's most fertile agricultural regions.

Roads came late to the lower Fraser Valley because the lands bordering the river were covered by tall trees, swamps, and marshes. **New Westminster,** at the head of navigation for deep-water vessels, became the region's major port and served as capital of British Columbia until 1868, when the provincial legislature moved to Victoria.

After the budding city of Vancouver, on ice-free Burrard Inlet, was chosen as the terminus of the transcontinental railway, the lower Fraser River became a rather polluted industrial zone of salmon canneries and lumber mills. The marshy north bank of the river in Burnaby and South Vancouver and the islands of the delta were diked by farmers—many of them Chinese—who raised produce for the Vancouver market as well as for railroad dining cars and ocean liner dining rooms.

Vancouver's origins lay with the timber trade. Three lumber mills came into being along Burrard Inlet during the early 1860s, supplying spars and masts for trading vessels and navies around the world. (City of Vancouver Archives)

Today many of these farms survive, despite urban encroachment. The cupolas of gundhwaras (temples) rising above the river are the heritage of Sikh immigrants, who came from India to work in logging camps and lumber mills. Today, with the arrival of immigrants from Hong Kong, tall condominium and apartment buildings are changing the face of the lower river, especially in the former farming community of Richmond.

■ RICHMOND

Richmond, on Lulu Island, is separated from Vancouver by the north arm of the Fraser River, but you'll see very little but fields and farms as you cross the island on the BC 99 freeway. Until recently, much of Richmond was agricultural. During the glory years of salmon canning, when sockeye were incredibly plentiful, Japanese fishermen settled at Steveston Harbour, at the southwestern tip of the island, near the banks the salmon had to cross as they entered the south channel of the Fraser. Chinese produce stands lined the Steveston Highway and other island roads; a small Chinese commercial center, with shops and restaurants, sprung up near the intersection of the Westminster Highway and No. 3 Road.

When huge shopping malls became popular, land inside Vancouver city limits was too expensive and the malls moved south to the dairy pastures of Richmond. Inexpensive land also attracted Chinese investors who left Hong Kong to avoid the takeover of the British crown colony by China.

Since the middle of the 1980s, Hong Kong money has thoroughly transformed Richmond. Large—and very fancy—homes now crowd into pastures where black-and-white cows grazed not so long ago, and highrise condominiums are replacing barns and silos. **Aberdeen Centre** in northwest Richmond was the first major Chinese mall outside Asia. Though it is somewhat "North-Americanized" with a bowling alley at its south end serving "fusion" fast food, it mostly has purely Chinese shops, from fishmongers to ginseng dealers, from news vendors to video outlets, with nary an English sign to be seen. A cash machine offers users a choice of written instructions in the British Columbia's three "official" languages: English, French, and Chinese. During Chinese New Year and at other important events, lion dancers invade the shops as they step to the sound of gongs, drums, and firecrackers.

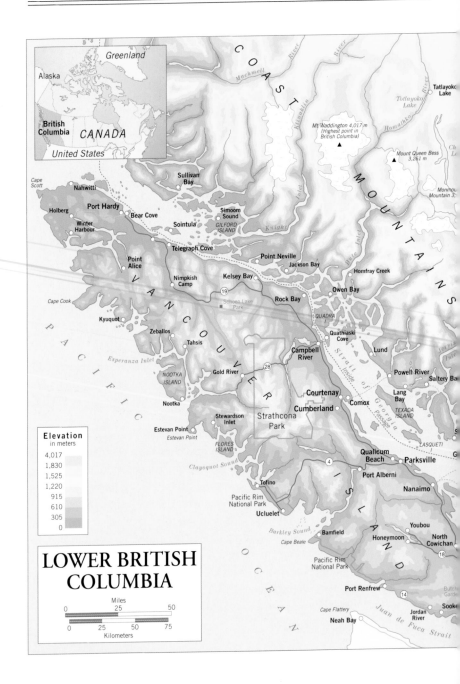

Greenland

Alaska

British
Columbia CANADA

United States

C O A S T

Macmell

River

River

Columbia

Totlayoko
Lake

Tatlayoko
Lake

Mt Waddington 4,017 m
(Highest point in
British Columbia) ▲

Homathko

Monmou
Mountain 3,

Mount Queen Bess
3,261 m ▲

Ch
L

Cape
Scott

Nahwitti

Sullivan
Bay

M O U N T A I N S

Holberg

Port Hardy

Bear Cove

Winter
Harbour

Simoom
Sound

Sointula GILFORD
ISLAND

Knight

Inlet

Telegraph Cove

Point
Alice

Point Neville

Jackson Bay

Bute Inlet

Homfray Creek

Nimpkish
Camp

Kelsey Bay

Owen Bay

V A N C O U V E R

Cape Cook

19

Schoen Lake
Park

Rock Bay

QUADRA

Kyuquot

Zeballos

Tahsis

Quathiaski
Cove

Strait

Lund

P A C I F I C

Esperanza Inlet

NOOTKA
ISLAND

Gold River

28

Campbell
River

of

Inside

Powell River

Saltery Ba

Lang
Bay

TEXADA
ISLAND

Georgia

Passage

Nootka

Courtenay

Comox

Cumberland

Stewardson
Inlet

Strathcona
Park

LASQUETI

Estevan Point

Estevan Point

FLORES
ISLAND

Qualicum
Beach

Parksville

Clayoquot Sound

I S L A N D

4

Port Alberni

Nanaimo

Tofino

Pacific Rim
National Park

Ucluelet

Barkley Sound

Bamfield

Cape Beale

Youbou

Honeymoon

North
Cowichan

18

Pacific Rim
National Park

O C E A N

Port Renfrew

14

Butch
Garde

Cape Flattery

Neah Bay

Juan de Fuca Strait

Jordan
River

Sooke

Elevation
in meters

4,017	
1,830	
1,525	
1,220	
915	
610	
305	
0	

LOWER BRITISH
COLUMBIA

Miles
0   25   50

0   25   50   75
Kilometers

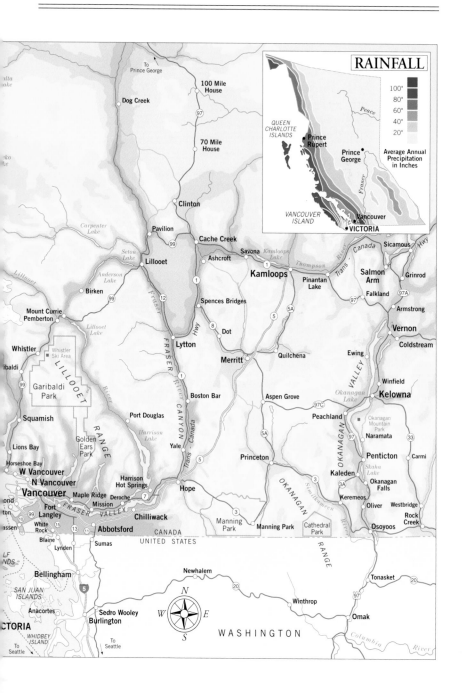

RAINFALL

100"
80"
60"
40"
20"

Average Annual
Precipitation
in Inches

QUEEN
CHARLOTTE
ISLANDS

Prince
Rupert

Prince
George

Peace

Canada

Fraser

VANCOUVER
ISLAND

Vancouver

VICTORIA

To
Prince George

Dog Creek

100 Mile
House

97

70 Mile
House

Clinton

Carpenter
Lake

Pavilion

99

Cache Creek

Savona

Kamloops
Lake

Sicamous

Hwy

alta
ake

Seton
Lake

Lillooet

Ashcroft

1

Kamloops

Thompson

Trans

Salmon
Arm

Grinrod

ko
ke

Lillooet

Anderson
Lake

Birken

99

1

12

Spences Bridges

Pinantan
Lake

97

Falkland

97A

Armstrong

Mount Currie
Pemberton

Lillooet
Lake

Fraser

Hwy

8

Dot

5

5A

Vernon

Whistler

Whistler
Ski Area

Lytton

Merritt

Quilchena

Ewing

Coldstream

ibaldi

99

LILLOOET

Garibaldi
Park

FRASER RIVER CANYON

1

Boston Bar

Aspen Grove

Okanagan
Lake

VALLEY

Winfield

Kelowna

Squamish

RANGE

Port Douglas

Harrison
Lake

Trans Canada

97C

Peachland

Okanagan
Mountain
Park

OKANAGAN

97

Naramata

33

Lions Bay

Golden
Ears
Park

Yale

5

Princeton

5A

Penticton

Carmi

Horseshoe Bay

W Vancouver
N Vancouver
Vancouver

Harrison
Hot Springs

Maple Ridge

Deroche

Kaleden

Skaha
Lake

Okanagan
Falls

ond
ton

99

Fraser

Mission

7

Hope

3

OKANAGAN

Keremeos

3A

Oliver

Westbridge

10

Fort
Langley

VALLEY

Chilliwack

Similkameen

River

Rock
Creek

assen

White
Rock

15

13

11

Abbotsford

Manning
Park

Manning Park

Cathedral
Park

Osoyoos

Blaine

Sumas

CANADA

UNITED STATES

RANGE

Lynden

LF
NDS

Bellingham

Newhalem

Tonasket

20

SAN JUAN
ISLANDS

5

20

97

Anacortes

Sedro Wooley
Burlington

Winthrop

Omak

N
W   E
S

CTORIA

WHIDBEY
ISLAND

To
Seattle

WASHINGTON

Columbia

River

To
Seattle

The **Yaohan Centre** one block north, off No. 3 Road, is even larger and has more important shops, including a very upscale supermarket with both Chinese and Japanese foods. This is a great place to buy fresh and unusual vegetables, great seafood, take-out sashimi and sushi, and rare Asian dainties. For those in a hurry, there is a food court where diners indulge in such fast-food delicacies as suckling pig on a bun, Chinese oyster omelet (the parent dish of San Francisco's "hangtown fry"), and durian milk shakes.

All of these new malls have ample parking; the **Parker Place**, a few blocks south, has additional parking on the roof. That's important to know, because **Floata**, one of the area's most popular restaurants, is in the center, and there are always traffic jams in the regular lot. Parker Place has two other attractions: a large Buddha in the parking lot—always surrounded by flower offerings—and a superb tea shop, **Arteas Chinese Tea** at 1545-4380 No. 3 Road. Look for objects made from jade in the jewelry shops—the selection is very good, because B.C. is the world's top supplier of jade.

Parker Place II next door is a maze of small shops connected by narrow hallways. There's no barrier between the two places, but the narrow aisles tell you immediately when you've stepped from one into the other.

The **Richmond Public Market** south of the Westminster Highway near No. 3 Road has mostly Chinese vendors, with food booths, vegetable and fish mongers, knick-knack merchants, and fast-food restaurants. It's open daily, but Tuesday is "optional open" day when most stalls are closed.

If all that rich mall fare overwhelms you, restore the harmony of your digestive system at **Bo Kong,** a vegetarian restaurant that's as much a learning experience as a dining place *(see page 86).*

To reach the Richmond Chinese district, take the Steveston Highway west from BC 99 (just north of the Fraser River tunnel) and turn right on No. 3 Road (beyond the magnificent Chinese Temple on the left). Or take the Westminster Highway west from BC 99 to No. 3 Road.

■ STEVESTON

Steveston, a small fishing port on the south shore of Lulu Island, near the mouth of the Fraser River, looks as though it had sprung straight from the pages of a John Steinbeck novel. It has kept its unique identity even though several chic shops and restaurants have opened in recent years. Once a separate community, Steveston is now part of Richmond but has, so far, kept urban sprawl limited to the fringes.

Until World War II, Steveston was home to many Japanese fishermen. During the war, the Japanese were interned and their boats sold to Anglo fishermen for a song. A few shops stocking Japanese goods, and a take-out sushi bar, are reminders of the town's Japanese period. An old cannery and shipyard along the refurbished waterfront have been turned into museums. At the public dock in the boat harbor, you can buy fish right off the boat. Look for boats with awnings draped across the boom—a sign they are selling that day.

You reach Steveston by taking No. 1 Road south from the Steveston Highway. If you continue to the end of road, you can park your car in a small public lot and take a levee trail along the Strait of Georgia waterfront past a virtual wilderness of reeds and other marsh plants, where you hear no sounds other than the soughing of wind in the reeds, the trill of redwings and the chirping of sparrows, the screaming of sea birds, and the occasional putt-putt of a fishing-boat engine. Take No. 5 Road south for access to levee walks along the Fraser.

You can't miss a magnificent Chinese temple just south of Steveston Road. The red-and-gold structure has curved roofs decorated with dragons. Inside the great hall are golden images. Ancestor tablets are set up around the margins. Visitors are welcome (remember to remove your shoes before entering the building and to refrain from disturbing worshippers.) A tea room below the temple is a good place for sampling different Chinese teas. Tables in a courtyard garden have displays of miniature rock landscapes and pots of miniature trees.

Other sights of interest include the **Gulf of Georgia Cannery National Historic Site** at 12138 Fourth Avenue, which has exhibits about the British Columbia fishing industry from the days when salmon were plentiful and the industry boomed. The **Britannia Heritage Shipyard** on the Steveston waterfront, is a combination shipyard and park linked to the harbor by the Richmond trail system.

■ NATURE RESERVES

At **Richmond Nature Park,** 11851 Westminster Highway just beyond No. 5 Road (which is one block west of the BC 99 freeway), trails wind through a lowland of forest and bog. Look for wild cranberries, labrador tea, and sundew (an insect-eating plant). The Nature House has exhibits and interpretive programs.

South of the Fraser River, drive to **Reifel Migratory Bird Sanctuary,** located 9.6 km (6 miles) west of Ladner on Westham Island. Sandhill cranes, swans, bald eagles, and other birds can be seen here in season. Birdseed is for sale and there is an admission fee.

■ TOWNS AND SIGHTS ALONG HIGHWAY 99

As you travel north or south on BC 99, you can spot the houses of the town of **Surrey** to the east hidden among the trees on gravelly ridges left by continental glaciers as they withdrew. The flat lands in the foreground are farmland protected by an ordinance that allows urban expansion only on lands without value to agriculture.

Though workers in local vegetable fields often wear broad conical Chinese straw hats, Surrey's ethnic make-up is becoming largely East Indian, especially in its north end. Look for the gilded domes of two temples east of the freeway. Feel free to visit a temple, but maintain the respect due a place of worship. During mealtimes, local Sikhs and Hindus may invite strangers to a free meal—after the food has first been offered to the local sage or deity, who "consumes its spiritual essence."

❖

White Rock, a typical beach town just north of Semiahmoo Bay (which is in the U.S.), has lots of sand, beachfront restaurants, and resort shops. In very warm summers, the beach looks much like a Southern California beach; in cold or

(above) A popular event at Harrison Hot Springs is the annual World Championship Sand Sculpture Contest. (opposite) Wonder Years Antiques in Spuzzum along Highway 1 in the Fraser River Canyon.

inclement weather, visitors bundle up and take long hikes along the tidal edge or enjoy a pint in a local pub.

❖

New Westminster, once the bustling capital of British Columbia and a busy river port, is today primarily a bedroom community of Vancouver. The grim, crenelated walls of the British Columbia penitentiary rose above the river here, until they were torn down in the mid-1980s to make room for condominiums.

New Westminster Public Market occupies a huge, modern building on the Fraser River quay, west of downtown New Westminster and just a block from the SkyTrain terminal. Downstairs are a profusion of food shops: delis, produce vendors, cheese- and fishmongers, et al. Upstairs are shops and restaurants ranging from fast-food eateries to fancy stuff. All have window seats for river watching (tugs, barges, log rafts, and an occasional freighter). Tugboats tie up at the wharf outside and an old sternwheel dredge, the *Samson V,* is permanently berthed at the quay (open weekends). The market is open daily. There's ample free parking. To get there, take the SkyTrain from downtown Vancouver to New Westminster or follow Marine Drive east until you see the market on your right. You can't miss it. From Highway 99, take the Annacis Highway north across the new Alex Fraser Bridge to New Westminster. Follow this road until you see the market.

Enjoy a meal or drink on a riverside terrace and watch the water flow by, or take a tour of the river. Between May and October, **Fraser River Connection** will give you a paddlewheeler tour of the river from New Westminster to Fort Langley; (604) 525-4465.

❖

Fort Langley is a must for history buffs. This fort, consisting of a wooden palisade and half a dozen odd buildings (most of them reconstructed, except those on the river side, where the bluff was cut off by a modern highway), was once the most important British stronghold in the Pacific Northwest. Founded in 1827, a dozen years after Hudson's Bay Company headquarters had been established at Fort Vancouver (now Vancouver, Washington), it is the oldest white settlement along the inland waters. Fort Langley predates Victoria, British Columbia's oldest city (founded as a fort in 1843).

Fort Langley was founded not so much as a military post (though the HBC put up a couple of bastions, with guns, to keep Americans at bay) but as a trading post and supply house for the inland waters from Puget Sound to southeast Alaska. It was here, by the way, that one of the Northwest's great industries got its start: salmon packing.

The fort has very friendly and knowledgeable tour guides. To reach Fort Langley take the Trans-Canada Highway (Route 1) east from Vancouver towards Hope. Follow signs to Fort Langley National Historic Park. The fort is open from 10 A.M. to 4:30 P.M.

Visitors and worshippers are welcome at **Westminster Abbey,** a starkly modern Catholic monastery rising high above the Fraser River (follow signs; the entrance is in back, away from the river).

❖

Sixty-four-kilometer (40-m)- long **Harrison Lake,** is one of several long and narrow fjord-like lakes cutting through the spine of the mountains. Others are Stave Lake and Pitt Lake to the west, also accessible via BC 7. The westernmost of these lakes, Indian Arm, stretches north from Burrard Inlet. Tall mountains shield Harrison Lake's beaches from inclement weather. Harrison Hot Springs is a small resort community at the southern end of the lake, just north of BC 7, with a large resort hotel. A public pool fed by natural hot springs invites bathers at the venerable **Harrison Hot Springs Hotel** (rooms can range from plain to luxurious, depending on whether you lodge in an old or new part of the hotel); 100 Esplanade *(see page 85)*.

The historic **Kilby Store and Farm** in nearby Harrison Mills gives you a glimpse into British Columbia farm life during the 1920s, with a country store, farm kitchen, dairy house, barn, orchards, and fields. 215 Kilby Road, off BC 7— follow signs—Harrison Mills.

A road runs south from Harrison Lake to TCH, Route 1. You might want to visit **Minter Gardens** at exit 135 in Rosedale, a 26-acre estate with several theme gardens, among them a Chinese, English, fern, fragrance, and rose garden, and a giant evergreen maze in a style once popular on English estates.

■ FRASER RIVER CANYON

The Fraser River Canyon is one of the most beautiful of Northwest places, especially now that the new Coquihalla Highway (opening a more direct route between Vancouver and Kamloops) has siphoned off much of the heavy truck traffic. The canyon takes on a mystical quality on rainy or foggy days, when the tall cliffs tumbling down to the raging river look incredibly romantic.

About half-way up the canyon is dramatic **Hell's Gate,** where the river gushes through a narrow chasm. You can take an aerial tram down the cliff to an observation deck or you can hike down a dirt road to the river. Spectacular.

■ TO THE EAST

From Hope, where the Fraser Canyon begins, you can take the **Crow's Nest Highway** (Highway 3) east to the **Okanagan.** On the way you'll pass through **Manning Park**—a great place for alpine hikes—and Keremeos, where the cherries are particularly fine in season. The road ends in **Osoyoos**—where the locals make believe, by way of architectural embellishments, they're in Southern California (that retirement-home dream slumbering in every Canadian's heart). If you have time, here's a great loop trip: Seattle north to Vancouver; from Vancouver east on the Trans Canada Highway (Route 1) to Hope; from Hope on the Crow's Nest Highway to the Okanagan; then south across the border to the Okanogan on Highway 97 and back to the west side by either the North Cascades or Stevens Pass Highway. Allow at least three days for the loop so you have time to enjoy the sights.

Sunrise over Deer Lake in Sasquatch Provincial Park.
(opposite) A view down the Fraser River Canyon in the Hell's Gate area.

OKANAGAN VALLEY WINERY TOUR

■ EAST FROM THE FRASER VALLEY

Among the high points of visiting British Columbia's Okanagan Valley are the approaches: no matter how you drive there, the road will be incredibly scenic. If you take BC 3, the Crow's Nest Highway, east from the Fraser Valley, you'll soon find yourself in an alpine landscape of tall peaks, deeply glaciated canyons, and colorful wildflower meadows alternating with dense forests. The scenery changes from forests to grasslands and bare rocks, as you cross the divide between the coast and the interior, but it remains beautiful.

The approaches from the south are equally beautiful—via WA 20, the North Cascades Highway, and US 97 north to the border, or by taking US 97 north from Interstate 90. If you come from the south, you'll get a surprise as soon as you cross the border. The American Okanogan Valley is a sparsely populated region of orchards and range land; the Canadian Okanagan Valley is not. (Note that Americans and Canadians spell the name of the valley differently.) Just north of the line sprawls the city of Osoyoos, a retirement mecca. Don't be surprised when you see a profusion of whitewashed arches and red tile roofs rising above sandy beaches. The town decided on a Spanish theme for its architecture (because it's so far south). On a sunny day, it makes you feel like you've been suddenly dropped into Southern California.

But as you head north, you're soon back in the farm country. Besides growing grapes, the Okanagan is British Columbia's fruit basket. In early summer, roadside stands sell cherries; in summer they're loaded to their canvas roofs with peaches; in fall, at grape harvest, it's apple time. The valley even has its own apple: the crisp, reddish-purple, tart-sweet Spartan, which was developed here in the 1920s. Its cultivation has spread to the U.S., but it is nowhere better than here in the valley of its birth. Do yourself a favor. Stop at a roadside stand and buy some. This brings us to a curious customs law. While you cannot usually bring fruits from Canada into the U.S., you are allowed to bring in British Columbia apples. By the box, if such is your desire. But you cannot bring Washington apples into British Columbia. It's against the law.

The Okanagan Valley is exceptionally scenic and gets prettier as you drive north. That's because it is a deep trough carved by a continental glacier. Places where the glacier encountered soft rock, and scoured deeper, are now filled with water. A chain of deep lakes, connected by the Okanagan River, stretches intermittently north from the U.S. border to the head of the valley near Armstrong. Mountains rise steeply to heights of 1,800 to 2,000 meters (6,000 and 7,000 ft) from the waters of the largest of these lakes, appropriately called Okanagan, leaving little land for cultivation or settlements along its shores.

But without the mitigating influence of this lake, which has never been fathomed and is too deep to freeze over in winter, viticulture would be all but impossible in the valley. Even so, some growers have been known to bury their vines to protect them from killing freezes.

■ FIRST PLANTINGS

British Columbia's first grapes were planted in the 1860s, near Okanagan Mission on the lake's east shore, by Charles Pandosy, an oblate missionary, for religious use and personal consumption. The padre left no record about the quality of his wines.

Until the late 1980s, the British Columbia wine industry limped along with low-quality, high-alcohol wines. While a few vintners, most notably George and Trudy Heiss at Gray Monk, planted quality grapes in the early 1980s, the tide did not turn until 1988, when a free trade agreement, plus a GATT ruling against Canada's protective tariffs, took effect. Until then, British Columbia vintners made wine from the cheapest fruit available: berries, apples, and hybrid grapes guaranteed by the Canadian government to withstand the severe winters. The agreement broke the power of the grape marketing board to set prices and to force wineries to buy everything the growers produced. Competition from American wines intensified. With wineries free to set their own quality standards for grapes, they could now pay premium prices for high quality grapes. Almost overnight 2,400 acres (two thirds of the British Columbia vineyards) were pulled up and replanted with European *vinifera* varieties—the vines that have made the wines of California, Oregon, and Washington famous. To make good wine from these more expensive grapes, the wineries also brought in professionally trained winemakers.

Less than a decade later, the results are spectacular. British Columbia wine promoter Jurgen Gothe declared, "We don't have to apologize anymore." He's right. The Okanagan Valley is worth exploring for its wines. Many wineries are still in the early development stage—as they were in California in the 1950s and in the Northwest in the 1970s. Keep your eyes open for signs as you drive along. You may discover a winery no one has, as yet, heard about. Be sure to call wineries for directions.

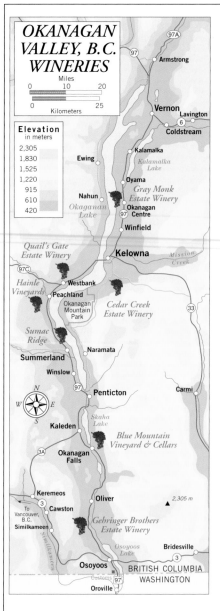

OKANAGAN VALLEY, B.C. WINERIES

Miles
0   10   20

0   25
Kilometers

Elevation
in meters

2,305
1,830
1,525
1,220
915
610
420

■ WINERIES

Gehringer Brothers Estate Winery
At the southern end of the valley between Osoyoos and Oliver on BC 97 is the turnoff road (326th Avenue) for Gehringer Brothers Estate Winery. This winery makes some very good riesling and, if conditions are right in late fall, an ice wine (wine made from the intensified juice of grapes frozen on the vine); (250) 498-3537.

Blue Mountain Vineyard & Cellars
Located a few miles to the north in Okanagan Falls, this winery makes very good sparkling wine, as well as pinot noir, pinot blanc, and pinot gris. While most red wines made in this valley lack varietal character, the Blue Mountain pinot noir has a tasty share of it; off Hwy. 97 on Allendale Rd.; (250) 497-8244.

After Penticton, BC 97, the main north-south highway, runs along the western shore of Lake Okanagan through a landscape alternating between steep cliffs and fertile alluvial fans.

Sumac Ridge Estate Winery
Just north of the small town of Summerland, you'll see a sign for this winery. Don't turn around when you see golf links. You haven't strayed. This pioneering winery was established in

A view of the Okanagan Valley.

1981 in the clubhouse of a golf course. Grapes were planted between the fairways. (Look for yellow-bellied marmots in the rough—they predate the golf course.) Sumac Ridge has gained a good reputation for its sparkling wines and gewurztraminer, and for a hybrid red called chancellor. It's quite good, though its taste will not remind you at all of, say, Sonoma merlot. A small restaurant at the winery serves simple food and has a deck where you can enjoy the wines outside on a sunny day; (250) 494-0451.

The next town up the road is called Peachland, because peaches are what the area is famous for. There are also a few wineries high above the lake on benchlands.

Hainle Vineyards

This winery makes very good pinot blanc, a good pinot noir and chardonnay and was the first winery in B.C. to make ice wine; (250) 767-2525.

At Westbank, BC 97C comes in from the west. This is the fast road to the coast, via Merritt and the Coquihalla toll road (BC 5).

Quails Gate Estate Winery

In the town of Westbank, Quails Gate produces chardonnay and pinot noir and makes a late-harvest botrytis-affected wine from the German optima grape. To reach the winery turn east on Gellatly Rd., then north on Boucherie Rd.; (250) 769-4451.

BC 97 crosses the lake to Kelowna, the valley's largest city, on a floating bridge. Look for Ogopogo, purported to be a monster of the Loch Ness variety that has been spotted here occasionally. Kelowna is the cheapest place in the valley for food and lodging.

Cedar Creek Estate Winery

Off BC 97, Pandosy Street runs along the east side of the lake and takes you 14 km (8.4 mi) south to this winery, located near

A tasting room in the Okanagan Valley.

the site of the mission where Father Pandosy planted B.C.'s first grapes. Cedar Creek makes very good pinot blanc, gewurztraminer, and pinot auxerrois, a somewhat obscure French white wine grape that seems to have found its home in the Okanagan Valley. There's also a quaffable "Proprietor's Reserve" white; (250) 764-8866.

Gray Monk Estate Winery

A true pioneer of B.C. wine, this last winery on our tour occupies a splendid site north of Kelowna in **Okanagan Centre,** high above the lake. For more than a decade, Gray Monk has made the valley's most exciting wine. Starting in 1982, vintners George and Trudy Heiss revolutionized both grape-growing and winemaking techniques in the valley. They succeeded with planting where government-paid experimenters did not, and set the stage for the production of high quality vinifera wines in the Okanagan Valley. The winery takes its name from a name of the pinot gris grape in the Heisses' native Austria. Of course, pinot gris is among the best wines made by winemaker George Heiss, Jr., as well as an excellent pinot auxerrois and rose called "Rotberger;" (250) 766-3168.

❖

North of here, the vineyards give way to pastures and fields. In spring, the sandy soils of the Armstrong region produce excellent asparagus.

The bounty of a roadside fruit stand serves as a testimony to the abundant produce of British Columbia's interior valleys.

Pinot noir grapes, a varietal that has proved particularly well suited to the Pacific Northwest.

■ TRAVEL AND CLIMATE

■ GETTING THERE

Most visitors to British Columbia arrive by car and cross into Canada at the Blaine border crossing (one of the few that is open 24 hours). North of the border, Interstate 5 changes to BC 99 but remains a freeway all the way to the Vancouver city limits. Because British Columbia has laws protecting its sparse farmlands, the road traverses a landscape of green pastures and fields, though you can spot suburban housing developments among the trees on gravelly ridges east of the freeway. About 10 miles north of the border, BC 10 turns west to the Vancouver Island ferry terminal at Tsawwassen.

The delta of the Fraser River has fallen victim to development, but east of New Westminster, the valley is still a pastoral idyll. To the north and east, the tall, craggy peaks of the Coast and Cascade mountains rise straight from the valley floor. To the south, in northwest Washington, snow-capped Mount Baker towers over fir-clad foothills. The river winds placidly through green meadows and cottonwood and birch forests. The **Trans-Canada Highway** (TCH) Route 1, a four-lane freeway, is the main route running east through level farmlands. Because of the proximity to the Vancouver metropolitan area—and because few travelers linger in this quietly beautiful landscape—there are few lodging facilities and restaurants of note. Scenic BC 7 skirts the rocky northern bank of the river, meeting the TCH west of Hope. Side roads lead to mountain lakes and to Harrison Hot Springs, the valley's major resort. Several two-lane highways—BC 11, 13, and 15—run from the TCH south to the border crossings at Sumas, Lynden, and Blaine.

NOTE: Speed limits and distances in British Columbia are posted in kilometers, not miles!

■ CLIMATE

The weather in the lower Fraser Valley tends to be a few degrees milder and less rainy than that in Vancouver; the upper valley is hotter in summer and colder in winter with heavy snowfall near the mountains. Heavy rain melting the mountain snows can cause severe flooding of the lowlands in the fall and spring and lead to the closure of roads. Frigid northeasters can sweep down the valley in winter and freeze up creeks and ponds. Once or twice during the last century the weather turned so cold that the Fraser River froze to its mouth—quite definitely an uncommon occurrence.

■ ACCOMMODATIONS AND RESTAURANTS

☎   For chain lodgings see toll-free numbers on page 352.

$$ For room and restaurant price designations see page 352.

✭   Means highly recommended.

CHILLIWACK

X **La Mansione Ristorante.**
46290 Yale Rd. E; (604) 792-8910
The name of this restaurant, like the food, is a mixture of languages. But the mixed culinary metaphors work well in this Tudor-style mansion. The restaurant has an extensive selection of wines by the glass—which comes in handy when you're exploring the different flavors of B.C. wines. $$

FORT LANGLEY

X **The Bedford House.**
9272 Glover Rd. (near the Fraser River at the turnoff for Fort Langley Park); (604) 888-2333
A pretty restaurant in a 1904 house with a view of the river. The food is traditional, of the rich, continental ilk. But such dishes as broiled salmon with hollandaise sauce can be perfect. $$

HARRISON HOT SPRINGS

☎ **The Harrison Hotel.**
100 Esplanade Ave.; (604) 796-2244
This hotel rises above the southern end of long, fjord-like Harrison Lake, on the site of an older hotel that was built in 1885 but burned down in 1926. There's good reason for a such a large hotel at the edge of the wilderness: the hot springs. The sprawling hotel complex with its extensive gardens, tennis courts and indoor (32 and 39 degrees C) and outdoor pools (32 degrees C) is about as close to luxury as you get at Western hot springs. $$$

X **Black Forest.** ✭
180 Esplanade Ave.; (604) 796-9343
British Columbians seem to associate steaks with Germany's black forest, for there are several steakhouses by that name in the province. This is one of the better ones. $$-$$$

KEREMEOS

☎ **Cathedral Lakes Resort.** (Call for directions); (250) 226-7560
This resort is very remote—you'll have to drive 21 km on a gravel road to a pickup point where the lodge's 4 x 4 will pick you up. Then it's another hour over an even rougher road. Once you're there, however, it's all worth it. The lodge is in the heart of Cathedral Lakes Provincial Park and has some great hiking, canoeing, and fishing. The land rises from 1,800 to 2,400 meters, and on clear day you can see Mt. Baker, Mt. Rainier, and the Kootenays. The park is a wildlife refuge where an occasional grizzly or cougar may cross your trail. (A local woman was killed near Princeton by a cougar in August of 1996 while trying to shield her six-year-old son from an attack.) $$

LADNER

☖ **River Run Floating Cottage.**

4551 River Rd.; (604) 946-7778
This cottage, docked among houseboats, has some very nice amenities: a claw-footed tub, a wood-burning potbelly stove, and cooking facilities. Chances are that ducks and geese will drop in for dinner. (A hot breakfast is delivered to the cottage.) In season, look for salmon leaping in the river and for bald eagles patrolling the banks. Two one-bedroom cottages on shore have wood-burning stoves. **$$**

MANNING PROVINCIAL PARK

☖ **Manning Park Motel.**

Hwy. 3; (250) 840-8822
This rather plain motel is part of a roadside development inside the park that also has a restaurant, a coffeeshop, and cabins. It is close to hiking and riding trails. In winter there's downhill and cross-country skiing. **$$**

PRINCETON

✕ **The Apple Tree Restaurant.** ⚹

255 Vermilion Ave.; (250) 295-7745
This excellent small restaurant in an unlikely spot is a perfect place to break up the drive between Vancouver and the interior. But the food here is so good you'll want to brave the Crows Nest Highway over and over again, just so you can eat here. There's an excellent wine list with selections from the nearby Okanagan Valley wineries. **$**

QUILCHENA

☖ **Quilchena Hotel.**

Hwy. 5A North; (250) 378-2611
This very quiet, somewhat seedy cattle-country hangout is quite popular with urbanites escaping the city noise and lights, even though the comfort and ambience are just a step above summer camp. **$$**

RICHMOND

Hong Kong money is pouring into town at such a rapid rate that new restaurants are springing up every month. Food standards are very high, even at the take-out places in the glitzy new shopping malls. At any of these malls you can have an incredible gourmet meal just by buying food at different take-out counters. There's a noodle house serving very inexpensive food at almost every major street corner. Or drop by a barbecue house, pick up the fixings for a picnic, and head down to the levees.

✕ **Bo Kong.** ⚹

8100 Ackroyd Rd.; (604) 278-1992
This is a vegetarian restaurant that's as much a learning experience as a dining place. Be sure to taste the five-spice bean-curd roll stuffed with mushroom, the tofu and eggplant, the hot-and-sour thick soup, and the bean-curd skin roll with black bean sauce. **$-$$**

✕ **Floata.** ⚹⚹

Parker Place Shopping Centre, 1425-4380 No. 3 Rd.; (if you can't find a parking space in the crowded parking lot, try the roof); (604) 270-8889

This elegantly appointed restaurant has been popular from the day it opened. Be prepared for a long wait if you come for dim sum. But it's worth it. The selection is very diverse and very tasty. The friendly staff will point out special tidbits. **$$**

X **Steveston Seafood House.** ★★
3951 Moncton St.; (604) 271-5252
The outside of this regional favorite is a bit drab, and the decor is old-fashioned in a 1950s way, but the service and the food are excellent. Don't let cutesy menu names like "Jonathan Livingston Seafood," and "The Contented Sole" turn you off. The ingredients are fresh and the preparation is perfect. Portions are huge. **$$**

X **Sun Sui Wah.** ★
Alderbridge Pl., 4940 No. 3 Rd.; (604) 273-8208
This elegant restaurant is an extension of a very successful Hong Kong chain. Dim sum is especially diversified and interesting. **$$**

X **Top Gun Chinese Seafood House.** ★
Aberdeen Centre, east of No. 3 Rd., 2110-4151 Hazelbridge Way; (604) 273-2883
This is a large, very popular restaurant with great seafood and exceptionally good dim sum. You can tell the immigrant Chinese clientele is affluent. Kids spotting friends on the other side of the dining room take out their personal cell phones and call them. **$$**

A Chinese market offers a variety of delicious, fresh seafood.

V I C T O R I A

■ HIGHLIGHTS

Inner Harbour
Empress Hotel
Crystal Gardens
British Columbia Royal Museum
Thunderbird Park
Parliament Buildings
Government Street Shops
Store Street Waterfront
Bastion Square
Fisherman's Wharf
Beacon Hill Park
Chinatown
Craigdarroch Castle

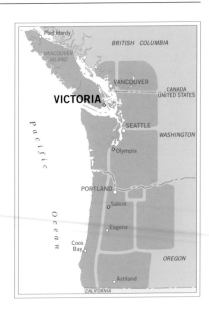

■ SETTING

VICTORIA SPRAWLS ACROSS A LOW, ROCKY HEADLAND at Vancouver Island's south-eastern tip, at the base of the Saanich Peninsula. The city has an interesting, much indented waterfront, with a tidily walled-in harbor downtown, a not so tidy fishing harbor further out, and an even less tidy "Gorge," which is what locals call the long northwestern arm of the harbor that almost cuts Victoria off from the hinterland. Its lower reaches lap against the seawall of an interesting "old town."

Some locals like to think of Victoria as the "southernmost" city in Canada, which it is not, since Windsor, Ontario, is about as far south as the Oregon–California stateline (about 42 degrees north). Even so, many retired civil servants have settled here because they like the mild "southern" clime with its low rainfall (Victoria is in the rain shadow of the Olympic Mountains and Insular Range).

■ HISTORY

Victoria was founded in 1843 as a fur-trading fort by the Hudson's Bay Company on Camosun Harbour, a natural port. By 1858, Victoria had made a transition from a sleepy outpost to bustling metropolis almost overnight, after gold was discovered on the Fraser River. The town's 500 residents were quickly outnumbered by the 25,000 miners who streamed into town to buy licenses and supplies. Their tents covered the waterfront and lined up along Front Street for a mile. During their short stay, many miners liked what they saw, and they settled in Victoria when they returned from the diggings—quadrupling the city's population by 1859 to some 2,000 people.

So many of these new settlers were Americans, the celebration of the Fourth of July soon took precedence over the Queen's Birthday—which, during Victoria's reign, was almost a sacred holiday. So how did the city get to look as "British" as it does now? Through what we would now call "psychological warfare." The British government went all out to make the capital of British Columbia look as "British"

Victoria in 1859 was growing rapidly due to the influx of thousands of would-be miners. (B.C. Archives and Records Service)

as possible, mainly in the design of government buildings, to avoid secession to, or annexation by, the United States. It's exactly that "British" look that makes Victoria so appealing to American visitors today. But it didn't necessarily satisfy 19th-century Victorians.

In 1868, Victoria residents (those mostly of non-British origin) signed a petition to U.S. President Grant, asking him "to receive British Columbia into the American Union." While nothing happened, the petition may have paved the way for the favorable terms the British Columbians got in 1871, when they joined the Canadian Confederation.

Because the railroad from eastern Canada ran only to Burrard Inlet on the mainland, Vancouver became the province's dominant port. But because Victoria has remained out of the mainstream of industrial development, it has preserved its 19th-century character and charm.

■ EXPLORING THE CITY

Victoria has more sights than you can handle in a day—you should plan to spend at least a weekend in town. What makes Victoria unique, in the eyes of many visitors, is its Inner Harbour, compact and stone-walled, like no other port in western North America. What makes the city easy to explore is that most of the town's attractions are either on the Inner Harbour or within easy walking distance. Tubby little ferries connect several landings along the harbor; every morning at 10:00 A.M. they "dance" on the water—to music, of course. Flower baskets have brightened up lampposts at the harbor and around town since 1937. Every August, a huge barge, topped by a band shell, is towed into the Inner Harbour for the annual free concert by the Victoria Symphony—which attracts as many as 40,000 people.

The tall stone edifice of the Parliament Buildings to the south of the basin and the stone facade of the **Empress Hotel** (721 Government Street) to the east give focus to the harbor. But the solidity of the Empress is a bit deceiving. Before its construction, the "James Bay flats" occupied the site where the hotel stands. They were filled in, and the masonry is supported by pilings driven through the mud. A large arch towards the north marks a spot where the pile drivers could find no ground to support the pilings—so they simply bridged it over. If the Empress and the Parliament Buildings seem to have similar stylistic features, that's because they were designed by the same architect, Francis Rattenbury. Unlike the Empress,

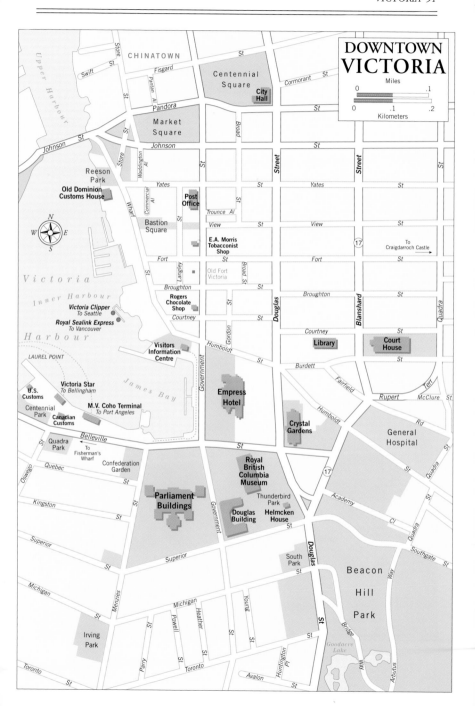

DOWNTOWN VICTORIA

Miles

0 .1

0 .1 .2

Kilometers

Upper Harbour

CHINATOWN

Swift St

Store St

Fisgard St

Pandan Al

Pandora St

Centennial Square

City Hall

Cormorant St

St

Broad St

Market Square

St

Johnson St

Johnson St

Waddington Al

Reeson Park

Old Dominion Customs House

Store St

Commercial Al

Yates St

Yates St

St

Wharf St

Post Office

Trounce Al

View St

View St

St

Bastion Square

E.A. Morris Tobacconist Shop

N W E S

Victoria

Langley St

Fort St

Old Fort Victoria

Fort St

Broad St

St

Inner Harbour

Victoria Clipper
To Seattle

Royal Sealink Express
To Vancouver

Broughton St

Rogers Chocolate Shop

Courtney

Broughton St

Gordon St

St

Douglas St

Blanshard St

Quadra St

Harbour

LAUREL POINT

Visitors Information Centre

Humboldt

Courtney St

Library

Court House

St

St

Burdett

Fairfield

Rupert

McClure St

Terr

U.S. Customs

Victoria Star
To Bellingham

James Bay

Government St

Empress Hotel

Humboldt

Rd

Centennial Park

M.V. Coho Terminal
To Port Angeles

Canadian Customs

Crystal Gardens

General Hospital

Belleville

Quadra Park

To Fisherman's Wharf

Confederation Garden

St

Royal British Columbia Museum

17

Quadra St

Oswego St

Quebec St

St

Parliament Buildings

Government St

Douglas Building

Thunderbird Park

Helmcken House

Academy

Cl

Quadra St

Kingston

St

St

Superior

Superior St

South Park St

Douglas St

Beacon

Southgate St

Michigan

Menzies St

Michigan

Heather St

Young St

Hill

Way

Irving Park

St

Powell

Parry

St

Toronto

St

Huntington Pl

Park

Goodacre Lake

Kew

Arbutus

Toronto St

Avalon St

To Craigdarroch Castle

however, the legislative house sits on solid rock.

For the "British" experience in Victoria, you might want to indulge in high tea at the venerable Empress or the **Crystal Gardens,** a huge glass conservatory behind the Empress at 713 Douglas Street. The Crystal Gardens building is built above the former mudflats. But instead of driving piles, architect Percy James floated the glass-roofed structure on a two-and-a-half-foot-thick slab of concrete. The Crystal once had a giant saltwater swimming pool surrounded by palms; now it is a conservatory housing many exotic flowers and birds.

The Royal British Columbia Museum (still known to insiders by its old name, the British Columbia Provincial Museum) is the one place you absolutely don't want to miss. It has a superb collection of totem poles and Indian artifacts, plus a number of historical exhibits (life in the cold interior, a 19th-century street), and a series of superb natural habitat displays. A dramatic, life-sized model of a Nootka whaling canoe, with the harpooner about to strike a whale, greets you as you enter the vast lobby, which is large enough to display several totem poles. The museum has an excellent bookstore with books on Native tribes and B.C. history, as well as a good selection of Native jewelry, masks, and other art objects. The museum

The Empress Hotel graces Victoria's picturesque Inner Harbour.
(opposite) High tea at the Empress Hotel.

underwent a major restoration in 1996, and is located at 675 Belleville Street; (250) 387-3014.

Just behind the museum, the tall totem poles of **Thunderbird Park** reach for the sky. They stand next to a scaled-down Kwakiutl longhouse built by chief Mungo Martin in the garden of the **Helmcken House**, the oldest house (1852) in Victoria still standing on its original site in its original condition. Dr. J. S. Helmcken was a crusty pioneer medical doctor and politician.

The **Parliament Buildings** on the south side of the Inner Harbour were completed in 1987, using local materials as much as possible. The exterior is made of stone quarried at tiny Haddington Island neat Port McNeill in the northern inland passage. The gilded statue atop the main copper-covered dome is not of Queen Victoria, but of Capt. George Vancouver, the first navigator to circumnavigate Vancouver Island. Statues of Sir James Douglas, who chose the location of Victoria, and Sir Matthew Begbie, the "hanging judge," flank the entrance. Be sure to take a close-up look at the buildings' details. Figures from British Columbia's past and grotesque stone faces decorate the exterior walls. Inside, the ornate woodwork is trimmed with gold and silver leaf. Visitors are welcome inside and may take one of the free guided tours of the buildings. The public may also watch the Assembly, when it is in session, from the galleries overlooking the Legislative Chamber. Located at 501 Belleville Street; (250) 387-3046.

Further west on Belleville Street, beyond the C. P. R. Steamship Terminal completed by Rattenbury in 1924 (and now housing a wax museum), is where the Port Angeles ferry and the passenger ferries from Bellingham and Seattle dock. A path from the Inner Harbour winds around **Laurel Point** to the west. Look for the tall masts of fishing trollers. A short stroll down side streets will bring you to **Fisherman's Wharf,** where purse seiners, gillnetters, trollers, and halibut vessels now occupy the place where it is believed Sir James Douglas first landed. Further down the harbor, freighters load lumber, and visiting cruise ships dock—a fraction of the ship traffic that passed through after World War I, when Victoria was Canada's second busiest harbor.

Back at the Inner Harbour, from the **Visitor's Information Centre** on the waterfront at 812 Wharf Street, you get a good view of the **Welcome Totem,** the tallest totem pole in the world at 55.6 meters (182.5 ft) seen across the harbor at Songhees Point. It was erected in 1994 for the Commonwealth Games.

Government Street, the wide street between the Empress and the harbor ran over a wooden trestle, where the stone causeway rises now, when it connected the stockade of the fort to the new residential areas to the south. Today, the section north of the Inner Harbour is downtown Victoria's prime shopping area. Here you'll find everything from top hats to heavy woolen sweaters knitted by Cowichan Indians, and from tartans to sweets. **Rogers Chocolate Shop** at 913 Government Street was established in 1885 by an American fruit dealer. It moved into its present (1903) building in 1918. Be sure to taste the famed Victoria creams. **E. A. Morris Tobacconist Shop** at 1116 Government Street was established in 1892 (when Morris advertised in the *Colonist* that he "imported cigarettes for ladies"—a daring proposition back then). Its inside is virtually unchanged since a 1910 renovation, with its fine wood craftsmanship, beveled glass, and onyx columns. Cigars are kept moist in a walk-in humidor with a damp brick floor; they may be lit at a perpetual flame burning in an onyx column.

An alley leads to **Bastion Square,** which takes its name from one of the bastions of Fort Victoria. The first city jail stood here; condemned criminals were publicly hanged in the square until 1870. The turreted old courthouse at 28 Bastion Square was built in 1889—the first concrete building in Victoria.

A 15-minute walk east on Fort Street to 1050 Joan Crescent will take you to **Craigdarroch Castle,** a lavish mansion built in 1890 for coal magnate Robert Dunsmuir, who died before the elaborate structure was finished. Craigdarroch now serves as a museum of turn-of-the-19th-century living.

To the north of Bastion Square on Fisgard Street is a small but interesting **Chinatown.** Fan Tan Alley, which claims to be the narrowest street in Canada, takes its name from former gambling dens, now replaced by shops. From here, it is an easy walk to the Gorge waterfront.

The **Old Dominion Customs House** on Wharf Street was built in 1876; the nearby seawall still has iron rings where sailing ships used to tie up. The old buildings along this waterfront once served as ship chandleries and warehouses.

Walk south down Douglas Street (east of the Empress and the R. B. C. Museum) to **Beacon Hill Park,** where some of southern Vancouver Island's native vegetation survives amongst plantings of shrubs and flowers, mostly because the city of Victoria didn't have enough money in the early days to "improve" the park. Horse races were once held here, and in 1878, guns were installed in Finlayson and

Macauley Point to help defend Victoria, in case those pesky Americans to the south thought of attacking. Gunpowder stored in a shed became a source of civic disquiet. European skylarks released here in 1888 and at later dates on the Saanich Peninsula adapted to the local climes and have spread to the San Juan Islands.

The rocky southern slopes of Beacon Hill Park rise sufficiently to allow for great views across the water. The lighthouse offshore is on **Trial Island.** Riptides along the shore are very powerful. In 1923, they pulled under the tug *Tyee,* and four crewmen were drowned.

Butchart Gardens 21 km (13 miles) north of the city on Highway 17 dates back to 1904 when estate owner Jennie Butchart decided to transform part of her limestone quarry into a sunken garden; (250) 652-4422.

(above) The exquisite Butchart Gardens. (opposite) Victoria is a city for walkers. In the warm months, flowers bloom in flower pots attached to light poles along downtown sidewalks.

■ TRAVEL AND CLIMATE

■ GETTING THERE

Victoria's location at the southeastern tip of Vancouver Island makes the capital of British Columbia a bit more challenging to reach than mainland cities. But it's definitely worth the effort. You'll have to take a plane, boat, or ferry to reach Victoria since no bridge crosses the Inland Passage to Vancouver Island from the mainland. Dress warmly if you plan to cross by ferry and want to stand on the deck.

By Car Ferry

From Vancouver area the B.C. Ferry leaves from Tsawwassen south of Vancouver and travels to Swartz Bay north of Victoria. For information and reservations call (604) 669-1211. These ferries are faster than the Washington State ferries, go more often, and cost half as much. The terminal is about a half-hour drive from Victoria.

From Anacortes the Washington State Ferry departs from Anacortes (on Fidalgo Island south of Bellingham, Washington) to Vancouver Island. The terminal is about a half-hour drive from Victoria; (250) 464-6400.

From Port Angeles (on the Olympic Peninsula) take the Black Ball car ferry *Coho.* The ferry unloads in the harbor; (360) 457-4491 or (250) 386-2202.

By Passenger Ferry

From Bellingham, WA: For information call (360) 738-8099.

From Seattle, WA: For information call (800) 888-2535; for reservations call (206) 448-5000.

By Air

The airport, about half an hour north of town, has scheduled national and international flights, and charter planes will take you almost anywhere. *(For more about B.C. travel by air and rail see page 354.)*

■ CLIMATE

Victoria enjoys more sunshine than mainland places, because the city lies in the rain shadow of the Olympic and Insular mountains. Spring comes early and autumn lingers. Winters are generally mild.

■ ACCOMMODATIONS AND RESTAURANTS

☎   For chain lodgings see toll-free numbers on page 352.

$$ For room and restaurant price designations see page 352.

✷   Means highly recommended.

☎ **Abigail's.**
906 McClure St.; (250) 388-5363
Just four blocks from downtown, this
Tudor country inn exudes comfort of an
old-fashioned kind in rooms that are
thoroughly up-to-date. **$$$-$$$$**

☎ **Admiral Motel.**
257 Belleville St.; (250) 388-6267
This basic motel on the Inner Harbour's
tourist strip has unexpectedly reasonable
lodging rates. **$-$$**

☎ **Beaconsfield Inn.**
998 Humboldt St.; (250) 384-4044
Just two blocks from Beacon Hill Park,
this 1875 mansion (restored in 1984)
makes wandering Anglophiles feel like
they've come home. **$$$-$$$$**

☎ **Bedford Regency.** 1140 Government
St.; (250) 384-6835 or (800) 665-6500
Since you don't get much of a view be-
cause of the hotel's downtown location,
go for a room with fireplace and jacuzzi.
Easy walking distance to shops, restau-
rants, the Inner Harbour and other local
attractions. **$$$$**

☎ **The Captain's Palace.**
309 Belleville St.; (250) 388-9191
The turreted mansion was built in 1890.
A decade ago it had a restaurant and one
suite; now it's expanded into several ad-
jacent buildings. **$$$**

☎ **Chateau Victoria.**
740 Burdett Ave.; (250) 382-4221 or
(800) 663-5891
A conventioneer's hotel near the Inner
Harbour and the Royal British Columbia Museum. Ask for a room near the
top of the 19-story pile to take advantage of the great view. **$$$$**

☎ **Coast Victoria Harbourside.**
146 Kingston St.;
(250) 360-1211 or (800) 663-1144
This luxury hotel near Fisherman's
Wharf has great views and parking for
both cars and boats. **$$-$$$**

☎ **The Empress.**
721 Government St.; (250) 384-8111 or
(800) 441-1414
This stately chateau-type hotel has dominated the Inner Harbour since 1908. It
has fine water-side views, and the hotel
balcony is the best place from which to
listen to the Victoria Symphony's annual
free performance on a barge moored in
the harbor. The high tea is sufficiently
arch to please a critical duchess. (Reservations required.) **$$$$**

☎ **Holland House Inn.**
595 Michigan St. (two blocks behind
the Parliament Buildings); (250) 384-
6644
This elegant house, set apart from the
motley crowds by a picket fence, is the

perfect urban hideaway—a home away from home. The breakfast alone is worth a stay. **$$$**

Laurel Point Inn.
680 Montreal St. (west side of Inner Harbour); (250) 386-8721
This angular structure (designed to give the rooms as much of a view as possible) sits at a strategic point on the Inner Harbour on the headland. The water-side rooms are a great place for watching the arrival of boats and floatplanes. **$$$**

Oak Bay Beach Hotel.
1175 Beach Dr.; (800) 668-7758
For many folks this grand Tudor-style pile is too far from downtown and its attractions. But the rooms are comfortable, some have a great view of Haro Strait, and there's a cozy snug where you can sit by the fire. **$$$-$$$$**

Ocean Pointe Resort. 45 Songhees Rd.; (250) 360-2999 or (800) 667-4677
This resort sits west of the bright-blue Johnson Street drawbridge across the harbor. Ask for a room with a view. The pudgy little harbor ferries connect you with the other shore. **$$$**

Olde England Inn.
429 Lampson St., Esquimalt; (250) 388-4353
Attractive to those who want to indulge in a touch of "old country" atmosphere, even if it's a tad corny. **$$$$**

The Prior House.
620 St. Charles St.; (250) 592-8847
This grand old mansion once served as the home of the Lieutenant Governor, the Crown's rep in British Columbia. It sits in a quiet neighborhood, away from the bustle of downtown. **$$$**

A period room in the Olde England Inn.

✕ **Barb's Place.**
310 Lawrence St.; (250) 384-6515
The locals like to hang out at this basic take-out stand at Fisherman's Wharf. That's because the fish and chips are about as fresh and crispy as you can get anywhere. Grab one of the two dockside picnic tables or head for the grassy park nearby. Closed in winter. $

✕ **Camille's.** ✭
45 Bastion Square; (250) 381-3433
This romantic basement restaurant may well serve the best food on Vancouver Island. There's a good selection of wine to go with the dishes. The place is very popular with locals. Reservations advised. $$

✕ **Chez Daniel.**
2524 Estevan Ave.; (250) 592-7424
This is traditional French dining at its best—flavorful and very rich. The locals love it. The wine list is about as good as it gets here. Reservations advised. $$$$

✕ **Empress Room.**
721 Government St.; (250) 384-8111
Reservations advised. For that ultimate shot of British atmosphere, dinner here is a must. The wine list is extensive. The waiters know they're holding up the flag of the British Empire. $$$-$$$$

✕ **Spinnakers Brew Pub.** ✭
308 Catherine St. (west via Johnson Street Bridge, or by passenger ferry from the Inner Harbour); (250) 386-2739
One of British Columbia's oldest brew-pubs is also its most popular one. The beer is great, the food is tasty, and the views across the water are splendid. $$

The Olde England Inn has a replica of the Anne Hathaway Cottage; it houses a small museum.

VANCOUVER ISLAND

■ HIGHLIGHTS

Fort Rodd Hill
East Sooke Park
Botanical Beach
West Coast Trail
Pacific Rim National Park
Strathcona Provincial Park
Nootka Sound
Fort Rupert and Alert Bay

■ LANDSCAPE

THE WEST COAST of Vancouver Island is one of the wildest and most beautiful places on the Pacific Coast: it is a rugged landscape of high mountains and deep fjords. Steep rock faces soar straight from the water to the clouds. Lowland woods and slopes tangle with the trees. The mosses and ferns of a temperate rainforest make the hinterland virtually impregnable. This is a world where the sea melts into the land and the land into the sky along fuzzy margins. Nothing seems real. Land and sea, mountains and clouds, men and animals, lose the defined edges of their being and blend into the landscape. In this misty world, it's difficult to distinguish the real from the supernatural. It is a silent world, the sounds muffled by the thick canopy of moss. Often the only sounds you hear are the dripping of water from the foliage, the chirping of forest birds, and the croak of a raven.

Roads touch the outer shore only at Port San Juan, Ucluelet, and Tofino. The eastern part of the island is a bit gentler and amenable to limited agriculture, but even here fertile fields are so rare that the island could most likely not survive on its own produce alone.

GEOLOGICAL HISTORY OF VANCOUVER ISLAND

The Insular Mountains are the tips of massive granite batholiths that buckled and took great portions of seabed with them as tectonic forces pushed them above the sea. They reach their greatest height and complexity at the island's center, in Strathcona Park. Here the Golden Hinde (2,202 meters, 7,219 ft) towers over a mountain kingdom of alpine peaks and glaciers. Elevations diminish from this point along the mountain chain, with no peaks higher than 1,525 meters (5,000 ft) northwest of Nimpkish Lake or southeast of Cowichan Lake.

Alberni Basin, near the island's center, disrupts this tidy mountain pattern. The wide basin runs 40 kilometers (25 mi) northwestward past Port Alberni, parallel to the mountain spine. Its east side rises dramatically in the sharp escarpment of an old fault line along the western edge of the Beaufort mountain range.

On northern Vancouver Island the mountains subside into the Nahwitti Lowland, whose low rounded hills seldom top 600 meters (1,800 ft). The Sasquatch Basin of sedimentary rock between Port McNeill and Port Hardy stays under 300 meters (1,000 ft) in elevation.

Along the west coast, the narrow Estevan Coastal Plain, deeply cut by fjords, separates the mountains from the ocean. For the 272 kilometers (170 mi) it extends along the coast, the "plain" seldom rises above 46 meters (150 ft). The Long Beach region comprises a major section of this plain. The mountains' eastern flank is bordered by the Nanaimo Lowlands, a strip of low country running down the Coast past Victoria to Jordan River, and including the Gulf Islands—which were cut off from Vancouver Island by glacier-scoured channels.

During periods of heavy glaciation, rivers of ice flowed into the Strait of Georgia (the "Georgia Depression") from mountain valleys on the island and in the Coast Mountains. The longest of these sunken valleys, the Alberni Inlet, is some 343 meters (1,125 ft) deep and reaches more than 64 kilometers (40 mi) inland, to the city of Port Alberni at the foot of the Alberni Basin.

This basic island geography is much obscured by steep-sided canyons, mountain ridges, very tall trees, mist, and fog. So don't be upset if you don't recognize all of these patterns right away. Relax and enjoy the scenery as it unrolls much like the scroll of a Chinese landscape painting.

(following pages) Sunset at Green Point in Pacific Rim National Park.

The island is dominated by the jagged, snow-covered peaks of the Insular Mountain Range which runs along its spine; strips of lowland lie along the east and west coasts, and large regions of low rolling hills lie at the northern and southern tips.

■ HISTORY

The native population of Vancouver Island is divided into three major language groups: the Coast Salish of the southeastern coast and the Gulf Islands, the Kwakiutl (Kwakiulth) of the north-central and northeastern coast, and the Nootka (sometimes called West Coast People) of the west coast. These groups shared a similar culture, lived in cedar-planked longhouses, and traveled over salt water in canoes carved from giant cedar logs. The Kwakiutl carved totem poles, which the Salish and Nootka rarely did. The Nootka traveled far to sea in their canoes, hunting seals and whales. On one of these excursions, in 1788, they beheld massive objects, larger than whales. Resembling floating houses, with strange wings spread to

The Kwakiutl village of Humdaspe on Hope Island off Vancouver Island's northern tip was photographed by Edward Dossetter in 1881. (American Museum of Natural History)

the wind, these odd-looking structures drifted from the ocean mists towards their shores. According to eyewitness reports preserved in Nootka oral history, the men reported after their hurried return that they had met fish looking like white men sailing across the sea in their houses.

*O*ne white man had a real hooked nose, you know. And one of the men was saying to this other guy, "See, see . . . he must have been a dog salmon, that guy there, he's got a hooked nose.". . . "Yes! We're right. We're right. Those people must have been fish. They've come alive into people. . . . So they went ashore and they told the big Chief: "You know what we saw? They've got white skin. But we're pretty sure that those people on the floating thing there, that they must have been fish. But they've come here as people.

The exploring expedition of British seafarer Capt. James Cook had arrived on the Northwest Coast. While Cook had found a safe harbor for his ships, he missed many of prominent landmarks, including the mouth of the Columbia River and Juan de Fuca Strait.

Nuxalt dancers from coastal British Columbia were photographed in 1886 in their elaborate masks and costumes. (Royal B.C. Museum)

Because of the roughness of the rocky coastline and because of the foggy, drizzly weather and rough seas, the region gave up its secrets slowly. For a decade and a half, neither Cook nor the explorers and fur traders following in his wake learned that Vancouver Island was not part of the mainland.

In 1792, British navigator George Vancouver sailed around the island and proved that it was indeed separate from the mainland. After the Spanish withdrew, Nootka and the west coast of Vancouver Island once again became a backwater. But the inland passage Vancouver had discovered became a busy place for local shipping—a role it has not relinquished 200 years later.

■ JUAN DE FUCA STRAIT

The coast west of Victoria has secluded beaches, some spectacular scenery and, at times, a lot of rain. BC 14, the Sooke Road, was authorized by governor James Douglas in 1852 to open up the western lands along the coast of Juan de Fuca Strait and to connect existing farms to the fort at Victoria.

Just west of Victoria is **Fort Rodd Hill,** built in 1895 to defend British Columbia against a feared U.S. naval attack. The guns are gone, but the batteries are still there. On a clear day they provide great views of the Olympic Mountains on the other shore of Juan de Fuca Strait. On the fort grounds is **Fisgard Lighthouse,** the oldest (1860) operational lighthouse on Canada's west coast. The military complex to the east is the **Canadian Forces base at Esquimalt,** the West Coast headquarters of the Canadian navy. It was established as a naval station in the 1850s by the British during the Crimean War.

Further down the road is **Royal Roads Military College,** the former Hatley Park estate of coal baron James Dunsmuir (heir to father Robert's fortune). The beautiful grounds with their elaborate gardens are open daily to the public.

A detour along **Metchosin Road** leads through pretty farm country, interspersed with beaches and great views of the Strait. (BC 14 runs inland.) Metchosin Road also leads to **East Sooke Park,** a headland at the southernmost point of Vancouver Island. The park is a wilderness of twisted trees, of hiking trails through the forest, good swimming beaches, and the spectacular views so common on this coast. Trails also lead to secluded coves. (Don't leave valuables in your car: vandals and thieves can be rather active.)

Sooke Region Museum, east of the town of Sooke, has an interesting collection of Indian and pioneer artifacts, plus a restored pioneer cottage. Sooke is a small town on Sooke Harbour, a quiet bay. The first independent settler on the island, Capt. Walter Colquhoun Grant, established a farm at Sooke in 1849. But the captain was no farmer. He soon followed the lure of gold to California and later returned to England and served in the Crimean and Indian military campaigns.

Whiffen Spit makes for a nice hike across the narrow mouth of the inlet. It ends at a narrow channel almost beneath the bluffs of East Sooke Park. The spit is a great place for seabird watching. Occasionally seals, sea lions, orcas, and dolphins drop by.

West of Sooke, the highway becomes rough and twisted, with many one-lane log bridges (watch out for logging trucks). BC 14 is not a fast highway even at the best of times, and it can get quite clogged up with traffic. But who's in a hurry? Sit back, relax, and take that lead foot off the accelerator. This road becomes rather lonely west of Sooke, but that doesn't mean you'll be stranded if your car breaks down. I was once pulled from a ditch (when I had foolishly forgotten to set my hand brake) by several students, who, after they had lifted my car back on the road, inquired what province I was from. I told them, "one of the American provinces," which they thought a good joke. In the meantime, I had asked a motorist to call the CAA (Canadian Automobile Association) for assistance from Jordan

The Olympic Mountains rise above Juan de Fuca Strait.

River, the nearest community; instead, the proprietor of the Jordan River pub came out to help.

The coast west of Sooke has many parks and trails to the beach. There's a pleasant pub at **River Jordan** , halfway between Sooke and Port Renfrew, and not much else. **Port Renfrew** is an old B.C. Forest Products company town that has been livened up in recent years. The **West Coast Trail** of **Pacific Rim National Park** starts here. This is a trail for experienced hikers only. It started out as the West Coast Life Saving Trail, which was established after the American steamer *Valencia* ran aground on this treacherous rocky coast in January of 1906. Of the 154 persons aboard, 117 lost their lives. A grisly finale was added in the following summer when local Indians discovered one of the *Valencia's* lifeboats floating in a sea cave approximately 183 meters (600 ft) from the wreck. The boat held the bodies of eight survivors of the wreck, who had died of exposure after the boat had been swept into the cave over a huge boulder blocking the entrance.

While the trail has been somewhat improved in recent years, it is still very wet and slippery and demands exceptional backcountry skills, especially when it comes to fording swollen creeks and rivers. The grand scenery makes it all worthwhile. The trail ends in Bamfield on Barkley Sound.

Botanical Beach at the mouth of Port San Juan has an exceptional aggregation of sculpted sandstone and marine life that is exposed during summer low tides.

■ FROM VICTORIA TO NANAIMO

Shortly after leaving Victoria, TCH, Route 1 crosses **Goldstream Provincial Park.** Gold was found here in 1885, but today's most valuable assets are the coho salmon returning to the Goldstream River each November to spawn. A trail leads to Niagara Creek and to the top of Niagara Falls, a spectacular 30.5-meter (100-ft) cascade. The toughest part of the drive comes as the road winds its way up the sheer rock cliff of the **Malahat** to a 353-meter (1,156-ft) summit above the deep waters of Saanich Inlet.

At the **Native Heritage Centre** in **Duncan** you can watch women knit the famous Cowichan sweaters. The sweaters are hand-knit in one piece, from naturally dyed wool that still has its lanolin. There's also an open-air carving shed where Native carvers create totem poles. Currently there are 66 totem poles in and around Duncan—even though totem-pole carving is not one of the traditional crafts of the local Cowichan tribe of Salish Indians; 200 Cowichan Way.

The small town of **Chemainus** lost its lumber mill, the town's only major employer, in 1981. The town hired artists to paint murals that told the story of the town—which now have become a major visitor attraction.

The 49th parallel passes through **Ladysmith**. This is where the U.S.–Canadian border would be, had the treaty of 1846 not excepted southern Vancouver Island. **The Crow and Gate Neighbourhood Pub** north of Ladysmith on Yellow Point Road adds the perfect British touch to the region. With its rose-arbor entrance, lawns, and duck pond it could have been lifted straight from the English countryside. Inside, there's a blazing fire in the fireplace, a dart board, and a collection of English magazines. The pub fare is excellent.

Nanaimo has preserved a bastion (1853) from the old Hudson's Bay Company fort. Nanaimo's value to the company was not in furs, but in the coal that was found here and fueled HBC steamers. Robert Dunsmuir became the island's richest man when he took over the mines. The **Nanaimo District Museum** at 100 Cameron Road has a replica of a coal mine entrance.

■ Traveling to the Outer Coast

The Trans-Canada Highway turns east at Nanaimo and travels via ferry to the mainland. BC 19 continues up the east side of the island. BC 4 branches off north of Parksville and takes you first to Port Alberni at the head of the Alberni Channel and eventually, after many twists and turns, to the outer coast at Long Beach and north to Tofino. A branch road goes south to Ucluelet. The road is some 150 km (94 miles) long; plan on at least two and a half to three hours' driving time.

Thanks to the **Alberni Channel**, a long, steep-walled fjord that cuts into the island from Barkley Sound for some 64 kilometers (40 mi), the timber town of **Port Alberni** has a deepwater port. Roger Creek Park in the center of town has a popular swimming hole right in the creek.

On Tuesdays, Thursdays, and Saturdays (and Fridays and Sundays in July and August), the *Lady Rose,* a 30.5-meter (100-ft) vessel built in Scotland in 1937, departs from Harbour Quay at the foot of Argyle Street in Port Alberni and travels down the Inlet to to **Bamfield**, on the southern shore of Barkley Sound. This just has to be the most romantic boat ride in the Northwest—traveling down the steep, rock-walled fjord on a boat that once plied the stormy coasts of Scotland. En route, the boat makes side trips to the **Broken Islands** (where kayakers and canoeists can have themselves dropped off and picked up). From early June to mid-September, the *Lady Rose* and the *Frances Barkley* make trips to Ucluelet via the Broken Islands. For the latest schedules and fares call (250) 723-8313.

The only other way to reach Bamfield, a pretty village with wooden walkways and flower boxes overhanging a fjord, is over a rough logging road which leads to the eastern shore of the inlet that cuts the village in half. Only the *Lady Rose* docks at both sides. That can lead to complications, as one resident learned in the mid-1980s, after the logging road first opened: he had bought a lawn tractor and did not want to pay—what he considered to be—"outrageous" freight charges of the *Lady Rose*. When he reached Bamfield, he learned that there was only one way to carry his tractor across the inlet—on the *Lady Rose*. "We charged him the full freight rate," said the mate.

If you decide to drive to the Pacific Coast, the road becomes rather scenic after Port Alberni; cliffs along the road have polished faces and lateral striations left by glaciers. The road follows the short but pretty Kennedy River to Kennedy Lake, the island's largest. The lake is almost at tidewater level, and shortly after you reach it, you arrive at **Long Beach**, the largest unit of **Pacific Rim National Park.** Here dense, often boggy forests grow right up to an 11-kilometer (7-mi) -long, flat beach of hard-packed sand, where the only sounds you may hear are the roar of the breakers and the croaking of ravens. Watch for gray whales playing in the surf.

Seaplanes in the harbor of Nanaimo (above) may be rented for flight-seeing trips to view Vancouver Island's scenery—such as this coastal area near Tofino (right).

The road turns south to Ucluelet and north to Tofino. **Ucluelet** is a fishing village on a protected bay where Native Americans had lived for thousands of years. It is close to the Broken Islands and to banks where migrating salmon feed. Until 1959, when the road from Port Alberni was completed, it could be reached only by boat or floatplane. If you're not interested in fishing or kayaking, you might want to take a nature cruise to the coast and the Broken Islands. Few things are more dramatic than having the boat nose up to a sea lion rock right where the ocean swells run into the calm waters of the bay. The rise and fall of the waves is tremendous: at one moment, you're staring an annoyed sea lion right in the eye, and the next instant you're looking at huge sea anemones clinging to the rock.

It's easy to understand why the **Broken Islands** in Barkley Sound, the central unit of Pacific Rim National Park, are so popular with kayakers and divers. Not only are they beautiful, all 98 of them, but they possess a rare mystic quality. Native villages once lined the beaches of quiet sandy coves where canoes were drawn up onto the sand. Today the villages are gone, but some of the land still belongs to the natives. Tread with respect wherever you go.

As you drive north to **Tofino**, you may notice sea kayakers tumbling about in the surf. Don't try to emulate them in a rental kayak. It takes a lot of experience to do that sort of thing. Tofino, a hamlet on the southern edge of **Clayoquot Sound**, has a huge airport, left over from World War II, when Tofino was a major air base. Today, it is the only commercial airport of the region.

Tofino is a fishing port and jumping off place for kayakers, with beachfront resorts, motels, and bed-and-breakfasts. To get away from the crowds, you can take a water taxi to hot springs north of town.

Clayoquot Sound was a favorite place of American and British fur traders, who dealt with the clever local chief, Wickaninnish. Some Americans came to grief in their dealings with Native people. John Kendrick's *Lady Washington* was unsuccessfully attacked in 1791, but in 1811, the Astorian's *Tonquin* was captured. After the British government was established on the coast, Indian attacks were dealt with harshly: when the trading vessel *Kingfisher* was captured and its crew murdered by Clayoquot Sound Indians, the naval vessels *Sutlej* and *Devastation* destroyed nine Indian villages and 64 canoes by shelling. Permanent European settlers arrived in 1875 to build the first trading post on Stubbs Island just offshore. Today, many "counterculture" squatters live on remote islands of the sound.

■ QUALICUM BEACH TO CAMPBELL RIVER

Qualicum Beach north of Parksville is the most popular bathing beach on the island. The water here and among the islands gets quite warm in the summer. This has had the benefit of causing Pacific oysters—which need warm water to spawn—to reproduce in such great numbers that Puget Sound oyster growers have come up here to collect oyster "seed" (that is, spat, the young oysters) to restock their farms. Many tidal rocks are covered with oysters. Unfortunately, these are barely edible during the summer spawning season but are at their best in late fall and winter, when hardly anyone likes to poke about the beach to collect them. Perhaps that's why they're still plentiful.

Courtenay and its twin sister **Comox** attracted the first white settlers in 1862— New Zealanders who had been lured to British Columbia by the Fraser River gold rush but decided to farm instead. In 1876, the first wharf was built and the navy established a training base on the spit. Since then the area has depended largely on the military for its support.

The **Forbidden Plateau** to the east got its name from a story told by the local Indians: fearing an attack by the Cowichans, they hid their families on the plateau. After the attackers were beaten off, the Cowichans searched for their families, but could not find them. They surmised that "skookums," evil spirits, had thrown them off a cliff, and the plateau became taboo. Today it is an all-season mountain recreation area, with subalpine wildflowers gracing the higher elevations in summer. A car ferry runs between Courtenay and Powell River on the mainland.

Campbell River, half way up the island from Victoria, is famous for its giant trees and huge king salmon—both of which are history. Offshore is **Quadra Island,** separated from Vancouver Island by **Discovery Passage** (so named by George Vancouver in 1792). This narrow defile, which is plagued by treacherous winds, tides, and whirlpools, is the main passage north. It was made even more dangerous by the Euclataw band of Kwakiutl, who had driven the local Salish Indians from the their Cape Mudge village early in the 19th century, and by Ripple Rock.

The Euclataws raided and exacted tolls from Indian and white trading parties using the passage to and from Victoria. They stopped only when the the British, utilizing the gunboat *Forward,* subdued the tribe.

Ripple Rock stood right in the middle of the narrowest part of the passage. Its

two summits were just below the water, in easy reach of ships' hulls, but also, potentially, of bridge piers. The rock had to be removed to make shipping safe, but the idea incensed islanders, who feared that with Ripple Rock removed they'd never get the government to build the bridge to the mainland promised them in the 1871 federation agreement. To remove the rock, a shaft was drilled on nearby Maude Island, followed by a tunnel under the seabed, and a "raise" to within a few feet of the rock's tips. After two and a half years of boring, 34 boxcars full of explosives were packed into the cavity. In April of 1958, the rock was blown up. Despite dire warnings, the blast did not cause a *tsunami* to race down the coast of Vancouver Island.

■ THE ROAD TO NOOTKA SOUND

BC 28 runs from north of Campbell River to Muchalat Inlet, an arm of Nootka Sound. Seventy-two kilometers (45 mi) west of Campbell River, you'll pass Strathcona Park Lodge and Outdoor Education Centre on Upper Campbell Lake at **Strathcona Provincial Park.** Strathcona Park has Vancouver Island's highest mountain, the Golden Hinde at 2,200 meters (7,218 ft), and Canada's highest

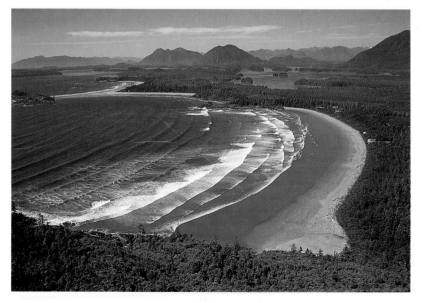

(above) Floating homes in Tofino Harbour. (opposite) Chesterman Beach near Tofino is typical of the many perfect coves that line the west coast of Vancouver Island.

waterfall, at 440-meter (1,144-ft)- high Della Falls. The park also has trees that were old when Capt. James Cook landed on the coast.

From **Gold River,** the ferry *Uchuck III* takes passengers north of Nootka, where Captain Cook landed in 1788, along the rugged west coast of Vancouver Island, to the very remote old village of **Kyuquot.** Passengers spend the night at a bed-and-breakfast and return the next day; (250) 283-2325.

■ CAMPBELL RIVER TO PORT HARDY

The road north from Campbell River to Kelsey Bay was built during World War II to facilitate troop shipment in case an invasion threatened from the north (Yorke Island in Johnstone Strait was fortified at that time). The road north from Kelsey Bay to Port Hardy was not completed until the third quarter of the 20th century. Until then, ferries connected Kelsey Bay to Beaver Cove in the north; from here a road continued to Port Hardy. As you drive north, keep a lookout for the resident pod of orcas living in Johnstone Strait.

Port McNeill was named after an American skipper in the employ of the HBC, who was famous for the subterfuges he used to avoid becoming a British citizen. The Kwakiutl village of Alert Bay is a short ferry ride from Port McNeill. It is well worth visiting for the **U'mista Cultural Centre,** an excellent museum; (250) 974-5403.

In *Guests Never Leave Hungry,* Kwakiutl chief James Sewid talks about the problems the builders faced in 1965, when they erected a large ceremonial house. After a giant forklift was unable to lift the huge beams, Sewid successfully used the traditional Indian method of rocking up the logs on a tower of eight-by-eight timbers. ". . . . that big log just rolled into the grooves that we had made for it. It was really quite easy and we did both of those logs inside of a day."

Fort Rupert, on Beaver Harbour, was established by the Hudson's Bay Company in 1849 to protect coal miners working the local seams. After the fort was built, a part of the Nahwitti tribe of Kwakiutl Indians moved here. The Edward Curtis film *In the Land of the War Canoes* was filmed here. Today, the village is one of the best places to buy Native art.

Port Hardy is the terminal for the ferry to **Prince Rupert** on the northern mainland, just below the Alaskan border. (Ferry reservations should be made well in advance.) Port Hardy was named after the commander of the British ship-of-the-line *Victory*, on whose deck Horatio Nelson died during the Battle of Trafalgar. (Nelson's last words were, "Kiss me, Hardy.")

From Port Hardy, several roads run to harbors on Quatsino Sound, the northernmost fjord on Vancouver Island's west coast. **Coal Harbour** was a whaling station in the 1950s. **Cape Scott Provincial Park** is a one-and-a-half-hour drive on a gravel road north of Port Hardy. A 20-minute walk through old-growth forest takes you to scenic San Josef Bay. At San Neck, you can look down both coasts of the island. Call the Chamber of Commerce for directions and information on other hikes in the region; (250) 949-7622.

■ TRAVEL AND CLIMATE

■ GETTING THERE

Much of Vancouver Island is very rugged, with steep forest- or brush-covered slopes. Beyond the main highways, be advised that most backcountry roads are not paved, and some that are paved don't stay that way for long, due to heavy logging truck traffic. If you're planning to take a logging road into the back-country, check the signs posted at the road entrance for the hours during which it is open to the general public.

By Car Ferry. Ferries run between Victoria and Port Angeles, between Sidney and Anacortes (this run may be cancelled), and between Swartz Bay and Tsawwassen on the lower B.C. mainland; *(see page 98 for details).* Ferries also connect Nanaimo to Horseshoe Bay north of Vancouver and to Tsawwassen on the lower mainland; and Courtenay to Powell River on the Sunshine Coast. Car ferries travel to the Gulf Islands and from the islands to the mainland.

■ CLIMATE

The climate is generally rather wet and cool all year long on the island's west coast, which faces the open Pacific. Inland shores are sheltered by the Insular Range from Pacific storms and by the Coast Mountains from the cold weather of the interior, making them pleasantly warm in summer. The people living here in aboriginal times were a hardy bunch. They wore little or no clothing even in winter and walked barefoot on the snow.

■ ACCOMMODATIONS AND RESTAURANTS

⊞   For chain lodgings see toll-free numbers on page 352.
$$ For room and restaurant price designations see page 352.
✶   Means highly recommended.

CAMPBELL RIVER

⊞ ✕ **Strathcona Park Lodge.**
On Hwy. 28, 45 km west of Campbell River at the edge of Strathcona Provincial Park; (250) 286-8206
You expect a place a step above a summer camp and what you get are surprisingly comfortable cabins. Meals are served family-style. $$

✕ **Royal Coachman Neighborhood Pub.**
84 Dogwood St.; (250) 286-0231
The food can be quite ambitious in this informal blackboard-menu restaurant that's very popular with local diners. No reservations, so get there early. $-$$

COMOX/COURTENEY

⊞ **Greystone Manor.**
4014 Haas Rd.; (250) 338-1422
This elegant 78-year-old house overlooks Comox harbor. Shared baths. $$

⊞ **Kingfisher Beach Resort.**
4330 S. Island Hwy.; (250) 338-1323 or (800) 663-7929 in British Columbia, Oregon, and Washington.
This comfortable motel among the trees overlooks the Strait of Georgia, and has spacious rooms with simple but comfortable furnishings. $$

✕ **Old House Restaurant.** ✶
1760 Riverside Ln., Courtenay; (250) 338-5406

This nicely restored 1938 house set among trees and flower gardens serves some of the best food on Vancouver Island. Upstairs is a formal dining room, with linen and fresh flowers on the tables and a pricey menu. The downstairs decor is more casual and the fare is simpler. Expect the freshest local seafood, vegetables, fruits, and herbs, plus locally raised meats. Reservations for parties of six or more. $$

LADYSMITH

⊞ **Yellow Point Lodge.**
3700 Yellow Point Rd.; (250) 245-7422
The main lodge of this classic resort was rebuilt in 1986 after a fire destroyed the original lodge. But the place is still as laid-back and comfortable as ever. $-$$$

✕ **Crow and Gate Neighborhood Pub.** ✶
2313 Yellow Point Rd.; (250) 722-3731
With its rose arbor entrance, duck pond, and backyard patio, this pub looks like it's been lifted straight from the British countryside, and it feels like it too. An easy walk from Yellow Point Lodge. $

MALAHAT

⊞ **The Aerie.**
600 Ebedora Ln.; (250) 743-7115
This luxurious inn some 120 meters above Malahat Summit is the most luxurious "eagle's nest" you'll ever encounter.

There's an indoor pool, an outdoor tennis court, and a helipad in case you need to arrive or leave in a hurry. The breakfasts have a local reputation for excellence. **$$$$**

NANAIMO

⊞ Coast Bastion Inn.
11 Bastion St. (downtown, a short drive from the ferry terminal and train and bus stations); (250) 753-6601 or (800) 663-1144 in the U.S.
All rooms of this comfortable hotel have views of the restored 19th-century Hudson's Bay Company bastion on the harbor front. **$$$-$$$$**

⊞ ✕ The Dorchester Hotel.
70 Church St.; (250) 754-6835 or (800) 661-2449
This 1880s hotel has been restored so thoroughly you'd be hard pressed to tell its age. The rooms are comfortable; most have views of harbor or the bastion. The restaurant, Cafe Casablanca, is very popular with the locals. **$$**

✕ The Grotto.
1511 Stewart Ave.; (250) 753-3303
A Nanaimo institution for more than 30 years, the Grotto remains popular for its fresh, barbecued shrimp, and its gourmet burgers. **$-$$**

✕ Old Mahle House. ✯
Cedar and Heemer Rds.;
(250) 722-3621
This very popular restaurant makes its reputation with fresh, locally produced ingredients transformed through the artistry of the kitchen. The wine list is impressive for this part of the island. Reservations advised. **$$**

QUADRA ISLAND

⊞ ✕ April Point Lodge and Fishing Resort. ✯✯✯
900 April Point Rd.,; (250) 285-2222
Operated for 50 years by the friendly Peterson family, this is one of British Columbia's top resorts. It's so perfect, in a laid-back, rustic fashion, it's hard to describe. You'll have to experience it. This is also one of the best lodges for chartering a fishing boat and guide—if the salmon are running. **$$$-$$$$**

⊞ ✕ Tsa-Kwa-Luten Lodge. Kwakiutl tribe. Lighthouse Rd., Quathiaski Cove,; (250) 285-2042 or (800) 665-7745
The design of this lodge, built by the Cape Mudge band of Kwakiutl, was inspired by traditional longhouse design. The rooms are, however, modern and very comfortable. The dining room specializes in freshly caught local fish. During the summer, the lodge puts on a weekly buffet of regional foods, which is followed by traditional dances. **$$$**

PARKSVILLE

⊞ Roadhouse Inn.
1223 Smithers Rd.; (250) 248-2912
This small Swiss-style chalet has basic but comfortable rooms. **$-$$**

PORT HARDY

⊞ Glen Lyon Inn.
6435 Hardy Bay Rd.; (250) 949-7115
The modern rooms of this pleasant motel have full views of Hardy Bay. Don't be surprised if a bald eagle drops by. A short ride from the ferry terminal. **$**

SIDNEY

⛨ Borthwick Country Manor.
9750 Ardmore Dr.; (250) 656-9498
A modern (1979) Tudor-style house
with very comfortable rooms. $$-$$$

✕ Blue Peter Pub and Restaurant.
2270 Harbour Rd. (4.8 km north of
Sidney); (250) 656-4551
Better than average pub food, a sunny
deck, and a great view across the harbor
make this place a local favorite. $

✕ Deep Cove Chalet. ⚹⚹⚹
11190 Chalet Rd. (between Victoria
and the Swartz Bay ferry terminal);
(250) 656-3541
A French country restaurant, presided
over by chef Pierre Koffel, with food as
good as anything you might find in
France, in a spot more beautiful than
the French countryside. $$$

SOOKE

⛨ Ocean Wilderness.
109 Coast Rd.; (250) 646-2116
A large (nine-room) log cabin on five
forested beachfront acres makes for a
perfect retreat. $$$

⛨ Point No Point Resort.
1505 West Coast Rd., Hwy. 14 (24 km
west of Sooke); (250) 646-2020
Rustic cabins on a wild seashore make
for a perfect getaway. It can be so quiet
here that all you'll hear is the crashing of
the surf and the cry of seabirds. $$$

⛨ Richview House.
7031 Richview Dr.; (250) 642-5520
This small B&B has the kind of atmos-
phere the Sooke Harbour House down
the road used to have before it became
famous and snooty. $$$

⛨ ✕ Sooke Harbour House. ⚹ ⚹
1528 Whiffen Spit Rd.; (250) 642-3421
The old 1931 clapboard farmhouse has
been turned into a luxury lodge. Some
old-timers liked the place better in the
old days when the place was smaller and
more laid back. Some folks love the new
rooms (in a separate building), some
claim it's more like a waterfront theme
park than an inn. The food served in the
restaurant can be inspired or it can be
downright strange. $$$$

✕ Good Life Bookstore and Cafe.
Downtown Sooke; 2113 Otter Point
Rd.; (250) 642-6821
The food is not fancy in this somewhat
eclectic bookstore-restaurant, but it can
be as good as anything you can get local-
ly. $$

UCLUELET / TOFINO

⛨ Canadian Princess Fishing Resort.
The Boat Basin, Ucluelet; (250) 726-
7771 or (800) 663-7090
It started with an old Canadian survey
ship that was turned into a basic fishing
lodge. Now more commodious rooms
on shore have added to the comfort.
The galley serves good food; a ship's
mast goes right through the dining
room. Charter boats take fishermen to
the salmon banks and non-fishing visi-
tors on tours of the Broken Islands in
Barkley Sound. $$-$$$

⛨ Chesterman's Beach Bed and Breakfast.
1345 Chesterman's Beach Rd., Tofino;
(250) 725-3726
A comfortable place on a long, sandy
beach perfect for bonfires. $$$

▥ ✕ **Himwitsa Lodge and the Sea Shanty Restaurant.**

300 Main St. (across from the main dock), Tofino; (250) 725-2017 (lodge) or (800) 899-1947; (250) 725-2902 (restaurant)

A Native-run lodge with restaurant and art gallery right in the heart of the village. **$$**

▥ **Middle Beach Lodge.**

400 McKenzie Beach Rd., Tofino; (250) 725-2900

A modern, comfortable lodge set on rocks above a private beach south of Tofino. **$$**

▥ **Pacific Sands Beach Resort.**

1421 Pacific Rim Hwy., Tofino; (250) 725-3322 or (800) 565-2322

A rustic motel with basic furnishings and fireplaces just north of Pacific Rim National Park. **$-$$**

✕ **Whale's Tale.**

1867 Peninsula Rd., Ucluelet; (250) 726-7453

A rustic no-frills restaurant serving fresh local seafood. **$$**

✕ **Wickaninnish Restaurant** (and lodge)

Long Beach, 16 km north of Ucluelet; (250) 726-7706

A dramatic setting on a three-km-long unspoiled beach makes this place very popular with visitors. The food is good, but the service can be uneven at the height of the summer tourist rush. Reservations advised for seven or more. Closed mid-October to mid-February. **$$**

I S L A N D S

■ HIGHLIGHTS

Pastoral Islands
Ferry Rides
Sunny Beaches
Wildflower Meadows
Scenic Hiking Trails
Comfortable Lodges
Good Restaurants
Fishing, Crabbing,
 Beachcombing

■ LANDSCAPE

ISLANDS ARE SPECIAL PLACES, miniature continents with moods uniquely their own. In the Pacific Northwest, with its misty days and foggy nights, you sometimes wonder if they are *terra firma* at all, or whether they float this way or that at the whim of the tide.

The inland waters of the Pacific Northwest, between the southern end of Puget Sound and the Canadian Inside Passage, have hundreds of islands of various sizes, shapes, and elevations. Some are little more than reedy sandbars in river mouths; others have peaks that rise straight from the water for almost 3,000 feet. Some are so close to shore, they have been tied to the mainland by bridges. Others are separated by deep, swift-running tidal channels or saltwater straits. Those can be reached only by boat, ferry, airplane, or floatplane.

What really sets these islands apart is their exceptional beauty, which expresses itself in dramatic cliffs where eagles soar, lush seaside meadows, gnarled trees, and multicolored wildflowers clinging to seemingly infertile rocks. The islands have valleys and mountains, forests filled with bird song, and leafy glens where the tiny island deer browse. Even a species of prickly pear cactus *(Opuntia fragilis)* grows here. Beaches can be pebbly or sandy, but all are scenic. Offshore, seals haul out on sandbanks, and orcas patrol the deep channels.

Sunset over Canada's Gulf Islands as seen from Ruckles Park on Salt Spring Island.

The islands are visited by ducks and swans, herons and hawks, humans and whales. Many islands are settled; some have picturesque villages—more often than not near a ferry landing—and a few have resorts for visitors. Many have camp-grounds and ample beaches or meadows where boaters (or hikers) can haul out and pitch a tent.

■ ISLAND HISTORY

The most beautiful of the Pacific Northwest's islands lie north of Juan de Fuca Strait, between the northwest Washington mainland and Vancouver Island. These islands were once part of Vancouver Island, from which they were separated by the grinding action of continental glaciers during the last ice age. Because the ice—some 3,000 feet thick—pressed the land down into the earth's crust, the islands have been rising slowly ever since the ice melted. Humans moved in as soon as the islands were free of ice.

Excavation of ancient shell middens proves that the islands have been inhabited for at least 5,000 years. But in Indian days, these were summer settlements only. According to Ken Pattison writing in *Milestones on Vancouver Island,* "None of these native visitors established permanent settlements in the Islands, and the first recorded settlers were a group of American Negroes who had purchased their free-dom in the U.S. and applied to Sir James Douglas for permission to settle on Salt Spring Island [in 1859]."

The islands were stopping off points for Nanaimo and Cowichan Indians from Vancouver Island; for Salish, Musqueam, and Tsawwassen from the mainland of present-day British Columbia; and for Lummi and Samish from present-day Washington State. The visitors used them as summer homes, camping in shelters of woven mats, and as a sort of natural supermarket, taking salmon and halibut from the reefs and harvesting camas root and berries on the land.

Perhaps the islands were not settled permanently because they were regularly raided by Haida, Tlinkit, and Kwakiutl warriors from the north out to capture booty and slaves. (The Tlinkit name for Puget Sound was the same as their term for slave.) In 1858, northern Indians—reportedly Stikine Tlinkit from Southeast Alaska—raided a Lummi summer village on the east shore of West Sound on Orcas Island. According to contemporary reports, the beach was soon littered with "over a hundred bodies." The site of that ill-fated village has ever since been known as "Massacre Bay." These raids continued long after Americans and British had settled along the inland waters and did not cease till the latter half of the 19th century. The Canadian Gulf Islands and the American San Juans belong to two different political jurisdictions. Back in 1846, when the Oregon Territory was divided between Britain and the United States, it was decided that, south of the 49th parallel, the border should run down the middle of the main channel between Vancouver Island and the mainland.

The vagueness of that diplomatic language caused a bit of grief back in the late 1850s, when the British decided that Rosario Strait, not Haro Strait as previously agreed upon, was the "main channel" separating the British from the American Domain. War almost erupted between the two nations when an American settler shot a Hudson's Bay Company pig that had been raiding his San Juan Island potato patch. This so-called "pig war" remained an *opera buffa* episode because cooler heads prevailed, leading to a joint occupation of San Juan Island by British and American troops until 1872, when the German emperor—who was asked to settle the dispute—awarded the San Juans to the United States.

■ GULF ISLANDS

The best way to explore this archipelago, which lies north of the San Juan Islands just off the eastern shore of Vancouver Island, is to travel there by car-ferry, boat, or kayak, and explore by bicycle or on foot. Island roads are limited and most parks and campsites are accessible by sea. Bald eagles, murres, pigeon guillemots, harlequin ducks, and an occasional puffin can be seen over or in island waters. Gnarled madronas (called arbutus trees by British Columbians), Garry oaks, and Douglas firs make dramatic statements atop cliffs and hills. Writers, artists, craftspeople, weekend cottagers, and retirees make up much of the resident population, which is augmented by heavy influxes of weekend and summer visitors.

■ GABRIOLA ISLAND

Seven-mile-long Gabriola Island is a residential island a 20-minute ferry ride southeast of Nanaimo (and almost a suburb of that city) and the northernmost of the Gulf Islands. It has few facilities for visitors. Yet there is one attraction well

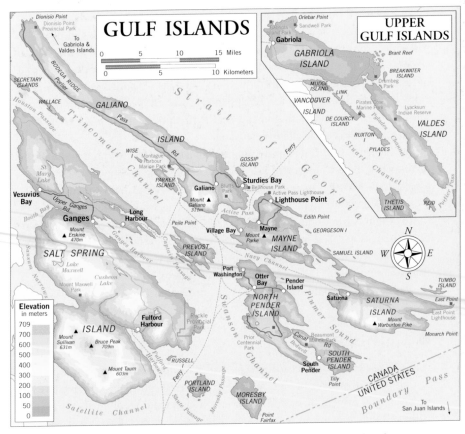

worth seeing: the famed Galiano Gallery on Descanso Bay, a 300-foot-long, 12-foot-high, spectacular sandstone formation near Malaspina Point that looks like petrified surf and sea foam. It shows what power the sea has when it exerts its full force to hollow out rock. (The Galiano Gallery is also sometimes confusingly called "Malaspina Gallery," by British Columbians, because it is near Malaspina Point, and perhaps because of a famous picture of the gallery published in Malaspina's *Voyages*.)

■ GALIANO ISLAND

Galiano Island is the first stop after the Tsawwassen ferry crosses Georgia Strait, and it retains much of the rustic character of its densely forested hillsides, towering bluffs, wildflower meadows, and sheltered harbors (only in these bucolic islands would anyone think of describing a harbor as "rustic"). Trails along **Bodega Ridge** wind through old-growth forest, past wildflower meadows, and open up to great views of the Olympic Mountains to the southwest. From **Bluffs Park** and **Mount Galiano** you can watch tide rips swirl through Active Pass and observe bald eagles as they scan the channel for fish or carrion.

This long, skinny sliver of rock is considered by many to be the most scenic of the Gulf Islands—perhaps because residents have fought to keep it unspoiled. It lies between two famous salmon fishing areas, Porlier Pass on the north, separating Galiano from Valdez Island, and Active Pass on the south, separating Galiano from Mayne. The latter is also an incredibly scenic as well as busy shipping and ferry lane.

Cormorants nest on the rocks and small islands separating Montague Harbour from Trincomali Channel. **Montague Harbour Marine Park** has campsites, a picnic area, floats, a boat launch, and sheltered swimming beaches. Bellhouse Provincial Park at Sturdies Bay overlooks Active Pass.

Galiano Island has resorts, a nine-hole golf course, and barely 1,200 residents, one gas station, but no bank, and only a few stores, all clustered at the southern end. Restaurants are scarce. La Berengerie restaurant is about as gourmet as things get around here. The pub fare at the Hummingbird Inn at the junction of Sturdies Bay and Georgeson Bay roads is a less expensive alternative. **Dionisio Point Provincial Park** at the north end of the island has challenging trails and primitive camping.

■ MAYNE ISLAND

Mayne Island is pastoral in a woodsy way. Middens of clam and oyster shells have been dated back 5,000 years, showing the island has been visited seasonally for a long time. Mayne was a stopover point for miners headed to Fraser River and Cariboo gold fields. By the mid-1800s it was the commercial center of the inhabited Gulf Islands. Farms and orchards were established by the Japanese in the 1930s and worked until their owners were interned during World War II. Farms and orchards still prosper, but there's no longer anything Japanese about the island. A farmer's market is open on Saturdays during harvest season. There's a ferry dock at **Village Bay,** and a trail to the top of **Mount Parke** (look for the carved wooden archway marking the entrance). It's a short 15-minute hike to the highest point on the island. From here you are rewarded with great views of Active Pass,

Vancouver Island, and the Strait of Georgia. Miner's Bay has a tiny museum of local history in the small former jail, the Plumbers Pass Lockup. Nearby St. Mary Magdalene Chapel was built in 1898.

Active Pass Lighthouse at the end of Georgia Point Road was built in 1855 and still operates. The grassy grounds are open to the public on afternoons and are great for picnicking.

■ NORTH AND SOUTH PENDER ISLANDS

These two islands are normally treated as one because they are connected by a picturesque 297-foot bridge. **Port Washington** on North Pender is the largest settlement and has the ferry terminal; **Bedwell Harbour** is the Canadian Customs Port of Entry for air and sea craft entering Canadian waters from the south.

The numerous coves and harbors on South Pender now attract pleasure boaters. During Prohibition they were used by rumrunners—despite their proximity to the Canadian Customs office.

The Pender Islands have few facilities but many beaches. **Prior Centennial Park,** two miles south of Port Washington, has campsites. **Beaumont Marine Park**

A perfect vacation home rests on the shores of Mayne Island.

on South Pender has a fine swimming beach near Bedwell Harbour Village with its commercial marine facilities. Travelers who have left their car at home can rent bicycles. The Stand has the islands' best hamburgers.

■ SALT SPRING ISLAND

This island got its name from 14 salt springs discovered on its north end by officers of the Hudson's Bay Company, who thought the briny emissions of 3,446 grains of salt per Imperial gallon were a bit too salty. Salt Spring is the most popular and commercialized of the Gulf Islands. But don't let that scare you off. "Commercial" here means a gas station or two and a few stores, art galleries, and shops selling hand-made candles and tie-dyed T-shirts.

Twenty-nine kilometers (18 mi) long and 11 kilometers (7 mi) wide, Salt Spring is also the largest and most populous of Gulf Islands. It has a 160 kilometers (100 mi) of road and three hamlets: Fulford Harbour, Ganges, and Vesuvius Bay, each with a ferry terminal. The first thing you note when you land are the steep hills. The highest is 709-meter (2,325-ft) Bruce Peak. From the top you can enjoy panoramic views of islands and mountains without end.

Ganges Harbour on Salt Spring Island.

Two miles south of Ganges, **Mount Maxwell Park** also has views as well as picnic sites. The permanent population of a few thousand souls is more than doubled in summer months, but sheep ranching remains the island's most important industry. If you've ever tasted Salt Spring Island lamb, you know why. Seaside meadows with their abundant sprinkling of wild herbs put special flavors into that tender meat. If you don't eat red meat, you'll be glad to know that the island has 11 freshwater lakes stocked with bass and trout.

Ganges, the island's cultural and commercial center, is a pedestrian-oriented seaside village where you should drop in at the rather ramshackle Mouat's Mall, built in 1912 and still serving as community store. Many studios of local artists are open to the public. Pick up a tour map at the chamber of commerce on Lower Ganges Road.

Salt Spring Island has two **Saturday markets.** They're held between April and October—one on top of the hill next to the Harbour House, the other in the center of town on Fulford-Ganges Road near Centennial Park. Look for locally grown fresh produce, seafood, crafts, clothing, herbs, candles, toys, home-canned foods, et al. (If you're not equipped to cook while traveling, go for the berries, apples, and other fruits, and for smoked salmon and other smoked or pickled seafood).

Ruckle Provincial Park is an 1872 heritage homestead with extensive fields still farmed by the Ruckle family. This working farm/park has camping and picnic spots as well as trails leading to rocky headlands.

■ SATURNA

The most southeasterly of the Gulf Islands, Saturna lies to lee of Mayne Island. It's sparsely populated, difficult to reach, and has no overnight accommodations. So why bother? There's a scenic, 12-mile marine drive from the ferry terminal at Lyall Harbour to the East Point Lighthouse (open to the public). The east slope of Mt. Warburton Pike has an ecological reserve to protect a virgin stand of Douglas fir.

Every July 1st, on Canada Day, Saturna hosts over a thousand visitors at the annual Saturna Lamb Barbecue, which has become a tradition for residents of all the islands. And don't worry: Saturna Island lamb is as good as Salt Spring lamb—if not better.

■ OTHER ISLANDS OF THE GULF OF GEORGIA

Denman and Hornby islands north of Nanaimo are sometimes included among the Gulf Islands though they are quite separate, as are Quadra, Sonora, and Cortes Island of the Discovery Group at the northern end of Georgia Strait.

Denman has old-growth forests and long sandy beaches; Hornby, too, has spectacular beaches. Both islands have thriving communities of potters, sculptors, and wood carvers. Ferries leave from Buckley Bay near Comox/Courtenay.

■ QUADRA ISLAND

Quadra is separated from Campbell River by Discovery Passage (a 10-minute ferry ride). When the first fur trappers arrived in the region the island was part of the traditional territory of the Coast Salish. But these people were driven out by Kwakiutl moving south. The invaders built a fortified village at Cape Mudge. From here they raided Indian canoes traveling north and south through Discovery Passage and they exacted toll from white ships as well—until the provincial gunboat *Forward* shelled the village and stockade in 1860.

The **Kwakiutl Museum**, three miles south of the ferry terminal, has an outstanding collection of native masks, blankets, and carvings. Tsa-Kwa-Luten Lodge of the Cape Mudge band of Kwakiutl, a contemporary lodge overlooking Discovery Passage, serves a weekly buffet of regional foods in summer, followed by tribal dancing.

■ SAN JUAN ISLANDS

The San Juan Islands are a cluster of large and small tree-clad rocks scattered across the lower end of Georgia Strait in northwest Washington, just below the Canadian border. They are pleasurably reached by ferry, and blessed with a temperate climate, lovely countryside, quiet beaches, and fine vistas.

■ LOPEZ ISLAND

The first stop on the ferry run from Anacortes is Lopez, the flattest of the big islands. Its gentle topography has fostered agriculture since white settlers first arrived on the island in the 1850s. Farmers raise everything from sheep to llamas, and from kiwi fruit to wine grapes.

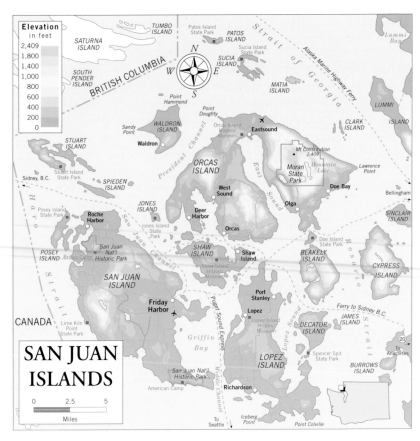

In summer, the island's 1,800 year-round residents are joined by throngs of vacationers who descend on Lopez every sunny weekend. Like the rest of the San Juans, Lopez struggles to hold onto its identity and remain a vital community.

Lopez Village, on the island's western shore, has a few good restaurants, a winery, a supermarket, and a great local history museum. From the ferry terminal you reach Lopez Village by following Ferry Road south about five miles. Along the way you will pass two splendid parks. Both **Odin County Park** and **Spencer Spit Park** are ideal spots to while away an afternoon hiking, beachcombing, picnicking, and even clamming.

■ ORCAS ISLAND

On the map, Orcas Island—the largest of the San Juans and the ferry's third stop—looks like a pair of well-worn saddlebags divided by the long, narrow body of East Sound. Up close, Orcas is lush and steep, and its roads are narrow and contorted. Luxury homes occupy much of the coastline, but along the island's one main road, the landscape remains mostly rural, or thickly forested with second-growth fir and alder.

At the end of the 19th century, fruit orchards and hop fields flourished in the fertile soil of Crow Valley, on the island's western side. All the crops went to market by boat, and as water transportation lost ground to railroads and then trucks, the island became commercially stranded. After irrigation projects converted the arid Wenatchee and Yakima valleys of eastern Washington into fruit-growing centers, most of Orcas Island's orchards were abandoned.

A handful of resorts—from posh Rosario to low-budget Doe Bay—as well as beautiful Moran State Park, draw hordes of visitors in summer. The massive hump of Mount Constitution, the highest point in the San Juans, rises 2,409 feet above

The Olga Store on Orcas Island.

sea level on the eastern side of Orcas Island. A steep, narrow road climbs to the mountain's summit. At road's end stands a watchtower built of hand-cut stone by the Civilian Conservation Corps in 1934-36. An open deck on top of the tower affords a spectacular 360-degree view. To the east, Mount Baker's snowy cone rises over the North Cascades. (In the San Juans, Baker is the peak of reference, as Rainier is from Seattle to Olympia.) The jagged ice-and-granite wall of the Cascades and the Canadian Coast Range closes out the eastern horizon. The Olympics are etched onto the western sky. Eagles soar a thousand feet below.

Mount Constitution is surrounded by **Moran State Park,** a forested 3,325-acre tract of land that covers most of Orcas Island's eastern lobe. The park includes isolated lakes, sandy beaches, and campsites. A few ancient spruce and fir—four or five feet in diameter—grow near the cool, mossy gorge of Cascade Falls, a short walk from the Cold Springs trailhead.

The park was the gift of shipyard tycoon Robert Moran, who served as Seattle's mayor during the fire of 1889, made a fortune building steamships for the Klondike gold rush, then retreated to the San Juans. Moran bought thousands of acres on Orcas, built a 19-bedroom mansion (today the centerpiece of Rosario resort) with two bowling alleys and an indoor pool in 1906, and in 1921, donated most of his land to the state.

During the Great Depression, the CCC (Civilian Conservation Corps) cleared the park's campsites and trails and built its stone gazebos, as well as the Mount Constitution Observation Tower and the stone guardrails along the mountain's treacherous, winding road.

■ SAN JUAN ISLAND

The most developed and second largest of the islands, San Juan is the last stop in U.S. waters on the ferry run from Anacortes, and the seat of San Juan County government. San Juan's National Historic Park, vantage points for whale-watching, restaurants, hotels, and campgrounds attract droves of fair-weather visitors who disembark at the town of Friday Harbor.

A few ribbons of two-lane blacktop cross the island from coast to coast, winding past the small farms of the San Juan Valley. The roads are confusing and poorly marked, but eventually they all lead back to Friday Harbor. Traffic—both cars and bicycles—fills them every summer. Many cyclists will tell you that the best way to enjoy the islands is to leave your car in Anacortes, take ferries between the islands, then bike and camp at your leisure.

Friday Harbor, with a population of 1,600, is the largest community in San Juan County. It was named for Joe Friday—not the "Dragnet" detective, but a Hawaiian shepherd who once lived here. Friday Harbor climbs the hill above the ferry landing and a neighboring marina. The town's brightly painted, remodeled, turn-of-the-19th-century homes have been converted into an assortment of chi-chi bistros, health food stores, and gift shops. A jumble of houses old and new, fashionable and funky, surrounds the business district.

Friday Harbor's **Whale Museum,** a yellow two-story building kitty-corner from the old brick courthouse on First Street, about three blocks north of the ferry dock, houses whale skeletons, models, and informational displays. Speakers in the stairwell broadcast what first seem to be the sounds of creaking docks and keening seagulls, but in fact are the recorded voices of local whale pods, often observed at Lime Kiln State Park on the island's west side.

American and British troops occupied San Juan Island jointly for 12 years in the mid-19th century, and American Camp, where the U.S. forces lived, and English Camp, the British stronghold on the island's north end, are now both administered as **San Juan Island National Historical Park.** (From downtown Friday Harbor take Spring Street west to Mullis Road. Turn left on Argyle, which will turn into Cattle Point Road and lead you to the **visitors' center.**)

American Camp occupies most of San Juan's southern tail, six miles south of Friday Harbor, and includes an information center, interpretive trails, two restored military buildings, and a few miles of public beach. The open plain around American Camp is honeycombed with rabbit warrens over which eagles, hawks, and owls glide, looking for dinner.

British Camp overlooks Garrison Bay, a sheltered inlet on the island's northeast corner, a 10-mile drive from Friday Harbor. A couple of neat, whitewashed buildings, including a two-room barracks with brick fireplaces, are scattered across the manicured lawn that slopes down to the bay. A blockhouse built of unpeeled, whitewashed logs stands at the water's edge.

The joint occupation was a peaceful affair, and relations between the occupation troops were friendly. The soldiers often attended holiday parties at each other's encampments and spent most of their time gardening, hunting, and maintaining their tidy settlements. The structures remain here thanks to the preservation efforts of a local named Jim Crook, who homesteaded the land following the departure of British troops.

A trail leads uphill from the parking lot, across the road and up to the British cemetery on the slope of Mount Young. Here lie the oak-shaded gravestones of eight Englishmen who died during the joint occupation. These men were casualties not of war, but of accidents. Above the graveyard are the steep, arid slopes of Mount Young, with meadows of tall, golden grasses, mossy slabs of exposed granite, and ancient, twisted oak trees.

■ SHAW ISLAND

Shaw Island, the ferry's next stop and the smallest of the four islands that it serves, is home to a few hundred permanent residents—among them a community of Franciscan nuns who run the ferry dock and the grocery store. Shaw's residents value their seclusion and have thus far resisted the tourist trade that thrives on the neighboring islands. Shaw offers neither restaurants nor overnight accommodations—the island's community plan forbids both.

(above) The seaside perch of the restaurant at San Juan Island's most famous hotel, the Roche Harbor Resort. (opposite) A spectacular view from the summit of Mount Constitution out across Rosario Strait to the islands and mainland. The towering volcanic cone of Mount Baker is visible in the background.

■ SUCIA ISLAND

Accessible only by private boat or floatplane, Sucia Island has the most widely sculpted of the San Juan Island sandstone formations. Surrounding several quiet coves, they are topped by red-and-beige-barked madrona trees that are so gnarled and twisted they look as if a gardener overdid it in placing them. But they grew that way—they're all natural. These rocks and trees alone are worth a visit. The eccentric beauty of the sandstone formations did not stop 19th-century entrepreneurs from quarrying them. Many of them ended up as paving stones on downtown Seattle sidewalks.

Some interesting remnants of the region's past have been found in **Fossil Bay:** a clay bank once yielded the perfect foreleg and hoof of a prehistoric horse. (The island is a state park and removing fossils is illegal.)

Kenmore Air in Seattle offers floatplane trips to Sucia; (206) 364-6990.

■ WALDRON ISLAND

Waldron Island has no public access, but it has numerous small rocky coves off its dramatically steep eastern shore where boats may anchor, as well as tiny beaches, unreachable by land, where kayakers may haul out and camp. Here the locals may see you, but they can't reach you. The steep sandstone cliffs near Point Disney were once quarried for the building stone that changed Seattle from a wooden city into a stone one.

■ TRAVEL AND CLIMATE

■ GETTING THERE

The scattered pieces of rock making up these islands are geologically part of Vancouver Island but were cut from the mother rock several millennia ago by deep-grinding continental glaciers. Today, they are politically divided into the Canadian Gulf Islands and the American San Juan Islands .

By Ferry. Car and passenger ferries travel among the Canadian Gulf Islands and among the U.S. San Juan Islands but not between the two island groups themselves. If you travel by car and ferry, you might want to plan a loop trip, boarding the Washington State ferry in Anacortes, Washington, and exploring the San Juan

Islands; continuing by Washington State ferry to Vancouver Island and Victoria; and from there taking a B.C. ferry to the Gulf Islands. Close the loop by taking a ferry from the Gulf islands to the B.C. mainland and the city of Vancouver. Be sure to bring your passport.

The terminals for ferries to these islands are little more than an hour's drive from Seattle or Vancouver. Active Pass between Galiano and Mayne Islands is the most scenic route in the islands, with the tide rips of the pass swirling around the ship, and the more than 2,000-foot-high peaks of southern Salt Spring Island looming above the channel's northwest shores.

British Columbia ferries from Tsawwassen on the mainland and from Vancouver Island (Swartz Bay, Nanaimo, and other docks) have regularly scheduled services. Since departure and arrival times are a bit confusing and since not all of the ferries go to or stop at the same islands, you should plan ahead, especially if you're planning to bring your car, and make reservations. For information and reservations call (604) 699-1211 in Vancouver and (250) 386-3431 in Victoria.

In the San Juan Islands, the four largest—Lopez, Shaw, Orcas, and San Juan—are served by the Washington State ferry from Anacortes or Vancouver Island. The rest can be reached only by private boat or plane.

By Air and Floatplane. Tiny air services using single-engine planes fly between the San Juan Islands and Bellingham and Anacortes. Floatplane companies offer scheduled and charter flights from Vancouver to the Gulf Islands.

■ CLIMATE

The San Juan and Gulf Islands lie in the rain shadow of the Olympic Mountains and the Insular Range and receive 29 inches of rain annually, compared to Seattle's 40 inches and Vancouver's 58. Summers are warm and winters are generally mild.

ISLAND DREAMTIME

Imagine yourself on a sandy beach of a quiet little cove. On the far shore, almost cutting off the bay from the strait, rise sandstone cliffs carved by the action of wind and water into weird shapes. Some resemble dragons, others look like petrified sponges, mushrooms, or giant fish heads.

Below the cliffs, the waves have cut deep tide pools. Their sides are encrusted with colorful lichen that all but match the mottled colors of sculpins, making them difficult to see. Limpets and snails crawl on tidal rocks, tiny crabs scurry among piles of seaweed, a large purple starfish clings to the side of a boulder.

Hidden in a dark crevice, you spot a tiny octopus, its tentacles barely hidden from the light. Octopuses are secretive and usually emerge only at night, when they stalk crabs and other prey. The inland waters of the Pacific Northwest are home to the largest octopus in the world (with an arm spread of more than nine feet and a weight of about 100 pounds). But this harmless monster is rarely encountered near the beach.

Ducks chatter as they dabble among the eelgrass in the shade of a large cedar whose flexible boughs hang out far over the water. Behind you tower tall firs, all but cutting off the view of the snow-capped Cascades to the east, where the glaciers atop the volcanic cone of Mount Baker glow pink in the setting sun. A robin trills its nightly song from a blackberry thicket as the booming hoot of a great horned owl echoes from the cliffs.

You've been fishing all day, and your boat is now safely anchored just offshore. Several kayaks are pulled up on the beach near you; an aluminum skiff rests in the sand further on. You've tidied up your campsite and spread out your sleeping bag. Now you're ready for dinner.

Fishing was good, today. You've caught a lingcod, a couple of rockfish, and three Dungeness crabs. A pot of saltwater you've set on the hot rocks of the campfire is beginning to boil. You drop in the crabs one by one. You spread the lingcod, Indian fashion, between sticks, brush it with butter, sprinkle it with salt and pepper, and set it up by the fire. You invite your neighbors for dinner. They contribute some pink scallops they gathered while diving and a pail of wild blackberries. As you open a bottle of wine, the sun sets behind Vancouver Island. You're in paradise.

A paradise like this can be found in many of the small coves of the Gulf and San Juan Islands. And you don't even need a boat to reach it. On many of the larger islands served by ferries, trails lead to hidden coves like this.

■ ACCOMMODATIONS AND RESTAURANTS: GULF ISLANDS

☎   For chain lodgings see toll-free numbers on page 352.

$$ For room and restaurant price designations see page 352.

✶   Means highly recommended.

GALIANO ISLAND

☎ ✕ **Galiano Lodge and Resort.**
134 Madrona Dr.; (250) 539-3388
This plush lodge sits right on Sturdies Bay and has great views of Active Pass and Mount Baker. Dinners are prepared with fresh local ingredients. $$$

☎ **Woodstone Country Inn.**
743 Georgeson Bay Rd.; (250) 539-2022
An elegant, albeit somewhat formal retreat in a beautiful pastoral setting of woods and green pastures. The dining room is as haute cuisine as cookery in the islands gets. House built 1895; four-room wing added in 1989. $$$

✕ **La Berengerie.**
Montague Harbour Rd.; (250) 539-5392
This small restaurant, the most popular place on the island, is run by a Paris-trained chef. The atmosphere is casual, the food excellent. Upstairs are five basic guest rooms. (closed in winter) $$

MAYNE ISLAND

☎ **Fernhill Lodge.**
Fernhill Rd.; (250) 539-2544
A comfortable, eclectically decorated hilltop retreat with uncommonly friendly hosts. $$$$

☎ ✕ **Oceanwood Country Inn.** ✶
630 Dinner Bay Rd.; (250) 539-5074
Casual, utterly comfortable bed-and-breakfast. This is the perfect retreat for a weekend, week, or month away from it all. The inn also has a splendid little restaurant with waterfront views and Northwest cuisine. Restaurant reservations required. $$$ -$$$$

SOUTH PENDER ISLAND

☎ **Bedwell Harbour Resort.**
9801 Spaulding Rd.; (250) 629-3212
Tucked away in a sheltered, woodsy cove, the resort has basic rooms and up-scale condominiums, a restaurant, and a full-service marina. $$

SALT SPRING ISLAND

☎ **Hastings House.** ✶
160 Upper Ganges Rd.; (800) 661-9255
This is about the most luxurious, best-run lodge in British Columbia. Dinners are always splendid; the Salt Spring Island lamb and the local salmon are particularly tasty. Reservations, jacket, and tie required in restaurant. (Closed in winter) $$$$

☎ **Old Farmhouse.**
1077 Northend Rd.; (250) 537-4113
A small, lovely, and very cozy inn in an old farmhouse. $$$$

☎ **Salty Springs Resort.**
1460 North Beach Rd.; (800) 665-0039
This is the only place on the island making use of the natural mineral springs. It has rustic ponderosa pine cabins with

fireplaces, and therapeutic whirlpool tubs tapped into the mineral springs. The resort is surrounded by 29 undeveloped acres and has saltwater views. $$$$

✗ **Moby's Marine Pub.**
124 Upper Ganges Rd.; (250) 537-5559
Pub food and good beer. $

✗ **Piccolo.**
108 Hereford Ave.; (250) 537-1844
Some of the best seafood in Ganges prepared with Scandinavian exuberance. Reservations advised. $$

S A T U R N A   I S L A N D

⌑ ✗ **Boot Cove Lodge and Restaurant.**
Follow signs from the ferry;
(250) 539-2254
A lovely lodge overlooking an oyster farm. Meals are made with fresh local ingredients, the rooms are bright and comfortable. $$

⌑ **Stone House Farm Resort.** 207 Narvaez Bay Rd.; (250) 539-2683
A pleasant neo-Tudor house with comfortable rooms and friendly innkeepers. $$-$$

■ ACCOMMODATIONS AND RESTAURANTS: SAN JUAN ISLANDS

L O P E Z   I S L A N D

⌑ **Blue Fjord Cabins.**
Elliott Rd. at Jasper Cove; (360) 468-2749
Two log cabins (each with a full kitchen) tucked away at the end of a dirt road guarantee the ultimate island privacy. $$

⌑ **Edenwild Inn.**
Lopez Village; (360) 468-3238
Eight rooms, each with bath, in a Victorian-style bed-and-breakfast in the heart of Lopez Village. An easy stroll from the scarce local restaurants. $$$

⌑ **Inn at Swift's Bay.**
3402 Port Stanley Rd.; (360) 468-3636
A former summer home has been turned into exquisitely elegant lodging, with suites and cabins. $$$

⌑ **McKaye Harbor Inn.**
McKaye Harbor Rd.; (360) 468-2253
This small two-story inn has the best views on Lopez Island. It makes a great home base if you're planning to kayak. $$

✗ **Bay Cafe.**
North end of Lopez Village, across from Zephyr Espresso; (360) 468-3700
Owner-chef Bob Wood specializes in ethnic dishes. Prices are reasonable, and there's usually at least one vegetarian option. The wine list is excellent and prices are reasonable. No wonder the place is popular with both residents and visitors. Reservations strongly advised. $$

O R C A S   I S L A N D

⌑ **Doe Bay Village Resort.**
Star Route 86, Olga; (360) 376-2291
"Funky" is the adjective used most often to describe the Doe Bay Resort. A former artists' colony, it offers some living spaces with kitchens and some without private showers or baths. Both guests and visitors can use the hot tubs. $-$$

⌑ **Rosario Spa and Resort.**
1 Rosario Way,, off Horseshoe Hwy.,

Eastsound; (800) 562-8820
The main lodge was built in 1905 by
Seattle shipbuilder Robert Moran after
he was told he had only six months to
live. The doctors were wrong. Moran
lived another 30 years. Now his opulent
copper-roofed dream house forms the
heart of the best-known lodge in the San
Juans. Upkeep can be inconsistent, so
check out rooms before moving in. $$$

⌂ **Spring Bay Inn.**
Obstruction Pass Trailhead Rd., Olga;
(360) 376-5531
Sunny bed-and-breakfast where the
friendly owners offer kayaking lessons
by day and cozy fires by night. $$$

⌂ **Turtleback Farm Inn.**
Crow Valley Rd. (10 minutes from the
ferry), Eastsound; (360) 376-4914
This place, with its woods, fields, and
pastures, seems to be everybody's fa-
vorite retreat. $$$

✕ **Christina's.**
North Beach Rd. and Horseshoe Hwy.,
Eastsound; (360) 376-4904
A homey restaurant on the waterfront.
The food is anything but rustic. Christi-
na's is the place for oysters from nearby
Crescent Beach, local rockfish and
salmon, and the freshest of vegetables
grown by Orcas Island gardeners. The
ambiance is casual; the food is elegant.
Yes, it's worth a ferry ride. Reservations
strongly advised. $$- $$$

✕ **Ship Bay Oyster House.**
Horseshoe Hwy. east of Eastsound;
(360) 376-5886
A great place to sample the local oysters. $$

SAN JUAN ISLAND

⌂ **Hillside House Bed and Breakfast.**
365 Carter Ave., Friday Harbor;
(360) 378-4730
A charming bed-and-breakfast overlooking Friday Harbor and Mount Baker.
Particularly impressive to avid birders
are mounted binoculars on the outdoor
deck. $$-$$$

⌂ **Roche Harbor Resort.**
4950 Tarte Memorial Dr., Roche Harbor; (360) 378-2155
Lodging is in the restored 1886 hotel
that forms the heart of the Roche Harbor. Rooms are small but cozy; cottages
and larger condos are available. $$-$$$

✕ **Duck Soup Inn.**
3090 Roche Harbor Rd.; (360) 378-4878
Great dishes made from fresh local ingredients. Good wine list. The best
place for sampling Westcott Bay oysters
if you don't like slurping them raw from
the shell at the oyster farm up the road.
Reservations advised. $$

✕ **Roberto's.**
205 A St., Friday Harbor; (360) 378-6333
A splendid little restaurant serving Ital-
ian-style food. Get there early or the
best of the night's dishes may have been
gobbled up by the locals. $$

✕ **Springtree Cafe.**
310 Spring St., Friday Harbor; (360)
378-4848
In fair weather you can truly talk about
"splendor under the elm tree" when you
sample the food. The vegetarian dishes
are best, but the seafood is also excellent.
$$

NORTHWEST INTERIOR

■ HIGHLIGHTS

Issaquah Alps
Skagit River Valley
North Cascades Park
Fidalgo Island
Whidbey Island
Apple, Cheese, and Oyster Tour

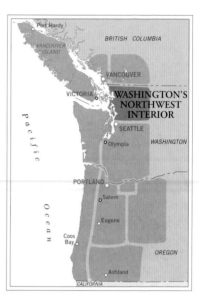

■ LANDSCAPE

THE CITIES OF THIS REGION ARE, on a clear day, always in sight of salt water and mountains. The relatively flat land on which they have been built was gouged out by rivers of ice that left deep valleys, which were then filled by gravels and clays left behind by the glaciers or by silt carried by rivers from the rugged Cascade Mountains, which form the eastern boundary of the region. The lower parts of these valleys—Puget Sound and its channels and inlets—are filled with water from the sea. The Cascades, from Snoqualmie Pass north to Canada, have been set aside as national park, wilderness, or national recreation areas. Hundreds of miles of hiking trails wind through wilderness areas, Ross Lake National Recreation Area, and North Cascades National Park. To the west, killer whales, ferries, kayaks, and sailboats travel through the channels of the inland sea to the islands.

■ NORTH CASCADES

The granite peaks of the North Cascades are far more rugged and ancient than the eroded hills south of Snoqualmie Pass. Drive into these mountains on a cloudy

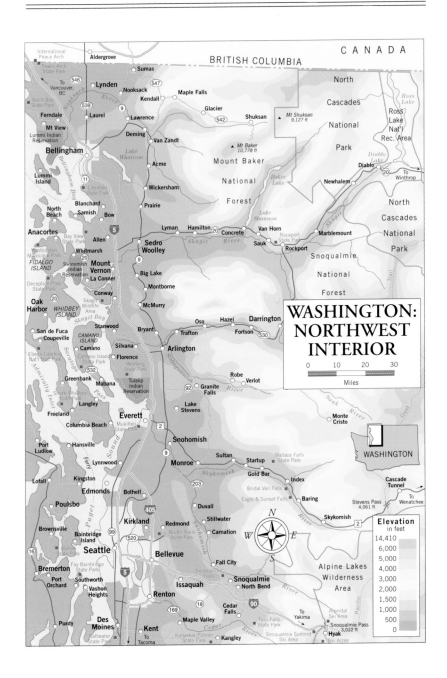

WASHINGTON: NORTHWEST INTERIOR

0   10   20   30
Miles

day, and the evergreens on the steep slopes look almost black, while the rock walls reaching for the clouds, like mountains in a Chinese landscape painting, seem to rise from earth to heaven. On the lower slopes in the heat of summer, the soil of the rocky trail may be dry as dust, while farther up patches of snow linger among wildflower meadows in full bloom with white or golden lilies, bright red-orange Indian paintbrush, and intensely purple lupines. As you climb higher, ridge succeeds ridge, their misty outlines towered over by the great, snowcapped volcanoes.

In the solitude of the mountains, hikers may not encounter any other humans, but they will always be in the company of wild animals—whiskeyjacks, juncos, buntings, pikas, chipmunks, ptarmigans, mountain goats, and, in rare instances, cougars. The heavy snows of winter, and the rock and ice of the high country, have not made the mountains inhospitable to wildlife. Wolves, once hunted nearly to extinction in the North Cascades, are making a comeback. Threatened northern spotted owls and marbled murrelets nest here. Salmon spawn in many of the rivers. Also present, but rarely seen, are grizzly bears, not at all surprising in mountains this rugged and wild.

Just north of Snoqualmie Pass, the half-million-acre **Alpine Lakes Wilderness**, a haven for hikers, fishermen, and backpackers, comes almost to the shoulder of the road.

■ SNOQUALMIE PASS

Despite its modest elevation, Snoqualmie Pass (3,004 feet) receives 35 feet of snow a year and offers skiing for all experience levels. Skiers head for the groomed slopes, Nordic trails, and warm firesides of ski areas like Alpental, Ski Acres, and Snoqualmie Summit.

In the foothills west of the pass, popular trails lead through the so-called **Issaquah Alps** or climb the steep southern slope of 4,167-foot **Mount Si**, the crag that looms over the upper Snoqualmie Valley. Nearby, the Snoqualmie River plunges 268 feet over a stone ledge at Snoqualmie Falls. The spot has always been sacred to the Snoqualmie Indians, who believe that the mists rising from the catch basin below ascend like prayers to heaven.

A hydroelectric powerhouse carved out of the solid rock below the falls has been producing electricity here since 1899. The steam train **Puget Sound & Snoqualmie Valley Railroad** runs along a scenic route between North Bend, at the base of Mount Si, and Snoqualmie, near the falls. Purchase tickets for the ride at the Snoqualmie Depot Museum on Railroad Avenue; (206/425) 746-4025.

■ EVERETT

Everett, a port 30 miles north of Seattle, lies on the shore of Port Gardner Bay, an inlet of northeast Puget Sound. Just south of town, **Boeing** manufactures 747s in the largest space under one roof in the world. The weekday tour of the plant, which allows visitors to view the huge aircraft in various stages of assembly, is arguably the premier industrial tour of the state; call (206) 342-4801.

A former mill town, Everett was platted in 1890. Frederick Weyerhaeuser subsequently built what became the world's biggest sawmill on its shore. Beautiful examples of building styles popular in the early decades of the 20th century decorate downtown. Within a few blocks you see the grand old wing of the Spanish mission-style courthouse with its clock and bell tower; the ornate art-deco brick of City Hall, and the massive, Romanesque Federal Building. Many of the mansions built by lumber barons still stand on Grand and Rucker avenues at the north end of town. Several blocks farther north on 18th Street are the marina and **Marina Village**—a string of waterfront restaurants and shops. It's here that you catch the ferry to **Jetty Island** for a day of picnicking, hiking, and bird-watching. Other sites in Everett include the **Everett Museum**, housed in a century-old brick building at 2915 Hewitt Street, and the **Everett Publick Market** at 284 Grand, a two-story structure consisting of shops, galleries, cafes, and an antique mall.

Northeast of Everett off WA 530 in the Cascade foothills lies the town of **Darrington,** originally settled by loggers from North Carolina. A **bluegrass festival** held here each July celebrates the town's Tarheel roots. In this scenic valley, dairy cattle graze in wet meadows with the crags and spires of the North Cascades rising behind them.

■ SKAGIT RIVER VALLEY

The jade green Skagit River rises in Canada and flows down through the North Cascades, entering Puget Sound in a wide delta southwest of the town of Mount

Vernon. Much of it is protected as the Skagit National Wild and Scenic River. At the river's mouth, the Skagit Wildlife Area provides habitat for whistling swans, snow geese, and other birds.

■ SKAGIT WILDLIFE AREA

To reach this birdwatcher's paradise, take the Conway–La Conner Road off Interstate 5 heading west. After winding past fields and farms, the road crosses a bridge to the top of the Skagit River levee. Look for signs directing you to the wildlife area. But before you go, look at the current hunting regulations: you're not going to see many birds on days open to hunting. But at other times, especially in spring, summer, and fall, this place is truly idyllic.

Ducks and geese are most common in spring and fall, when huge flocks stop here on their way to and from wintering marshes in California's Sacramento Valley. But many waterfowl, especially swans, stay here all winter. There's nothing more stirring than to watch a skein of trumpeter swans flying overhead, their melodic bugling drifting across the marsh. In summer, watch for goldfinches collecting thistledown for their nests. Swallows twitter in the air, the booming "oonk-

Mount Shuksan (above) is one of the many northern Cascade peaks which rise above the Skagit River Valley (right). The valley is one of the world's foremost tulip-growing regions.

ka-ch'oonk" of a bittern may resound from the reeds, a great blue heron may wade in the shallow water, carefully measuring each step, as it searches for frogs, fish, and muskrats. You may be startled by the rattling call of a kingfisher while listening to the melodious gurgling of a meadowlark. If your meditations are interrupted by a loud splash, hold still. The beaver that slapped its tail on the water to scare off the intruder will return to see if it worked, and it may slap again and again before deciding you may be harmless after all. If you're lucky you can see a beaver carry sticks and twigs to a lodge. And if you're really fortunate, a beaver may climb from the water, lumber up a bank, and begin cutting down a willow or cottonwood (often you can hear a beaver's gnawing long before you spot the animal itself). Or you might see a family of otters cruising a slough in search of crayfish. This is truly a magical place. Don't forget your camera and binoculars.

■ MOUNT VERNON

Mount Vernon, on Interstate 5, straddles the Skagit River. The town houses a natural-food co-op, where chef Peter Cady cooks, a Mexican grocery, two bike shops, a good bakery, and a small bookstore with an entire shelf devoted to UFO abductions. In spring, Mount Vernon bustles with visitors to its 10-day **Tulip Festival**, when daffodils and tulips paint the fields in bright yellows, pinks, and reds in late March and April. *(See page 360.)*

For a look at the Skagit River delta farmlands, turn off the freeway south of Mount Vernon and head west to **Conway**, a quiet hamlet with a white-steepled church built in 1916 and a tavern very popular with visitors.

Between Conway and La Conner, the delta spreads out in a patchwork of fallow and green fields. Farmhouses with their huge old barns sit by the side of the road at regular intervals; drainage ditches wind through the green fields. You can tell from far off that one old, whitewashed, clapboard building atop a levee is a country store, because it advertises the usual: "BAIT, AMMO, COLD BEER." On a clear day, white-topped Mount Baker dominates the landscape.

■ LA CONNER

La Conner lies along the eastern bank of the Swinomish Channel, a narrow inland waterway used as a sheltered marine passage from Bellingham Bay to Puget Sound. Quaint "olde tyme" boutiques, craft stores, and antique marts occupy the early 20th-century storefront buildings along La Conner's First Street. Visitors browse the trinket shops and dine al fresco in restaurants overlooking the channel.

La Conner's reputation as an "artists' colony" dates back to the late 1930s, when Northwest School painters Guy Anderson and Morris Graves took up residence in a dilapidated cabin here. It got a boost in the 1970s when novelist and pop philosopher Tom Robbins became the town's most famous resident. Fine old Victorian homes and churches stand on the cliff above the commercial district. The Skagit County Historical Museum sits atop the hill, at the end of Fourth Street. The two-story brick wedge of City Hall, built in 1886, rises above Second Street at the south end of town. Between the city hall and the high, orange arch of the painted steel bridge that spans the channel, fish-processing plants stand near the water in a jumble of green nylon nets and crab pots.

■ UPPER SKAGIT AND NORTH CASCADES PARK

The Skagit tumbles out of some of the state's most wild and beautiful country. Upstream from the vacation town of Rockport, the **Skagit River Bald Eagle Natural Area** attracts some 500 bald eagles every winter, when they come to feed on spawned-out chum and other salmon. Beyond the eagle refuge, WA 20, the North Cascades Scenic Highway, follows the river through **Ross Lake National Recreation Area,** a buffer zone between the northern and southern units of North Cascades National Park. Campgrounds, trailheads, lodges, resorts, and boat launches can be found here as well as in adjacent national forest lands.

The drive along the highway is invigoratingly scenic. Stop for the views from Goodall Creek Viewpoint and the Diablo Lake, Ross Lake, and Washington Pass overlooks.

North Cascades National Park is home to 1,700 species of plants, more than botanists have found in any other national park. The highway's climax is Washington Pass (5,477 feet), from which short hikes lead to spectacular views of Snagtooth Ridge, Cooper Basin, and the jagged peak of Liberty Bell.

The national park itself is a roadless wilderness accessible only by foot. Trails connect the national park and recreation area with the Pasayten Wilderness to the east, and to the Glacier Peak Wilderness and the Lake Chelan National Recreation area to the south. Water taxis take hikers up 24-mile-long Ross Lake to trailheads far north of the road. One trail leads to the nation's largest stand of old-growth western red cedar. But there are also short trails that start at campgrounds or the side of the highway and can easily be covered in a day or a few hours. Fishermen can rent boats and motors at the **Ross Lake Resort** or the **Diablo Lake Resort.**

Both Ross and Diablo lakes were created early in the 20th century by Seattle City Light power dams. The scenic trip up Diablo Lake ends at the foot of Ross Dam. A four-mile hike takes you to Cascade Pass and back, through acres of lupines and white-tufted beargrass. Water seeps out under glaciers, tumbles over boulders in gray streambeds, and drops down sheer vertical walls. In a nearby cirque filled with fireweed, dozens of nameless waterfalls cascade over granite cliffs.

■ FIDALGO ISLAND

Wooded and rural, with rocky outcroppings rising straight from the sea on one side and tideflats stretching across Padilla Bay on the other, Fidalgo Island is a very appealing place. Its only town, Anacortes, has the ferry landing for the San Juan Islands' ferry. But Fidalgo is more than just a ferry stop. It's an island worth exploring. The island is connected to the mainland by a bridge (WA 20) across Swinomish Channel, a winding saltwater slough. To the south of the highway lies

(above) Deception Pass between Fidalgo and Whidbey islands. (opposite) One of the many glacier-fed streams coursing through the forests of the Cascade Mountains.

the Swinomish Indian Reservation, a quiet, woodsy place with a Native village across the channel from La Conner.

Anacortes, at the island's northwestern shore has attractive parks and maritime views, the ornate 19th-century residential neighborhood of Causland Park, and an attractive old downtown area. A refurbished steam engine pulls cars and tourists through the town on the **Anacortes Railway** from the old Burlington Northern Depot. South of town, accessible by paved road, Mount Erie (1,270 feet) offers views of Campbell Lake, of Deception Pass (a churning saltwater channel, to the south) and, on clear days, of Mount Rainier and Mount Baker.

From the air, the rocky hill of **Washington City Park** looks like a sounding whale, half risen from the water. Mostly covered with a dense tangle of Douglas fir, cedar, madrona, and alder, broken now and then by clearings and meadows, the park rises from the waters of Rosario Strait to the rocky crest of Fidalgo Head. You can navigate it by a car on a narrow, 2.4-mile loop road, or you can explore it on one of the many trails winding through the woods.

On **Fidalgo Head,** grass-covered cliffs rise from the churning currents of Burrows Channel in a series of rocky steps to forested ridges. Bedecked with wildflowers in spring, they appear like well-tended rock gardens, though the artifice of man played no role in their creation. If the rocks here look different, that's because they are. Fidalgo Head is composed of serpentine and ultrabasic rocks, which also make up the southern part of Cypress Island, to the immediate north, and are akin to the dunite rock of the Twin Sisters at the edge of the North Cascades—but are totally unrelated to any other rocks found in the vicinity.

Twisted junipers crouch on the exposed rocks of Fidalgo Head. Their tangled roots grip the convoluted rocks, their gnarled branches reach defiantly into the sky with wind-burned tips. Hawks and bald eagles ride the updrafts of the cliff face on their never ceasing shore patrols.

■ WHIDBEY ISLAND

Across Deception Pass Bridge from Fidalgo Island lies Whidbey Island, the second longest island in the country. Lying in the Olympic rain shadow, Whidbey receives little rain even in the wet season. Sunny summer days attract many visitors. Farms, woods, and native prairies cover most of this peaceful island; towns are small.

Deception Pass State Park borders both shores of the channel that British navigator Capt. George Vancouver sighted in 1792. Hoping the rock-bound passage would lead to a secure harbor, Vancouver felt deceived and named it Deception Pass. Visitors to the park can hike, swim, fish, or go boating.

When you see strands of seaweed swirling in the tidal eddies of Deception Pass, consider yourself fortunate, for you are beholding the hair of a beautiful maiden of the Samish people who married the spirit of Deception Pass. Seeing the maiden brings good luck: you shall have wealth and ample food for the rest of your life.

Whidbey Island changes with the year, from the wildflower-covered meadows of spring to the wind-ruffled days of winter, when new colonies of lichen spread across the decaying concrete walls of the abandoned forts like so many colorful ice flowers. Not that you'd ever see many real ice flowers here. The climate is dry—with some of the lowest rainfall averages west of the Washington Cascades—and mild throughout the year. An occasional wild rose may bloom on New Year's Day; rain and snow never stay for long. Turquoise cabbage fields, Van Gogh–yellow wheat patches, lush meadows, and scattered copses of conifers cover the low, undulating landscape of the island's center. Plowed fields, black with the fertile loam of prairies, terminate in tall, sand bluffs crowned by sculpted trees and by weathered snags turned to bronze and pewter by sea breezes and salt air. One of the prairies has been preserved as **Ebey's Landing National Historic Park**. No recreational development will take place—the arable land has been leased back to farmers to insure the preservation of the prairie as farmland, in homage to the early settlers whose back-breaking toil first cleared the land for cultivation.

At the north end of this park, a small turnout marks the beginning of the bluff trail and beach walk to **Perego's Lagoon**. (The land just off the trail is private property, so respect the rights of the owners by treading carefully here.) The trail climbs along the leading edge of the prairie until it reaches a point of about 240 feet above the waters of Admiralty Inlet. The hilltop affords a sweeping view of the water and the Olympic Mountains to the west.

The lagoon and bluff take their name from George Perego, a Civil War veteran who homesteaded here in 1876. Perego never attempted to farm the land, and today it remains a wilderness—a windswept bluff, the lagoon, a low spit of sand, rocks, and driftwood. Many of the rocks are not native to the island. Carried here as ballast in sailing vessels, they were dumped onto the beaches before the ships loaded Puget Sound lumber. Ravens and bald eagles may fly past—and don't be surprised if you see a rare peregrine falcon zip by.

Much of Whidbey Island is a wildflower-lover's paradise in the spring, but the steep meadow at the head of Penn Cove is especially noteworthy. This is one of the few places west of the mountains where the wild blue flag grows in profusion.

From the head of Penn Cove you can drive along winding, scenic Madrona Drive to the **Captain Whidbey Inn,** a long, two-story madrona lodge on a wooded promontory. It is bordered on one side by Penn Cove and on the other by a secluded saltwater lagoon. The Captain Whidbey has a special kind of hospitality and charm now rarely found. Gracefully aged, surrounded by native shrubs and trees, it is the perfect hideout for those who wish to escape from the worry and stress of the world. The bar at the Captain Whidbey is a favorite hangout of local characters. Here you may think and talk, and after a relaxing day, doze off by the fire over a cup of mulled wine.

Continuing down Madrona Drive brings you to **Coupeville,** a village founded in 1852 and little changed since the late 19th century and well known for its art galleries, restaurants, and antique shops. The main street is lined by old buildings with false storefronts. A pier and a few historic houses perch above the tidelands on mussel-encrusted wooden stilts. (The oldest dates from the early 1850s.) On a

Kayaks for rent on Coupeville Pier, Whidbey Island.

Live music on a summer's weekend in Bellingham's Fairhaven district.

clear day, Mount Baker looms to the northeast, its white glaciers reflected in the waters of the cove. The best view is from the backroom at **Toby's Tavern** on the waterfront.

The Island County Historical Museum, next to the Alexander Blockhouse near the waterfront just off Front Street, offers a self-guided walking tour map describing many houses surviving from the mid- to late 1800s. Most of the old homes are still occupied, and all are carefully maintained by their present owners.

Whidbey Island pioneers built blockhouses in the 1850s to protect themselves from raids by marauding Indians (in 1857, a band of Tlinkit Indians from Alaska raided the homestead of Col. Isaac Ebey and took his head to avenge the killing of a chief by U.S. marines). Some of the log structures still stand in the town of **Coupeville,** founded in 1852 and known for its well-preserved Victorian-era downtown.

Another attractive walking village is **Langley** to the south, with galleries, restaurants, an excellent bakery, and small, well-stocked shops. For four days in late August, its Island County Fair brings together local agricultural exhibits, a parade, and logger competitions. **Fort Casey State Park** preserves fortifications built by the army in the 1890s, the **Admiralty Point Lighthouse,** and an underwater park.

■ BELLINGHAM

The last big town before the Canadian border, Bellingham was cobbled together in 1903 from four pioneer communities on Bellingham Bay. A town whose urban core has fallen on hard times since a mall opened north of town, Bellingham is a fishing port with a pulp mill and the **Western Washington University** campus high on Sehome Hill. From the freeway, all you see of Bellingham is the unfortunate strip mall. But there are highlights downtown that include the ornate, restored Mount Baker Theater and the **Whatcom Museum of History and Art,** a massive 1892 brick fantasy at 121 Prospect Street just north of Champion and the downtown's main thoroughfare, Holly. The collection includes Native American artifacts, exhibits on pioneering and logging, and Northwest contemporary art; (360) 676-6981. The museum faces Bellingham Bay and the fishing harbor from its perch atop a steep bluff. The park at the foot of the bluff has a waterfall and spawning beds for fish, where coho salmon spawn in the late autumn.

❖

Fairhaven, on the southern shore of the bay, is the most interesting Bellingham neighborhood. (You get there by taking Old Fairhaven Parkway off Interstate 5 west towards the water and turning right on 12th Street, then left on Harris.)

Fairhaven, it has been said by local street-corner sages, is a state of mind. Spiritually, Fairhaven has maintained its independence as a liberal enclave in a conservative city. Downtown Fairhaven is a collection of coffeeshops, bookstores, restaurants, and a pub, occupying venerable brick buildings. Beyond the core, it's a medley of cottages and gardens, of green woods bordering a purling creek, where salmon run in season, of wildflower meadows and, down along the bay front, sandstone cliffs, tideflats, boatyards, and fishing boats. Here the Alaska ferry docks at the site of what was once the largest salmon cannery in the world. In summer, passenger ferries carry visitors to the San Juan Islands and Victoria.

Sea ducks and river otters feed on the mussels covering the abandoned pilings; great blue herons patiently stand in the shallows, waiting for fish to swim by; crows and gulls patrol the shore, digging for clams and marine worms, and bathing in the brackish water of Padden Creek Lagoon. Sea lions and seals float by; now and then a bald eagle soars overhead. Walk the trail from the lagoon up to Padden Creek in November to watch chum salmon ascend the stream and spawn in the riffles. The salmon attract herons and otters.

Fairhaven has been settled for a long time: ancient shell middens and stone tools going back thousands of years prove that the mouth of Padden Creek has long been occupied by humans. History records one raid in 1854, when Haida Indians, visiting from northern British Columbia, swept down on the fledgling community and attacked a log cabin with little success, but paddled off with the heads of two hapless British coal miners. (Sehome to the north had a coal mine.)

A local historical society has put down plaques throughout the village, marking such historic sites as the city's drowning pool (for dogs only, it says, where the local constable killed stray pets); the shore where Fairhaven moored its prison (a barge); and the site of the town pillory. Yes, Fairhaven had a pillory as late as the 1890s. Plaques also tell you where Dirty Dan Harris, the city's founder, built his log cabin, and where the bunkhouse of Chinese cannery workers stood. Some gardens near the bunkhouse still have drainage ditches dug by the Chinese.

Fairhaven's residents are a motley lot: fishermen and college professors, poets, ship fitters, painters, and the sons and daughters of hippies who settled here in the 1960s. Most importantly, it's a friendly crowd, meeting at the **Colophon** at 1208 11th for breakfast; enjoying a picnic lunch in **Marine Park;** trysting on the bench outside the **Eclipse Bookstore** at 915 Harris; browsing the shelves of **Village Books** at 1210 11th; or enjoying a pint of porter at the **Archer Ale House** at the corner of Harris and 10th. In the evenings they crowd into **Stanello's** at 12th and Donovan for the best pizza in town or congregate at Post Point, to watch the red sun sink behind the San Juan Islands.

■ NOOKSACK VALLEY AND MOUNT BAKER

From Bellingham, WA 542 takes you east to 10,778-foot Mount Baker and the trails of the northernmost and wildest parts of Cascades National Park. *(See page 153.)*

Beyond Glacier, the steep cliffs hemming in the road rise higher and higher, the trees become taller and their branches more gnarled, the boulders in the north fork of the Nooksack River below the road become bigger. A few miles south on twisting Glacier Creek Road will bring you to the trailhead for **Coleman Glacier.**

continues page 166

APPLE, CHEESE, AND OYSTER TOUR

Apples, Washington's best known fruit, are the stars of this trip. While the first apple may have caused the expulsion of Adam and Eve from Paradise, today the coast of northwestern Washington and the eastern mountain valleys of the North Cascades form another Garden of Eden: warm valleys planted with blossoming trees that yield delicious fruit. As of this writing, mankind has been free to enjoy the apples here without incurring heavenly wrath.

Because of the difference in climate, different varieties of apples grow east and west of the mountains. Most people know about eastern Washington apples but are unaware that western Washington also grows great apples. A bonus for visitors is that these orchards are located in an exceptionally scenic area.

Apples and cheese have an affinity for each other. The region also has a native cheese that's just right to enhance the flavor of the locally grown fruit. While traveling from orchard to orchard, as an extra bonus, you'll be passing a shellfish farm where you can sample a variety of oysters, scallops, and clams.

Pleasant Valley Dairy

You start the tour in Whatcom County north of Ferndale by taking Grandview from Interstate 5 west to Kickerville and turning left. Pleasant Valley Dairy will be almost on your left.

The gouda and farmstead cheeses produced at this tiny dairy are made from raw cow's milk aged for a minimum of 60 days; they go very well with Whatcom and Skagit County apples. The dairy is open Saturdays only January through June and Monday through Saturday the rest of year. 6804 Kickerville Rd.; (360) 366-5398.

Cloud Mountain Farm

From Pleasant Valley, you drive to the first of the apple orchards on this tour by continuing south on Kickerville Road to its junction with Mountain View, then heading east to Ferndale (Mountain View turns into Main Street), turning right at Hovander Road which turns into West Smith Road after it crosses Interstate 5. Smith Road eventually runs into the Mount Baker Highway, State Route 542. A left turn brings you to the Nooksack River. Just north of the river, turn left onto State Route 9; turning right on Siper Road, right on Hopewell, and left on Goodwin brings you to Cloud Mountain apple farm. Look for a sign and apple trees on your right.

An orchard on the southwestern slope of Sumas Mountain, which grows such uncommon apples as Elstar, Jonagold, Melrose, Mutsu, and Idared. If you want your apples in concentrated form, without the roughage, you can buy freshly

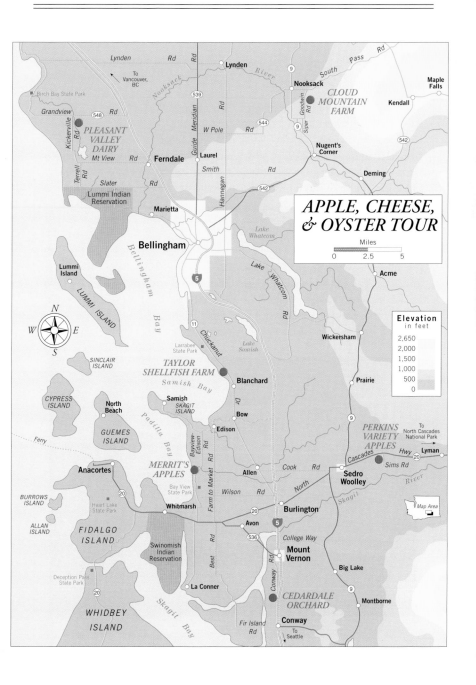

APPLE, CHEESE, & OYSTER TOUR

Miles
0   2.5   5

Elevation
in feet
2,650
2,000
1,500
1,000
500
0

Lynden Rd
Lynden
To Vancouver, BC
Birch Bay State Park
Grandview Rd
548 Rd
Kickerville Rd
Terrell Rd
PLEASANT VALLEY DAIRY
Mt View Rd
Ferndale
Laurel
Smith Rd
Slater Rd
Marietta
Lummi Indian Reservation
Bellingham
Lummi Island
LUMMI ISLAND
Bellingham Bay
SINCLAIR ISLAND
CYPRESS ISLAND
North Beach
GUEMES ISLAND
Ferry
Anacortes
BURROWS ISLAND
ALLAN ISLAND
FIDALGO ISLAND
Heart Lake State Park
Deception Pass State Park
WHIDBEY ISLAND
La Conner
Swinomish Indian Reservation
Skagit Bay
Best Rd
Whitmarsh
Bay View State Park
MERRIT'S APPLES
Bayview-Edison Rd
Padilla Bay
SKAGIT ISLAND
Samish
Samish Bay
TAYLOR SHELLFISH FARM
Larrabee State Park
Chuckanut Dr
Lake Samish
11
Edison
Bow
Blanchard
Allen
Wilson Rd
Avon
20
536
Conway Rd
Fir Island Rd
To Seattle
Conway
CEDARDALE ORCHARD
Mount Vernon
College Way
Burlington
5
Cook Rd
North
Wickersham
Prairie
Acme
Lake Whatcom Rd
Lake Whatcom
542
Deming
Nugent's Corner
CLOUD MOUNTAIN FARM
Nooksack
Lynden
9
South Pass Rd
Maple Falls
Kendall
542
Goodwin Rd
Super Rd
544
W Pole Rd
Meridian Rd
Guide Meridian Rd
539
Hannegan Rd
Nooksack River
Big Lake
Montborne
9
Sedro Woolley
PERKINS VARIETY APPLES
Cascades Hwy
Sims Rd
Lyman
20
Skagit River
To North Cascades National Park
Farm to Market Rd
Map Area

N W E S

pressed cider. 6906 Goodwin Rd., Everson; (360) 966-5859.

❖

Return to Bellingham via the Mount Baker Highway (State Route 542) and head south on Interstate 5 to the Chuckanut Drive exit (exit 250). Follow Chuckanut Drive along the very scenic shoreline south to Taylor United's Samish Bay Shellfish Farm *(also see page 224)*. After Chuckanut Drive leaves the mountain and heads south across the Samish River flats, look for the tiny Bow post office on your right and turn right to Edison. After the road winds through Edison, it changes its name to Farm-to-Market Road. Continue south to D'Arcy Road and turn right. Turn left on Bayview-Edison Road. The most scenic apple farm in Washington, Merrit's, is on your right, where the road reaches the top of the bluff.

Merrit's Apples

The Gravenstein and Jonagold orchards of this farm spread across a bluff above Padilla Bay and on a flat just a few feet above the saltwater shore, where eagles soar. On a clear day, with snow-capped Mt. Baker looming in the eastern sky, you think you've rediscovered the Garden of Eden. When you bite into one of the apples, you know you have. 896 Bayview-Edison Rd., Mount Vernon; (360) 766-6224.

The "Honesty Wagon" of Sunshine Orchards, to the east in the Lake Chelan area.

Golden delicious are the ideal storage apple and the perfect accompaniment to cheese and dessert wine.

Cedardale Orchard

If you're in a hurry, you can skip the northern leg of this tour and stock up on westside apples at Cedardale Orchard. Take the South Mount Vernon exit off Interstate 5, and you'll find the orchard south on the west side of the freeway on Conway Road. You can't miss the big barn and signs of the farm. Here you can sample the diverse flavors of Akane, Gala, Jonagold, Jonamac, Melrose, and Summered; (360) 445-5483.

Continue the tour by taking State Route 20, the North Cascade Highway, east from Burlington across the mountains.

Perkins Variety Apples

Your next chance for stocking up on apples comes on WA 20, the North Cascades Highway, three miles east of Sedro Woolley, at Perkins Variety Apples, where more than a 100 varieties of apples are grown, including Akane, Jonamac, and Melrose. 816 Sims Rd.; (360) 856-6986. Lay in a good supply. While there are blueberry bushes along the North Cascades Highway (in season, if you hit right), there are no more orchards till you reach the valleys on the far side of the mountains.

A short trail leads to the glacier's snout, where the ice pushes into the alders; a longer, steeper hike brings you to the glacier's side, where you can look down into the crevasses and listen to the ice as it grinds downhill. The scenery looks like it was snatched from an Alaska tourism brochure. Take a close look at the edges, where the ice meets the land—in midsummer this fertile verge is covered with pink and white wildflowers.

Back on the main road, your next stop is Nooksack Falls, reached by a short gravel road through the woods. Look at the dense, virtually impenetrable tangle of trees, shrubs, ferns, and deep mosses as you head down the slope. This is a typical western Washington forest. The tree-girded falls plunge over a rocky ledge 170 feet into a narrow canyon. This is a popular picnic site, but beware—the rock is unstable and there's real danger of taking an irreversible plunge. A nearby grove of cedars is thousands of years old.

If you're driving to Mount Baker in August or September, you'll see high-bush huckleberries by the road. The shrubs are about chest-high and have smallish light-green leaves and blue-black berries. (Always check with someone knowledgeable before you pick berries.)

Picture Lake near the end of the road, high up on the east slope of Mount Baker, has great picnic spots along its wildflower-bedecked shores. But as one of the most photographed spots in the state, it's almost deja vu. All because of dramatic, glaciated Mount Shuksan looming across the valley. The blueberries here grow on very low bushes, but they are very good and worth every stoop. They ripen from August till late fall. If the snow has melted, you can drive on to the very end of the road, past the ski area lodge, and hike along alpine ridges for good views of both Mount Baker and the glacier-cut valley of Baker Creek.

Mount Baker offers climbing, downhill skiing, and trails through the Mount Baker Wilderness.

■ TRAVEL AND CLIMATE

■ GETTING THERE

By Car. Interstate 5, the traffic artery of this region, has its scenic spots north of the Seattle suburbs and Everett. Green fields, pastures, and woods stretch from the freeway to the foothills of the snow-covered Cascade Mountains to the east and the waters of Puget Sound to the west. The blue peaks rising above the water are the mountainous San Juan Islands. On clear days, the massive snow cone of Mount Baker rises above the lesser mountains at its base.

From the Skagit Valley, you can look upriver into the heart of the northern Cascades. North of the valley, the freeway runs through rugged mountains and passes Lake Samish before it descends to Bellingham and the Nooksack River lowlands.

An even more scenic freeway, I-90, crosses the Cascades on Snoqualmie Pass. Narrow, winding, two-lane US 20 takes travelers east via 4,061-foot Stevens Pass. WA 20, the slowest but most scenic of the highways (closed every winter because of deep snow and avalanche danger), crosses 5,477-foot Washington Pass.

By Ferry. A car ferry crossing from Mukilteo, just south of Everett, takes you to the southern end of Whidbey Island. This crossing affords some spectacular views of the snow-covered Cascade and Olympic mountains. A two-lane highway running north along the island's spine takes you to the Keystone ferry landing, where you can catch the ferry to Port Townsend, to Anacortes, or the San Juan Islands (the landing can also be reached from Mount Vernon via WA 20), and eventually back to I-5.

North of Bellingham, narrow, two-lane WA 542 winds its way through the Cascade foothills into the chasm of the Nooksack River's north fork and up the slopes of Mount Baker.

■ CLIMATE

Weather here is usually wet in spring and fall and sunny and warm in summer (though on the average about 10 degrees cooler than Seattle.) Winters are generally mild, but on the uncommon occasions when the northeasters blowing down the Fraser River canyon turn south, the air can chill down in a hurry (while Lake Washington rarely freezes over, Lake Whatcom occasionally does).

■ ACCOMMODATIONS AND RESTAURANTS

☎   For chain lodgings see toll-free numbers on page 352.
$$ For room and restaurant price designations see page 352.
✶   Means highly recommended.

ANACORTES

☎ **Majestic Hotel.**
419 Commercial Ave.; (360) 293-3355
A small hotel housed in a renovated building in the historic downtown. Victorian furnishings in the lobby, antiques in the bedrooms, and a gazebo on the fourth floor. $$$

BELLINGHAM

☎ **Best Western Lakeway Inn.**
714 Lakeway Dr.; (360) 671-1011
Large and lacking in character, but includes a pool, sauna, and weight room. Conveniently located downtown. Children under 12 stay free. $$
☎ **Schnauzer Crossing**.
4421 Lakeway Dr.; (360) 733-0055 or (360) 734-2808
Elegant B&B near Lake Whatcom. $$$
✕ **The Archer Ale House.** ✶
1212 10th St.; (360) 647-7002

The main attractions here are the classic European brews and Northwest microbrews; good pub fare: Welsh pasties, hot wings, enormous slices of pizza. $
✕ **Boundary Bay Brewery Bistro.** ✶
1107 Railroad Ave.; (360) 647-5593
The decor isn't much, but the beer and food more than make up for it. The hearty dishes match the complex flavors of the microbrews. $
✕ **Colophon Cafe.**
1208 11th St., Fairhaven; (360) 647-0092
The fine Village Bookstore in historic Fairhaven houses this little cafe where the soups and sandwiches are tasty. $
✕ **Pacific Cafe.**
100 N. Commercial St.; (360) 647-0800
Next door to the ornate old Mount Baker Theater, the Pacific Cafe serves seafood and pasta with an Asian touch. The decor is somewhat Asian, too. $$

B O W

X **Oyster Bar.**
240 Chuckanut Dr.; (360) 766-6185
An elegant restaurant with stunning
views of Samish Bay. **$$**

X **Oyster Creek Inn.** ✕✕✕
190 Chuckanut Dr.; (360) 766-6179
The Oyster Creek Inn means more than
good food. Tucked into a green bend of
the road, away from the distracting salt-
water views, it is a perfect haven. The
menu stays the same from lunch through
dinner, which means you can drop in any
time between noon and 9:00 P.M. and
nibble food, sip wine, or quaff a micro-
brew. **$$$**

F A L L   C I T Y

X **The Herbfarm.** ✕✕✕
32804 Issaquah–Fall City Rd.;
(206/425) 784-2222
This small country restaurant serves
only a couple of prix-fixe luncheons and
dinners each week, and it can be devil-
ishly difficult to get a reservation. Chef
Jerry Traunfeld relies heavily on herbs
and vegetables from the restaurant's
kitchen gardens, and he buys everything
else from local producers. (The Herbfarm burned down early in 1997, but
local chefs organized a fund-raiser to
help rebuild it.) **$$**

G L A C I E R

X **Milano's Market and Deli.**
9990 Mt. Baker Hwy.; (360) 599-2863
A fun deli and sandwich place with
good pasta and reasonably priced wine,
on the way to and from Mount Baker. **$**

S N O Q U A L M I E

⊟ **Salish Lodge.**
6501 Railroad Ave. SE; (206/425) 888-
2556 or (800) 826-6124
A luxurious lodge from a bygone era—a
large stone fireplace, maple bookshelves,
overstuffed chairs, and an exposed-beam
ceiling. **$$$**

X **Salish Lodge Restaurant.**
6501 Railroad Ave. SE; (206/425) 888-
2556 or (800) 826-6124
The main dining room, overlooking the
falls, is strictly a linen-tablecloth affair.
$$$

W H I D B E Y   I S L A N D

⊟ **The Anchorage Inn.**
807 N Main St., Coupeville; (360) 678-
5581
Victorian-style bed-and-breakfast situat-
ed in the center of town, near the water-
front. Private baths in all the rooms and
expertly prepared breakfasts. **$$-$$$**

⊟ **Captain Whidbey Inn.**
2072 Captain Whidbey Inn Rd. at
Madrona Ln., Coupeville; (800) 366-
4097 or (360) 678-4097
An inviting inn built of madrona logs
with water views on one side, and forest
views on the other. **$$$**

⊟ **Inn at Langley.** ✕✕✕
400 First St., Langley; (360) 221-3033
A great waterfront lodge with fine views,
and its dining room serves the best food
on Whidbey Island. If you want to
know what Northwest food is all about,
this is the place to go. **$$$**

S E A T T L E

■ HIGHLIGHTS

Waterfront
Pioneer Square
Pike Place Market
Ship Canal
Chittenden Locks
Arboretum and Japanese Garden
Seattle Art Museum
Museum of History and Industry
University of Washington
Water Taxi Travel

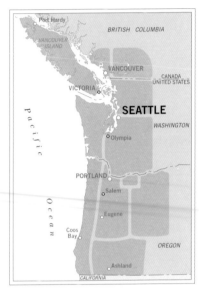

■ SETTING

SEATTLE IS A CITY SET AMONG saltwater
bays, lakes, and forested mountains. To
the west, the waters of Puget Sound lap up against piers and beaches, to the east it
is delineated by Lake Washington. On most days, you can see the craggy snow-
covered peaks across the sound from downtown Seattle, as well as the 14,410-foot
snow cone of Mount Rainier to the south; on a very clear day you can pick out
10,750-foot Mount Baker, to the north. The high-rises of the downtown business
district rival the city's hills for height and can be seen far up and down the sound
on a clear day.

While the pioneer founders of Seattle envisioned a city to rival the greatest cities
in the world (they originally named it "New York"), local residents think of it as a
collection of urban villages, each with its unique personality. Much of this has to
do with the way Seattle is spread out over several hills and valleys, and split into
sections by the Ship Canal, Lake Union, Green Lake, the Duwamish River, and
the massive concrete roadway of Interstate 5. On many days, the city is shrouded
in mist, its glass-and-steel monoliths rise from thick, gray fog banks, and seagulls
drift like ghosts between the downtown office towers and disappear in the low

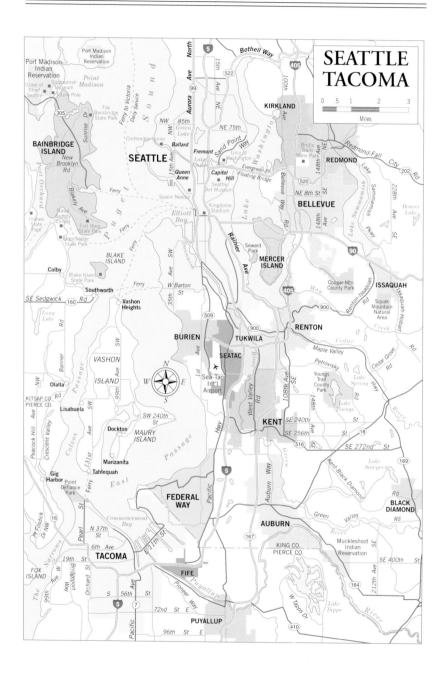

cloud mass. The lugubrious wail-honk of a ferry horn sounds somewhere beyond the shrouded waterfront as clean-cut citizens in Eddie Bauer raincoats clutch briefcases and paper cups of caffe latte, and wait for traffic lights to change.

But when the sun comes out, the sidewalk cafes on the piers and the picnic tables on the plank decks of Waterfront Park fill up with Seattle-ites who abandon their workday schedules with the speed of a sunburst. Sun brings out an uncommon levity in the residents of the gray city by the sound. On one sunny afternoon I watched a very staid looking businessman in a three-piece suit, briefcase in hand, raincoat draped over his left arm, walk up to the Waterfall Fountain downtown, glance around to make sure no associate was watching, stride into the fountain, and emerge on the far side slightly moistened, with a smile.

Of course, once you get to know Seattle, you'll learn that it hardly ever rains in summer, never mind how much residents moan and groan about the constant overcast. But perhaps Seattle-ites need the specter of rain to justify the energy they radiate. They never hold still for long and always are up to something, whether it's long walks or runs, sailing on the sound, or hiking in the mountains. Even the fishing they describe to you in a casual conversation is a high-energy sport. They don't just float a cork on a calm stream; no, they wade, and cast, and reel in, constantly. Maybe it's the Scandinavian work ethic that arrived with Norwegian, Swedish, Finnish, and Icelandic immigrants earlier in the century. Along with that energy and industriousness came a lighthearted, self-mocking humor. A favorite old folk song, "The Old Settler," goes as follows:

No longer a slave of ambition,
I laugh at the world and its shams,
As I think of my happy condition
Surrounded by acres of clams.

■ AMBITIOUS BEGINNINGS

The first settlers to put down roots in what is now Seattle, were a party of Americans from the Midwest under the leadership of Arthur Denny. While Denny never quite says in his autobiography what exactly made him pull up stakes, he does admit that he wanted to find a place where he would be the first to put down roots and make a killing in real estate. When his party reached Portland, Oregon,

Denny was dismayed to find a booming town of 2,000 people. He had come too late. That's when he heard about an unsettled place called Puget Sound.

The Dennys joined forces with the Terrys, who hailed from New York, and founded their new town at a sandy spit just south of Elliott Bay. They called it New York. It soon gained the epithet "Alki," a Chinook jargon word meaning "by and by," a name the site has kept to this day. The Dennys and Terrys soon discovered that in bad weather or at low tide, the exposed sloping beach of their townsite was a poor place from which to load ships. And load they did, since their income came from lumber they sold to ship captains who had sailed north from another enterprising place on the coast, San Francisco.

■ SEATTLE RELOCATED
Reluctantly, the settlers picked up their belongings and moved across Elliott Bay, a less desirable place if you wanted to surround your cabin with a vegetable and flower garden, but much more appealing to a commercial mind, since it bordered on a deep, sheltered harbor, where ships could sail up right to the shore. Here they built their houses on steep, overgrown hillsides rising above the bay. It was a wet

Regrading hillsides for construction projects was a laborious task for Seattle developers in the city's early days. (Museum of History and Industry, Seattle)

place, cut by deep ravines. Springs flowed down from the bluffs and dripped from the moss-covered trees, which turned trips to the hinterland into major expeditions of exploration. But the trees were soon cut down. Early pictures of Seattle show mostly stumps, not trees, between the cabins. The tree-cutting accelerated when Henry Yesler built and ran a sawmill that became the new city's main industry. Yesler used rocks carried as ballast on inbound ships to build a wharf hundreds of feet out into the bay, so the largest ships could unload on any tide. The site of that first wharf is marked by a plaque near Colman Dock, where the ferries from Bremerton and Bainbridge Island dock.

Yesler's dock was also the landing place for the early steamboats plying the waters of Puget Sound. One amusing anecdote tells of a group of legislators bound for Olympia on the *Eliza Anderson*. Wakened by what they thought was the steamer's whistle, they roused themselves from their hotel beds and stumbled down to the wharf on a dark, rainy morning, heading straight for the open door of a boiler room that promised warmth on this chill morning. But the "ship" didn't appear to move away from the dock. Checking his watch and noting that it was well past sailing time, one of the legislators tapped the fireman on the back and asked, "May I ask when we are going to pull out for Olympia?"

Yesler Way, the original "Skid Road," so called because of the log skids placed in the street to enable timber to be moved easily to the docks. Pioneer Square now exists where the flagpole appears in this photo. (Museum of History and Industry, Seattle)

Would-be fortune hunters crowd onto a steamer bound for Alaska during the Klondike Gold Rush of 1897. (Museum of History and Industry, Seattle)

"Olympia?" replied the fireman. "This sawmill don't run to Olympia." The legislators had mistaken the mill's boiler room for that of the steamer. By now, the *Eliza Anderson* had left, and the legislators had to return to the provincial capital by Indian canoe, a wet and chilly proposition at best.

■ ON TO THE KLONDIKE

A century ago, Seattle became the jumping-off place for prospectors heading to Alaska and the Yukon during the Klondike goldrush. The excitement was ushered in one day in 1897 by the arrival the ship *Portland,* which happily unloaded its "ton of gold" near Colman Dock. (A plaque now marks the spot.) Seattle's mayor at the time, W. D. Wood, was as enthusiastic as everyone else at the thought of getting rich and immediately deserted his post to join a shipload of eager-beavers going north.

An earlier Colman Dock on the same site served as the headquarters of the "Mosquito Fleet," the flotilla of boats that ferried passengers and freight around Puget Sound from the mid-19th century through World War II, making Seattle the hub of local trade. Then, every little community had its own dock; and vestiges of these—double rows of gray pilings—still march, two by two, into deep water at spots where steamboats used to call.

■ COLORFUL CHARACTERS, UNBOUNDED OPTIMISM

Early Seattle was a bit rough around the edges. It was a place of unlimited optimism, never mind that the streets could get so muddy, horses and wagons might get stuck. When the Northern Pacific Railroad decided to snub Seattle in favor of Tacoma, Seattle-ites decided to build a railroad of their own. They didn't get very far, but what they built sufficiently scared the railway moguls to hook up Seattle to the main line.

The town's early population was lively, to say the least. Indian women sold butter clams on the sidewalks of the business district, and saloons boomed, especially in the "Lava Bed"—the bustling red-light district south of Yesler's mill. One of early Seattle's more colorful characters was David "Doc" Maynard, who moved to Seattle after he was kicked out of more sedate Olympia. Maynard had married a widow he met on the Oregon Trail, without first getting a divorce from the wife he had left behind in Ohio. Things became tense when his first wife sailed into port, but the two supposedly settled matters amicably, and Maynard continued to live with wife number two.

Maynard was known as a man who always helped folks in need. He had filed a homestead claim on what is now downtown Seattle but died a poor man because he sold most of his land below its value and even gave it away, to help the budding city grow. Nard Jones reported in his book on Seattle that Maynard was given the largest funeral in the city's history when he died in 1873, and adds, "An unidentified citizen, whether friend or enemy is not known, stood up to say, 'Without Doc Maynard . . . Seattle would never have reached its present size. Perhaps, had it not been for Doctor Maynard, Seattle might not be here now.'"

One reason Maynard did not get along with civic-minded teetotalers like Henry Yesler and Arthur Denny is that he drank too much. In *Totem Tales of Old Seattle*, Gordon Newell and Don Sherwood record an argument Maynard had with Denny, when the latter asked him to attend a temperance lecture at Yesler's hall. "'Temperance!' Doc roared. "That's the only thing I believe in taking in moderation. In fact I'm a total abstainer."

Early Seattle may have had more citizens of the Maynard ilk than of the Denny and Yesler kind, because vice prospered well into the early decades of the 20th century, despite repeated civic campaigns to stamp it out.

By 1899, most of Seattle's 40,000 inhabitants lived and worked in the 50-plus blocks of one- and two-story clapboard buildings that then comprised downtown. The big fire of June 1889 burned most of Seattle's waterfront business district to the ground but spared the residences on the hill. The gutsy citizenry didn't sit around in Yesler's cookhouse complaining. No, these exemplars of industriousness set about rebuilding their town immediately. The new downtown that rose from the ashes of the old was made of brick, and its streets were elevated a full story above their previous level to solve the city's chronic sewage problem. Elevating the streets trapped many ground-floor storefronts below ground and created "Underground Seattle," which is now a major tourist attraction. *(See "Pioneer Square," following, for directions.)*

■ PIONEER SQUARE

The original 19th-century center of the city was Pioneer Square. This name applies both to the triangular cobblestone park on First Avenue, where James Street meets Yesler Way, and to the core of ornate brick and stone buildings at the south end of downtown, built mostly in the decade following the Seattle fire of 1889. The triangular "square" itself marks the site where Henry Yesler built the first steam-driven sawmill on the shore of Elliott Bay before the city extended its shoreline into the bay. First Avenue, then called Front Street, was the waterfront in those days, and logs cut from settlers' claims on the forested ridge above town were skidded down what is now Yesler Way to the mill. There they were sawed into boards that built the embryonic city of Seattle.

Yesler Way was the original Skid Road, a name that most of the country has long since corrupted to "skid row." It got its name from the logs which were skidded along its incline and because it marked the boundary between the city's business district and the Lava Bed red-light district to the south (called the Tenderloin after the fire, and now known as the Pioneer Square district). The homeless people and drifters hanging out in this area have long been a thorn in the side of civic-

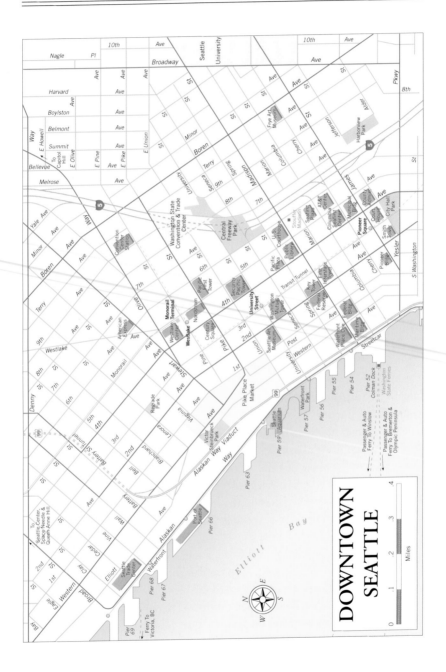

DOWNTOWN SEATTLE

minded improvers. But the "bums" have always been here, long before the influx of the current crop of homeless people. In this part of town, we might argue, it is the gentrifiers who are the intruders.

Today, Pioneer Square's preserved historic front gives a sense of historical continuity to an area packed with art galleries, bookstores, and missions serving the needy. **Elliott Bay Book Company,** at the corner of First and Main, is one of the area's most enjoyable hangouts: five rooms of books, two stories of exposed brick walls, creaky wood floors, literary readings nightly, and a downstairs cafe make this one of the most popular places in the area.

Visitors who want a taste of local color can sign up for the private **tour of Underground Seattle,** which starts at Doc Maynard's Public House at First Avenue and James Street, across from Pioneer Square. This restored pub with its carved back bar gives you a feel for what Seattle was like in the early days; the rock bands that perform here at night put you very much into contact with what's happening in Seattle right now. On sunny days, you can sit at one of the tables outside and watch Pioneer Square high and low life flow by (expect to be panhandled; it's a time-honored Seattle custom). The well-preserved facades of the buildings you'll see on the Underground Tour and the anecdotes told by your tour guide give you a glimpse of what Pioneer Square was really like in the old days.

❖

The **totem pole** that stands today in Pioneer Square is a newer version of a pole spirited away from a "deserted" Tlingit village on Tongass Island in southeast Alaska by a "goodwill committee" of prominent Seattle citizens in 1899. When the Tlingits learned where their missing pole had gone, they demanded, and received, payment for their purloined property. That's why Tlingit artists cheerfully carved a new pole when the original was severely damaged by an arson fire in 1938, for another payment in hard cash. The pole's figures, from the bottom up, represent a killer whale (orca), raven, and mink, telling the story of mink and raven, who go to sea in the belly of a killer whale. This is followed by a frog, the husband of the woman above him, who holds a frog child, symbolizing various intermarriages of the raven clan. The pole is topped by raven carrying the moon in its beak. Raven here represents a culture hero who brought light to the world by stealing the sun and moon from Raven-at-the head-of-the-Nass, who had kept them locked up in his lodge.

Steinbrueck Park, at the edge of the Pike Place Market, also has totem poles, but these are less authentic, having been created by two carvers of the Quinaults, an Olympic Peninsula tribe that did not traditionally carve totem poles.

Visitors intrigued by Seattle's role in the Gold Rush of 1897 will enjoy the exhibits at the Seattle unit of the **Klondike Gold Rush National Historic Park**, in the Union Trust Annex at 117 South Main Street.

❖

At the corner of South Main and Second Avenue South is the **Waterfall Garden**, an enclosed courtyard where the soothing sounds of a tall waterfall shut out the rest of the city. Tables and chairs placed near the water are usually packed at lunch time by workers from nearby offices.

A few blocks to the south the **Kingdome**, a baseball-and-football stadium shaped like a giant hamburger on a bun, is surrounded by restaurants catering to sports crowds.

Inland from the ball park, the **International District** holds the city's largest concentration of Asian restaurants, food stores, and social services. Asian Americans and even most Asian immigrants live elsewhere now, and Asian restaurants can be found all over the city—but some of the older, chiefly Chinese, social institutions remain. People still pour in to visit local restaurants and shops. International District businesses have been expanding eastward in recent years. Many of the new stores, restaurants, and professional offices are Vietnamese. Uwajimaya, at the corner of South Sixth and King, is a Japanese department store where you can buy everyday staples like rice, fresh vegetables and fish, as well as rare sake, kitchenware, garden tools, and Japanese fabrics, papers, and objets d'art.

■ DOWNTOWN AND THE CENTRAL WATERFRONT

From downtown hotels, it's only a short walk to the central business district. The white, 42-story spire of the **Smith Tower** was the tallest building west of the Mississippi when it was completed in 1914 (and it remained the tallest building in Seattle for 55 years). Now, it is dwarfed by highrises, the result of an office building boom in the 1980s that transformed the look and feel of Seattle's downtown. The city's contemporary highrise skyline stretches north from the Smith Tower, and includes a more recent "tallest building west of the Mississippi," the 76-story **SeaFirst Columbia Center**.

The downtown waterfront just down the hill is no longer Seattle's economic focal point, but the proximity of salt water remains vital to the city's character and history. Many of the old piers along the downtown waterfront have been transformed into shops, museums, restaurants, and amusements. **Harbor tours** depart from **Pier 55** every weekday and **Pier 57** on the weekends, giving visitors great views of the city's skyline, the docks of Harbor Island and the Ship Canal—a narrow waterway cutting a gorge from Shilshole Bay to Lake Union and Lake Washington. En route, the tour boats traverse the Ballard Locks, the world's second largest (only those of the Panama Canal are bigger). Many visitors stroll the mile and a half north to **Pier 70**, now a commercial complex, detouring over the harbor on the boardwalks and fishing piers of Waterfront Park, and returning on a vintage (1927) waterfront streetcar.

Next to the fireboat dock on Pier 54, children may enjoy seeing the small **firefighting museum**, and watching the fireboats stage weekly pumping drills. On Pier 59, they can get a sense of life beneath Puget Sound in the underwater dome of the **Seattle Marine Aquarium** or take in a film on the Omnidome's wraparound screen.

A short walk sorth of Pier 59 along First Avenue to the corner of University takes you to the **Seattle Art Museum**, designed in a flashy postmodernist style by Robert Venturi.

■ PIKE PLACE MARKET

At Pike Place Market (beyond the museum and First Avenue's few remaining pawnshops), stores and restaurants are grouped along a covered arcade overlooking Elliott Bay and in several buildings across Pike Place from the cliffside. A series of ramps and stairs leads to the "Hillclimb," a broad stairway flanked by shops and restaurants. These stairs go all the way from the cliff upon which the market is perched down to the waterfront (the Seattle Aquarium is just across the street). It's all very dramatic, and we suspect that the market's success is based in part on its spectacular setting. Beneath the arcade, the "down under" section of the market descends several stories to Western Avenue. Here are some of the market's more interesting shops, where you can buy a variety of goods from uncommonly inexpensive imported olive oil and exotic spices to folk art, old prints, books, and even parrots. The Main Arcade overlooking the bay and the open vendors' stalls on the other side of Pike Place and in Post Alley are the heart of the market. Farmers man the arcade's tables during the growing season between May and October, but the

market is fascinating at all times, because the fish vendors and the "high stalls" (merchants who are allowed to sell produce they do not themselves grow) are always packed with food.

The market is a riot of color: The fish stalls gleam with silver-scaled salmon and red rockfish, pearly squid and orange Dungeness crab, bright red shrimp and blue-black mussels. Plus clams, oysters, and giant geoduck clams. The produce stalls are piled high with red and green apples, golden pears, crimson cherries, purple plums, orange chanterelle mushrooms, cream-colored oyster mushrooms, brown shiitake and morels. In season, you'll find fresh strawberries, raspberries, blueberries, melons, apricots, peaches, nectarines, and quinces. This is truly special produce. Just smell and taste one of the ripe peaches for sale here and you'll agree. Cucumbers come in long and short varieties, green and yellow; eggplants are white or purple. A truly astounding variety of cabbages and other greens is for sale, many of them uncommon Asian kinds. The farmers, many of whom have recently immigrated from Asia, love discussing their produce. At the cheese shops you can buy uncommon locally produced cheeses, like the superb hard goat cheeses produced by Quillisascut and Sally Jackson. The butcher shops sell some of the city's best racks of lamb, pork chops, steaks, and sausages. The aroma of freshly baked

Pike Place Market is the place to go for produce and fresh seafood. (above and left)

breads wafts through the air. The market has bakeries specializing in French, Greek, and Chinese pastries. Restaurants cater to every taste, from plain sandwiches, spaghetti and meatballs, or dim sum to the freshest of fish cooked and sauced to perfection.

The northern end of the Main Arcade and the enclosed bridge across Western Avenue are taken up with craftspeople displaying a variety of handmade objects from silver bracelets to pottery fish platters and carved wooden bowls. Above all rise the strains of street musicians, a surprisingly harmonious medley of classic, folk, and jazz.

The market is one place where you see few people without a smile. Its mood is happy and invigorating. It's also exhausting. Relax and take it easy. Treat yourself to a cup of coffee or a glass of wine, grab a window seat and watch the freighters and fishing boats far below in Elliott Bay. Or buy the fixings for a picnic, head down the Hillclimb to Waterfront Park (just south of the aquarium), snag a table, and enjoy an al fresco meal.

Be sure to visit **Rachel, the Market Pig,** a life-sized bronze piggy bank at the Pike Street entrance of the arcade. It has served as a fundraiser for the market for more than a decade. Some folks have their picture taken astride Rachel.

The market has retained a few of its original shops. **Three Girls Bakery,** founded in 1912, sells wonderful breads and pastries, while **De Laurenti Specialty Foods Market,** founded in 1928, is a classic Italian deli with a great selection of old-world olive oils, wines, and cheeses.

The market began back in 1907, at a time when Seattle's forward-looking civic leaders and businessmen were influenced by socialist ideas, and thought of this as a way to eliminate the middleman. In 1970, the city of Seattle caught the nationwide redevelopment virus that replaced "beat up" but picturesque old downtowns with brutalist concrete structures. These plans were derailed by the single-minded opposition of a local architecture professor, Victor Steinbrueck (who is now memorialized by a grassy park at the market's north end) and a grassroots citizens' campaign. In 1971, Seattle voters passed an initiative to save the market.

Just a few blocks up Pine Street from the market lies Seattle's shopping and hotel district, with popular Westlake Park at its heart, at Fifth and Pine. Seattleites come here to shop at Nordstrom, a hometown store that has since expanded all across the country, and the Westlake Mall, or on a hot day, to stroll through the "waterfall" fountain.

■ REGRADE AND BELLTOWN

North of Pike Place Market, the streets run almost level to Seattle Center and steep, primarily residential Queen Anne Hill. The "Regrade" hasn't always been so flat. At the turn of the century, the rounded cone of Denny Hill rose 140 feet above what is today the more level neighborhood of Belltown.

The missing hill is a non-monument to city engineer Reginald Thomson, who wanted Seattle's downtown to stretch to the base of Queen Anne Hill and become one continuous, accessible business district, and, darn it, Denny Hill was in the way. Not only that, it was crowned with houses and topped by a luxury hotel. But Thomson was determined to flatten things out, and between 1902 and 1930, workmen sluiced Denny Hill into Elliott Bay. Today's Belltown—bounded by Queen Anne Hill, Pike Place Market, and First and Third avenues, is worth a visit for its boutiques, restaurants, nightclubs, and taverns.

Seattle Center is dominated by the **Space Needle,** the trademark structure built

The regrade of Denny Hill was a 28-year earth-moving project that cleared away some 140 vertical feet of a hillside. (Washington State Historical Society, Tacoma)

(following pages) View of the city from Queen Anne Hill. Mount Rainier looms in the distance.

for the 1962 *Century 21* world's fair, an event that drew both John F. Kennedy and Elvis Presley. According to the "Official 1962 World's Fair Guide," the Space Needle is 606 feet tall. Its legs are 500 feet high (which puts the restaurant at just above 500 feet and the Observation Deck a bit higher). There is an admission charge for the observation deck, but you ride free if you have a reservation for the restaurant. The top rides on a turntable mounted on a pair of twin rails and revolves 360 degrees once every hour. The kitchen-service-area core of the restaurant is 66 feet across; the donut-shaped restaurant itself is 14 feet wide. There are two high-speed elevators, but in case the power goes off, you'll be glad to know that you can escape down two stairways—each with 832 steps. The food at the restaurant does not match the view.

The 74-acre cluster of buildings and gardens that comprise the Seattle Center has something for everyone, from plays, operas, and concerts at the new Bagley Wright Theater to hands-on exhibits for kids, the Imax Theater, and big traveling shows at the Pacific Science Center. The **Seattle Children's Museum** is located in the basement of the Center House, and there are carnival rides at the **Fun Forest** amusement park. **Pro basketball games** by the Seattle Sonics are held in the newly restored Key Arena (until recently known as the "Seattle Coliseum"). Crowds jam the Northwest Folklife Festival on Memorial Day weekend and the annual Bumbershoot musical extravaganza on Labor Day weekend.

❖

The **monorail,** hailed when it was built as the transportation system of the future, but seen by many Seattle residents as more of a carnival ride, whisks people between Seattle Center and Westlake Mall, on the northern edge of downtown, in 90 seconds. But this advanced system of transportation may get a second lease on life: a recent petition drive was started to force the city to expand the monorail all the way to Sea-Tac Airport.

■ LAKE UNION

In the center of town, between Queen Anne and Capitol hills, lies Lake Union. Once a center of shipbuilding and repair, the lake is still home to commercial shipyards, a lot of marina space, and hundreds of houseboats, as well as some fairly generic waterfront restaurants. A pretty trail runs along the southern waterfront past lawns, restaurants, and docks where large yachts moor. From here you get a great view of the picturesque clapboard houses of the Wallingford neighborhood, rising on the lake's north shore above the greenswards of Gasworks Park; of the NOAA research fleet and rafts of houseboats moored on the eastern shore below wooded Capitol Hill; of sailboats crossing the quiet waters of the lake; and of the floatplanes landing here to pick up passengers and whisk them to Victoria, the San Juan Islands, or remote fishing spots in the mountains.

The **Ship Canal,** leading west from the lake to Puget Sound and east into Lake Washington, is a commercial waterway. Restaurants, shipyards, office buildings, and private marinas crowd the shore, while fishing boats, yachts, federal research vessels, and luxury houseboats share moorage. The houseboats moored along the eastern shore, once a kind of floating low-rent district, have gotten more upscale in recent times.

■ NORTH OF THE SHIP CANAL

At the **Hiram M. Chittenden Locks,** which raise boats from sea level to the level of Lake Union, look for the palm trees thriving in the park surrounding the locks. Beyond lies **Ballard,** home port for the bulk of the Alaskan fishing fleet, which has chugged north annually since the end of World War I to catch Alaskan salmon. Halibut boats, crabbers, and big-bottom trawlers make the northward voyage, too.

The colorful neighborhood of **Fremont,** across the ship canal from lovely Queen Anne Hill, has been "countercultural" for decades: the community's motto, in fact, is "De Libertus Quirkus"—the freedom to be peculiar. It has pleasant restaurants, pubs, clothing stores, and probably the best-known street sculpture in Seattle. The bronze pedestrians of *Waiting for the Interurban,* waiting at a bus stop near the Fremont Bridge since the 1970s, and the *Fremont troll* munching a Volkswagen under the north end of the Aurora Avenue Bridge, have recently been joined by a statue of Lenin someone "acquired" from a defunct East Bloc country. To get to Fremont, take Mercer Avenue off I-5, turn right (north) at the first light, then left (west) at the second light just before you get to Lake Union. Follow Westlake Avenue as it turns north along the lake. After you pass under the Aurora Street Bridge, turn right across the bright blue-and-orange Fremont Avenue drawbridge spanning the Ship Canal, and look for parking. You're there. Most of Fremont's shops and restaurants are within easy walking distance of each other.

■ FIRST AND CAPITOL HILLS

East of downtown, across the freeway, rise First and Capitol hills. One pleasant way to walk across to either is to follow paths through the shrubbery, flowers, and waterfalls at Freeway Park, a garden sanctuary built atop hectic Interstate 5.

The more southerly First Hill is sometimes called "Pill Hill" because it holds the city's largest concentration of hospitals, clinics, and medical offices. The **Frye Art Museum,** a conservative institution with a large collection of mostly 19th-century art, stands on the western slope. Seattle University—whose concrete and red-brick buildings soar above what is essentially a seedy neighborhood at the edge of Seattle's black ghetto—covers a good deal of the eastern slope.

Capitol Hill, just north of First Hill and reached by taking Denny Avenue uphill and turning left on Broadway, has old mansions and tree-lined residential streets, and some of Seattle's best espresso. Broadway is, for several blocks, the city's

(above) Hing Hay Park in Seattle's International District. (right) The Melbourne trolley transports passengers around downtown.

liveliest and most eclectic thoroughfare. A variety of local institutions stand on the hill, including Seattle Central Community College and the Cornish School of the Arts.

The excellent **Seattle Asian Art Museum** stands in Volunteer Park. The park also has a climbable old brick water tower that provides great views west over Puget Sound.

Martial arts movie megastar Bruce Lee lies in the large **Lakeview Cemetery** north of the park, and just north of Lakeview, in the little Grand Army cemetery, Civil War veterans are buried.

St. Mark's Cathedral, a blocky brick-and-concrete fortress with high, arched windows and a shiny copper roof, perches on the northwest edge of Capitol Hill. It is not one of the most beautiful gothic cathedrals in the country. Its bare, cavernous interior—soaring, vaulted ceilings, walls of raw concrete—was left unfinished to preserve the brilliant acoustics (which apparently would have been sadly diminished by a completed interior).

Near the Montlake Bridge on the Southern bank of the Lake Washington Ship Canal, just north of Capitol Hill and east of Lake Union, the **Seattle Museum of History and Industry** preserves pioneer artifacts, Boeing's first aircraft, and historical pictures of 19th-century Seattle. Nature trails branch out from here along Lake Washington's shore and to the Washington Park Arboretum.

The **Japanese Garden** is a delightful place to visit, with its water-lily-studded koi pond (where turtles haul out on rocks during sunny weather), waterfalls, shaded woodland walks, secluded benches, and seasonal displays of flowers. Groves of bamboo separate it from the arboretum, making this peaceful spot even more serene. An authentic teahouse is not open to the public but is reserved for *chanoyu* (Japanese tea) demonstrations. The resident calico cat, with a smile like a Buddha, loves being petted by visitors.

■ UNIVERSITY DISTRICT

West of Lake Washington and north of the Ship Canal lies the University District, home of Washington's largest school, the **University of Washington**. The campus is lovely, albeit less bucolic than it was when the ratio of buildings to trees was lower. The modern "U-Dub," as it's commonly called, rakes in more federal research and training money than any other public university in the United States.

The university also is known for big-time college football and highly publicized athletic scandals. Despite the scandals, UW "Husky" sports teams have kept their loyal fans. Since Husky Stadium is near the Ship Canal, many of season ticket holders arrive by boat.

The **University district** offers a sharp contrast to the tree-shaded campus. It is a boisterous neighborhood of small shops, restaurants, bookstores, and pubs, popular with locals (not all of them affiliated with the University) till late at night. This is the place to hang out if you have nostalgic memories of the late 1960s and early 1970s. University Way (locally known as "The Ave") is the heart of the district, busy until late at night with diners, pub crawlers, street musicians, and hawkers.

■ LAKE WASHINGTON AND THE EASTERN SUBURBS

Lake Washington was carved by the same great glacier that gouged out the basin of Puget Sound. The ship canal to Puget Sound, completed in 1916, was supposed to make Lake Washington a center for building and repairing ships. It didn't, although wooden ships were built there during World War I and even later, and a small fleet of Alaskan whalers wintered in Kirkland for a number of years. Now the lake is used primarily by pleasure boats.

Across the lake from Seattle, **Bellevue** was, half a century ago, a farming community locally famous for its annual summer strawberry festival. When the first floating bridge was completed across Lake Washington in 1940, suburban houses blossomed in the fields of pastoral Bellevue, at the eastern end of the bridge. After World War II, Bellevue became a classic Eisenhower-era bedroom suburb.

Kirkland, a small town on Lake Washington just north of Bellevue, has a pleasant waterfront with parks, pubs, and restaurants near the corner of Central Way and Lake Street. This is a surprisingly cozy shopping district in an area otherwise dominated by suburban malls.

The heart of the local software industry is Microsoft's headquarters campus in **Redmond.** There isn't much to see, even if you drive through, but Microsoft makes Redmond an epicenter of world software development.

Between I-5 and US 99, on the banks of the Duwamish River, stands **the headquarters of Boeing,** the world's largest manufacturer of aircraft. Boeing started in 1916, when William Boeing, an heir to Midwestern lumber money who had set up shop in Seattle to finish a yacht, decided to build airplanes. He built wood-

People enjoy a sunny day in Marina Park on the shores of Lake Washington.

and-fabric aircraft at first—his very first was a seaplane that made its maiden flight from Lake Union.

Boeing's backyard makes an ideal site for an aircraft museum. Stop by the **Museum of Flight**, at 9404 East Marginal Way South, for a history of U.S. and Pacific Rim flight. This is a dramatic museum, centered on the red barn where Bill Boeing built his first airplane. Inside a huge hall, airplanes—ranging in size from a biplane to a giant B-47—are suspended from the ceilings. Grounded, but here too, is the original Air Force One, in which U.S. Presidents from Eisenhower to Nixon flew. It's open to the public, with all the fancy trimmings in place—like Jackie Kennedy's makeup parlor and Lyndon Johnson's custom-made temperature controls. Would-be-pilots and nostalgic airplane buffs can touch other aircraft and crawl into their fuselages. A gift shop sells books, model airplanes, leather bomber jackets, and other hard-to-find nostalgia items; (206) 764-5720.

■ WEST SEATTLE

West Seattle, a community with a lively mix of Hispanic and Southeast Asian immigrants, is separated from the rest of the city by the Duwamish River, a salmon stream whose lower reaches are lined with shipyards, warehouses, and cement plants. Big orange gantry cranes load containers onto oceangoing ships. A bridge that soars above the river mouth connects West Seattle to downtown.

From Alki Point, where Seattle began, you can see the Olympic Mountains—on a clear day—rise a mile and a half above Puget Sound's western shore, and you may ponder the porpoises that occasionally play in the bow waves of state ferries, or the pods of orcas that sometimes swim down from the San Juans. On a rainy day, the mountains disappear and you see only shades of gray. If the sky is merely overcast, as it often is, the mountains may appear and disappear in the mist.

You reach Alki Point by heading south from the downtown Seattle waterfront on WA 99, and turning off onto the West Seattle Freeway (follow the signs) to Harbor Avenue SW. Harbor Avenue runs northwest along the shore of Elliott Bay

The 5,000th B-17 rolls off the assembly line at Boeing in 1943. The aircraft bears the signatures of all the company employees. (Underwood Photo Archives, San Francisco)

(be sure to stop at the beach for the great views of the downtown waterfront) and becomes Alki Avenue after it turns southwest. Look for signs directing you to Alki Point. If you get there at low tide you can see why this spot did not long remain the center of town. There are some interesting beach walks on this relatively un-spoiled shore.

■ TRAVEL AND CLIMATE

■ GETTING THERE

By Car. Seattle, spread out between two bodies of water, is a city of hills and lakes. The compact downtown business area is custom-made for walking, with the waterfront, hotels, restaurants, and shops in close proximity. Some hills are rather steep, but once you reach the tops you're rewarded with great views of salt water and snow-capped peaks. On clear days, Mount Rainier looms to the south. Interstate 5, the city's main traffic artery, vanishes into a concrete canyon as it crosses downtown. In places it's hidden beneath a park and the Convention Center.

By Air. Sea-Tac airport, half an hour south of downtown, has numerous national and international flights as well as excellent ground transportation to and from the city. Allow extra time for your luggage to arrive. Sea-Tac has a reputation for mixing up bags.

By Ferry. Seattle can be reached by car ferry from the Olympic Peninsula via Bremerton and from Bainbridge and Vashon islands in Puget Sound.

■ CLIMATE

Seattle is commonly warmer and gets less rain than other areas of western Washington. Annual precipitation averages less than 40 inches. July and August temperatures often reach the high 80s, but skies can be overcast for long periods of time (Seattle natives joke about having 200 days or more a year when they can't see the sun). Winter temperatures do not drop far below freezing, but unexpected snowstorms may shut down the city as early as November and as late as March. Between storms, the weather often turns balmy and trees burst into bloom.

■ ACCOMMODATIONS AND RESTAURANTS

☎   For chain lodgings see toll-free numbers on page 352.
$$ For room and restaurant price designations see page 352.
★   Means highly recommended.

BELLEVUE

☎ **Bellevue Club Hotel.** ★
11200 S.E. Sixth St.; (206/425) 454-
4424 or (800) 579-1110
This utterly luxurious hotel next to the
Bellevue Athletic Club is *the* place to
stay on the east side. Best of all, if you
stay here, you get to use the exercise
equipment at the club, one of the best
appointed in the state. $$$$

✕ **I Love Sushi.** ★ 11818 NE Eighth St.;
(206/425) 454-5706
Modern decor, no-nonsense chefs, and
the most exquisitely arranged sushi in
town. The Seattle location, though not
as spacious, offers pleasant views of Lake
Union at 1001 Fairview Ave. N;
(206) 625-9604. $$$

KIRKLAND

☎ **Woodmark Hotel on Lake Washington.**
1200 Carillon Pt.; (206/425) 822-3700
On the shores of Lake Washington, this
elegant hotel charms business and pleasure travelers with stunning views and
cozy rooms. A favorite feature is compli-
mentary late-night snacks. $$$

✕ **Yarrow Bay Grill & Beach Cafe.**
1270 Carillon Pt.; (206/425) 889-9052
The Grill is upstairs. The cafe is down-
stairs, close to the water. It's a casual, fun
place with great, easy-to-eat food. From
the windows and the deck there's a great
view of lake towards Seattle. Upstairs at
the Yarrow Bay Grill, the food is more
"haute," the view of the lake is higher,
and so are the prices. $$-$$$

SEATTLE

☎ **Alexis Hotel.**
1007 First Ave.; (800) 426-7033 or
(206) 624-4844
Small, understated, chic, and expensive.
Near the Seattle Art Museum and the
Pike Place Market. $$$

☎ **Four Seasons Olympic Hotel.** ★
411 University St.; (206) 621-1700
This was the classiest place in town
when it opened in the 1920s, and after a
1982 renovation, it is again. $$$

☎ **Inn at the Market.** ★
86 Pine St.; (206) 443-3600
This is a pleasant place, and many of the
comfortable rooms have views over El-
liott Bay, but the main attraction is the
location: right in the Pike Place Market.
$$-$$$

☎ **The Landes House.**
712 11th Ave. E; (206) 329-8781
Bed-and-breakfast near Volunteer Park
and once the private home of Seattle's
first female mayor. $$

☎ **Mayflower Park Hotel.**
405 Olive Way at Fourth Ave.; (800)

426-5100 or (206) 382-6991
A handsomely appointed hotel with European furnishings and Oriental rugs. Excellent service. $$$

⚏ **Meany Tower Hotel.**
4507 Brooklyn Ave.; (800) 899-0251 or (206) 634-2000
A pleasant, old-fashioned hotel, only a few blocks from the University of Washington campus. $$

⚏ **Sheraton Hotel.**
1400 Sixth Ave.; (800) 325-3535 or (206) 621-9000
A big hotel right near the Washington State Convention & Trade Center, the Sheraton takes in a lot of meetings and a lot of groups. The lobby features glass works by the ubiquitous local artist Dale Chihuly. $$$

⚏ **West Coast Camlin Hotel.**
1619 Ninth Ave; (800) 426-0670 or (206) 682-0100
Built in 1926 and remodeled in 1987, the Camlin has an elegant small lobby and plain but spacious rooms. One of the better bargains in downtown hotels. $$

⚏ **Westin Hotel.**
1900 Fifth Ave.; (800) 228-3000 or (206) 728-1000
The Westin's cylindrical twin towers give every room a view and plenty of light— or as much light as Seattle offers at any given time of the year. Bill Clinton has stayed here and had hamburgers delivered to his room from the McDonald's across the street. $$$

✕ **Anthony's Pier 66.** ✫
Pier 66 (The Bell Street Pier), 2201 Alaskan Way; (206) 448-6688
Under the inspired guidance of chef Sally McArthur, this bright new restaurant serves the best seafood on the Seattle waterfront. Which just goes to show that a great view and great food can go together. $$

✕ **Cafe Flora.**
2901 E Madison St.; (206) 325-9100
Flora serves vegetarian food that looks good and tastes good and would be worth going out of your way to eat even if it weren't good for you. $$$

✕ **Campagne.**
86 Pine St.; (206) 728-2800
An elegant French country restaurant right at the Pike Place Market, with a view out over Elliott Bay. Service is often slow and can be rude. $$$

✕ **Canlis.**
2576 Aurora Ave. N; (206) 283-3313
A fine-dining fixture in Seattle where steaks and oysters are the main draw. $$$$

✕ **Dahlia Lounge.** ✫
1904 Fourth Ave.; (206) 682-4142
Tom Douglas, the chef who owns the Dahlia Lounge, is one of the gurus of Pacific Rim cuisine. $$-$$$

✕ **Flying Fish.** ✫✫
2234 First Ave.; (206) 728-8595
With Chris Keff in the kitchen, this bright storefront restaurant serves some of the best seafood in Seattle. It's as close to San Francisco as a Seattle restaurant can get. $$

The Space Needle, originally built for the 1962 world's fair, has become a popular symbol of the city.

X **Fullers.** ✭✭✭
1400 Sixth Ave. in the Seattle Sheraton Hotel; (206) 4r7-5544
Chef Monique Barbeau understands the foods of the Northwest and the seasonings they require. This is a great place to linger over appetizers and to study the restaurant's splendid collection of Pilchuck glass art. $$$

X **El Gaucho.**
2505 First Ave.; (206) 728-1337
Fresh seafood, well-aged beef, and a regionally famous Caesar salad attract an upscale clientele to this new incarnation of Seattle's most elegant and romantic restaurant—in a former Sailor's Union building. $$$

X **Georgian Room.** ✭✭✭
411 University St. in lobby of the Four Seasons; (206) 621-7889
The food presentations are so beautiful, it's hard to tell whether you're dealing with Sear the chef or Sear the artist (he is very good at both professions), but you stop wondering with the first bite: this is beautiful food that tastes good. $$$

X **Metropolitan Grill.**
820 Second Ave.; (206) 624-3287
Best steaks in town, as well as very good seafood cooked and sauced to perfection. $$

X **The Painted Table.** ✭✭
92 Madison St. (in the Alexis Hotel); (206) 624-3646
Local artists display their works on the walls of this stylish restaurant while the Northwest artists in the kitchen turn out sophisticated regional fare. $$$

X **El Puerco Lloron.**
1501 Western Ave. (on the Pike Place Market Hillclimb); (206) 624-0541
People come for the kitschy Mexican-cafe decor and for some of the best Mexican food in Seattle. $

X **Ray's Boathouse.**
6049 Seaview Ave. NW; (206) 789-3770
Ray's isn't fancy, but no place in Seattle offers a better waterfront location. The seafood and wine are also quite good. The upstairs cafe has a better view and is cheaper. $$$

X **Rover's.** ✭ ✭ ✭
2808 E Madison St.; (206) 325-7442
Tucked away in a small house, this restaurant offers dining at its absolute best. $$$

X **Saigon Gourmet.**
502 S. King St.; (206) 624-2611
One of the International District's best dining spots is this informal yet superb Vietnamese cafe. $

X **Saleh al Lago.** ✭✭
6804 East Green Lake Way N; (206) 524-4044
This small, comfortably appointed place near Green Lake is Seattle's best Italian restaurant. $$$

X **Salty's on Alki.**
1936 Harbor Ave. SW, West Seattle; (206) 937-1600
Nicely prepared seafood and sweeping views of the city's skyline. $$-$$$

X **Santa Fe Cafe.**
Two locations: 2255 NE 65th St.;
(206) 524-7736 and 5910 Phinney Ave.
N; (206) 783-9755
Southwestern cuisine, blue corn tortillas, plenty of chiles, in two relatively
upscale settings. **$$$**

X **Sea Garden Restaurant.** ✶
509 Seventh Ave. S; (206) 623-2100
Highly acclaimed Chinese cuisine, prepared with only the freshest fish and
vegetables. **$$**

X **Shuckers.** ✶
411 University Ave.; (206) 621-1984
Just as one would expect from a restaurant tucked inside the Four Seasons
Hotel, Shuckers is refined and gracious.
Fabulous oysters. **$$**

X **Trattoria Mitchelli.**
84 Yesler Way; (206) 623-3885
An informal place with Italian food (and
good thin-crust pizza) in an old brick
building off Pioneer Square. Open late
and often crowded. **$$$**

X **Wild Ginger.** ✶✶
1400 Western Ave.; (206) 623-4450
The menu is delightfully and eclectically
Asian, with dishes from China, Thailand, Vietnam, Indonesia, and elsewhere. In its decor, Wild Ginger is a
classic Seattle restaurant with a clubby
setting. **$$**

FINE CUISINE IS NOTHING NEW

This observer traveled from San Francisco to Puget Sound in the late 1860's:

*I*f there is one thing, indeed, more than another among the facts of civilization which the Pacific Coast organizes most quickly and completely, it
is good eating. From the Occidental at San Francisco to the loneliest of
ranches on the most wilderness of weekly stage routes, a "good square meal"
is the rule; while every village of five hundred inhabitants has its restaurants
and French or Italian cooks. . . . When the Puritans settled New England
their first public duty was to build a church with thrifty thought for their
souls. Out here their degenerate sons begin with organizing a restaurant and
supplying Hostetter's stomach bitters and a European or Asiatic cook.

—Samuel Bowles, *Our New West,* 1869

OLYMPIC PENINSULA
WASHINGTON COAST

■ HIGHLIGHTS

Beaches
Rocky Shores
Olympic National Park
Ozette Village
Temperate Rainforest
Alpine Meadows and Peaks
Grays Harbor
Willapa Bay
Columbia River

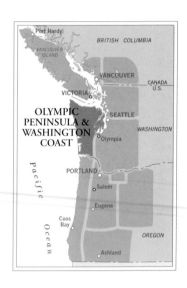

■ OLYMPIC PENINSULA
OVERVIEW

THE NORTHWESTERNMOST PART of the contiguous United States, the Olympic Peninsula, juts north between the Pacific Ocean and Puget Sound. Heavily glaciated, never crossed by any road, the Olympic Mountains form the peninsula's 7,000-foot-high spine. Short, swift rivers tumble from the mountains to the Pacific on the west, the Strait of Juan de Fuca on the north, and Hood Canal on the east. In west-facing valleys, temperate rainforests grow within a day's hike of glacial ice and the surf-thrashed rocks of Pacific beaches. **Olympic National Park,** which protects the mountains and rainforests of the peninsula's core, also has the nation's longest wilderness beach outside Alaska.

The human history of the Olympic Peninsula goes back at least 3,000 years. The oldest house foundations found during excavations at Ozette Village of the Makah people on the coast of the northern Olympic Peninsula date back some 800 years. Other objects showed that the Makah, along with the neighboring Quillayute, Quinault, and Clallam, had a culture that remained remarkably stable

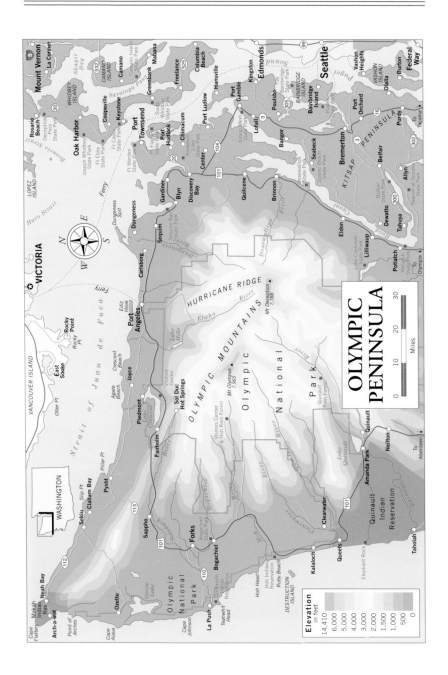

OLYMPIC PENINSULA

for centuries. The Makah and the other coastal tribes went to sea in large canoes, to hunt seals and whales. They fished for salmon and halibut and gathered wild berries. Their culture was rich in myths and dances.

Warfare among the tribes ended shortly after white settlers established their form of law and order. During the 20th century, the Olympic Peninsula has seen heavy logging and exhaustion of the salmon runs. But the heart of the peninsula has been protected from exploitation since Congress created Olympic National Park in 1938.

■ KITSAP PENINSULA

If you travel to the Olympic Peninsula from Seattle, a car ferry will take you to Bremerton on the **Kitsap Peninsula,** where a fleet of gray warships rides at anchor in Bremerton, a Navy-yard town since the late 19th century.

Makah Indians land a whale through the surf at Neah Bay. Sealskin floats hinder the whale from diving and keep it afloat after death. (Washington State Historical Society, Tacoma)

The Kitsap Peninsula is a low, deeply fjorded region of dense woods, small, picturesque harbor towns, and the U.S. Navy's largest West Coast shipyard and submarine base. The grave of **Chief Seattle,** for whom Seattle was named, overlooks Puget Sound at Suquamish on the Port Madison Indian reservation.

Nearby, along Liberty Bay, the town of **Poulsbo** plays up its Norwegian immigrant history. Its name means "Paul's Place" in Norwegian, and the town sponsors a Viking Fest in mid-May, the Skandia Midsommarfest in June, and the Yule Log Festival in November. The old mill town of **Port Gamble** overlooks the mouth of the Hood Canal, a glacial fjord on the far side of the Kitsap Peninsula. The white frame buildings evoke the Maine backgrounds of the founders of the Pope & Talbot Company, which sold lumber in Gold Rush San Francisco and built the first mill in the town of Port Gamble in the 1850s.

As you drive over the floating bridge across the flat, blue water of Hood Canal, it's hard to imagine that 80-mile-per-hour winds sank the bridge's predecessor in 1979. Even the new bridge, during severe storms, may be closed to traffic. The bridge is opened by pulling aside a float to let large ships pass through, and you may be delayed by black, ominous-looking Trident submarines slipping out to sea from the Bangor base to the south.

■ NORTHEAST OLYMPIC PENINSULA

North of the bridge is the resort town of **Port Ludlow**—famous for its boat harbor, golf course, and the Inn at Port Ludlow across the harbor on a sandy bar. The inn's restaurant serves the best food on the Olympic Peninsula. As you drive north towards Port Townsend, look around you. The woods and fields of this region were made famous by Betty McDonald in *The Egg and I.* Stop in Chimacum and ask where local heroes Ma and Pa Kettle lived.

Port Townsend is a special place, with its bookstores, restaurants, brick buildings downtown, and ornate Victorian homes on the bluff above. Port Townsend has a literary reputation and hosts writers' workshops. At the decommissioned military post of Fort Worden—setting for the 1982 movie, *An Officer and a Gentleman*—the officers' quarters and parade ground overlook the Strait of Juan de Fuca and trails lead through the woods to lonely bluffs and beaches.

(following pages) Point Wilson Lighthouse in Port Townsend has a fine view across the straits. Mount Baker is visible in the background.

On the road west from Port Townsend, stands of massive old cedar and fir still crowd the highway. In autumn, the red and yellow leaves of vine maple glow among the evergreens. Other spots along this road resemble Christmas tree lots—signs proudly proclaim model tree farms. Clear-cut and reseeded a decade ago, these patches of fir and alder are choked with salal and bracken, where deer and black bears browse. Rain-soaked pastures are punctuated here and there with ancient stumps six feet in diameter.

The highway town of **Sequim** ["SKWIM"] is noted for its burgeoning retirement population and its dry climate (it sits in the rain shadow of the Olympics). **Dungeness Spit,** possibly the largest natural sand spit in the world, juts into the Strait of Juan de Fuca, curving northeast for five and a half miles to the lighthouse at its tip like the claw of a giant crab. Seabirds bob in the sheltered waters of the bay and sea lions cruise along the exposed western shore. The coastal forest near the base and adjacent tidal zones are now protected as part of the **Dungeness National Wildlife Refuge,** home of some 250 bird species.

The harbor town of **Port Angeles** serves as the main gateway to Olympic National Park. The town has reasonably priced lodging (including one motel right on the harbor), several good restaurants, and ferry service to Vancouver Island, which lies to the north, across the dark, frigid waters of the strait. The late actor John Wayne berthed his boat here; short-story writer Raymond Carver and the poet Tess Gallagher lived here.

■ OLYMPIC NATIONAL PARK

Olympic National Park encompasses more than 1,300 square miles of wilderness in the heart of the Olympic Mountains. The surrounding land was set aside as forest reserve in 1897. Twelve years later, President Theodore Roosevelt established the Mount Olympus National Monument as a sanctuary for the later-named Roosevelt elk, which had been hunted nearly to extinction for their teeth (which were used as watch fobs). Under pressure from logging and mining interests, President Woodrow Wilson reduced the protected area by half in 1915, re-opening much of today's park to logging and homesteading. That ended in 1938, when Congress created the Olympic National Park. Since then, the park has been expanded to include the Queets and the Hoh river valleys. More recently, Congress added the coastal strip, the longest stretch of wilderness beach outside Alaska.

A deer pauses among the wildflowers on Hurricane Ridge in Olympic National Park.

❖

Olympic is the most geographically diverse of our national parks. Crowned by 7,965-foot Mount Olympus, clad in glaciers and towering over steep, green valleys, the Olympic Mountains exude a sense of grandeur. The park also embraces 57 miles of pristine seacoast, large swaths of lush, temperate rainforest, and a splendid array of wildlife, including black bears, mountain sheep, bald eagles, and more than 5,000 Roosevelt elk. With more than 600 miles of trails, the heart of the Olympics reveals itself best to travelers on foot or horseback. For auto-bound travelers and campers, a few spectacular roads probe fleetingly (never more than 20 miles) into the borders of the park, granting sublime mountain vistas of the distant Olympics, as well as access to alpine, beach, and rainforest trailheads. Motorists visiting Olympic will need to do some backtracking, especially if they visit more than one section of the park.

In the Olympics, you have to plan around the weather. Even in summer, the area experiences more rain or fog than sunshine. Beaches, tide pools, and rainforests embellish the west side of the peninsula, where the heaviest rains in the continental United States (up to 140 inches per year on average!) water massive forests of immense red cedar, Sitka spruce, and Douglas fir, many of them draped and thickly bound in mosses of a hundred shades of green. The main roads to the rainforest trailheads follow the Hoh River near Forks; the Queets River near the town of Queets; and the Quinault River, beyond Quinault Lake in the southwest corner of the park. Access roads to the Olympic beaches lead to Ozette Lake, La Push, and the southern stretch of coastline between Ruby Beach and Queets.

The park's grandest entrance winds 17 miles from Port Angeles to Hurricane Ridge, where you can look out over the Elwha Valley into the heart of the Olympics or north to the Strait of Juan de Fuca. There's a day-use lodge here, even a snack bar, but you can hike a long way without finding better views of the peaks. The Park Service keeps the road plowed in winter, and people drive up here for cross-country and downhill skiing.

Farther west along US 101, the road passes through low forests to scenic **Lake Crescent,** a lake surrounded by hills and perhaps best known to fishermen for its trout. Close at hand are the comfortable cottages of **Lake Crescent Lodge,** which were built for President Franklin Roosevelt's visit in 1937. Or "take the waters" in the three mineral water pools at **Sol Duc Hot Springs,** 12 miles south of Lake Crescent along a paved road.

■ ALONG THE WESTERN STRAITS

Beyond Port Angeles, narrow State Highway 112 winds west along the Strait of Juan de Fuca. South and east, a luminous blanket of snow caps the crumpled ridges of the Olympic Mountains, rising starkly from their surrounding forests. As you follow it along the coastline, curving around rocks and huge trees, you should not hurry—this is one of the finest coastal drives in the Northwest. Near Pysht, huge, mossy spruce trunks crowd the blacktop and along the Pysht River, epiphytes drip from maple limbs. Farther west, you see rocky headlands, sea stacks, and waves breaking on stony beaches.

Neah Bay is a sport-fishing village, where the occasional totem pole and housefront painting remind you that this is a settlement of the Makah nation. For centuries the Makahs paddled dugout canoes into the strait and the Pacific to hunt whales and halibut. Neah Bay was also the site of the first European settlement in Washington State. In 1792, Spanish colonists from San Blas, Mexico, arrived aboard the frigate *Princesa* at the bay they called Nuñez Gaona. They built a fort and a bakery and planted a small garden but abandoned the settlement after five months. The first Americans to stay here were traders arriving in 1850.

The **Makah Cultural and Research Center** displays artifacts recovered from the Ozette village site at Cape Alava. In part, the exhibits form a kind of hymn to cedar. Makahs used it for straight-sided boxes and for the wide, flat planks of their longhouses. (A modern reconstruction of a longhouse stands in the museum.) Cedar bark gave them material for woven mats, blankets, and hats. The wood was made into graceful, tapered canoe paddles; and above all, it was made into the canoes themselves. The museum contains modern versions of the smaller cedar canoes once used for seal hunting and daily travel, and the long canoes with flat bottoms and high prows used for whale hunting on the Pacific.

Perhaps the most startling display case holds a row of knife blades, some slate, some shell, and one of rusted metal. Metal! Five hundred years ago, Makah craftsmen were making blades out of metal. Where did they get it? Presumably from ships that drifted across the Pacific from Japan. In the mid-19th century, early settler James Swan found the Makah using copper taken from Asian shipwrecks. It is unclear how often living mariners—people from another world—drifted ashore with their wrecks, but a documented case of Japanese sailors surviving a shipwreck here happened in the early 19th century. The cultural center is located on State Highway 112, across from the Coast Guard base; (360) 645-2711.

❖

West of Neah Bay, **Cape Flattery**, the westernmost point of land in the coterminous United States, juts into the Pacific. From high ground, you can look south
along the misty coast, over the dark forest and the white line of breakers at the
edge of the continent, to the distant sculpture garden of sea stacks at Point of
Arches.

■ OZETTE LAKE AND NORTH OLYMPIC COAST

West of Sekiu on State Highway 112, a branch road winds southwest, following
the Hoko River toward Ozette Lake. The road ends at a ranger station on the
north end of 10-mile-long Ozette Lake. Two three-mile boardwalk trails from
Ozette Lake to the long wilderness beach cut through thick rainforest, where a
soft, green light seems to emanate from the trees and the earth itself.

Between the Makah reservation, on the extreme northwestern tip of the peninsula, and the big Quinault reservation south of Kalaloch, the whole Pacific coastline is part of the Olympic National Park, except for three small pockets of land

*An aerial view of Tatoosh Island (above). It is the northwesternmost point of the coterminous
United States, resting just off Cape Flattery. Hobuck Beach (right) in Mukkaw Bay is on the
Makah Indian Reservation.*

occupied by the **Ozette, Quillayute,** and **Hoh** reservations. Here ancient forests grow down to the shore. At low tide, the broad, sandy beach stretches out to small, wooded islands and surf-sculpted rocks that dot the shore. Drift logs seven feet thick attest the power of the ocean.

Cape Alava was the site of a Makah village for at least 2,000 years but was abandoned in the late 19th century. Ozette village, occupied for some 3,000 years, was built in succeeding layers. An early layer, sealed in by mud slides centuries ago and exposed by winter storms in 1970, provided one of Washington's most important archaeological sites. Wooden artifacts and woven baskets dating to the 1400s, perfectly preserved in their airless tomb, give a clear picture of traditional Makah life. The artifacts are preserved at the tribal museum in Neah Bay, and a replica cedar longhouse now marks the village site.

■ La Push

Fourteen miles west of the US 101 town of Forks lies the fishing village of La Push, close to the mouth of the Quillayute River on the tiny **Quillayute Indian Reservation.** The coast is magnificent: wind-warped cedar and hemlock and stands of lichen-whitened alder stand on steep clay banks overlooking the endless Pacific. Offshore, sea stacks—weird hives and spires of dark basalt—rise from the surf. **Second Beach** and **Third Beach** are reached by half-mile trails leading down from the road about a mile before town. The town of La Push lies on First Beach, a site occupied by the Quillayute for unknown centuries. Today, La Push is a collection of shabby, weathered houses, with one store, an old Shaker church, and a small harbor where a fleet of fishing boats bobs. Salmon fishing is the chief livelihood of the Quillayute people, as it has been for millennia. Charter boats leave from the harbor, too.

■ Rainforests

People come from all over the world to see the rainforest, and with good reason. The coastal valleys catch the prevailing winds from the Pacific, which carry rain and mist up the **Hoh, Queets, Quinault,** and **Bogachiel** rivers to the big spruce and cedar trees, the ferns, the mosses, the shrubs, the epiphytes. Everything is green—innumerable hues, shades, textures, and overlapping layers of green. There are no hard edges; everything is softened, enveloped, illuminated by moss. A thick carpet of moss covers the ground where roots create ripples in the green, and waves of moss seem to flow toward the trees. In fall, you may hear the high, tinny "bugling" of Roosevelt elk or see one of the big creatures slip through the trees.

The canopy of branches overhead is made up of multiple layers. Where light penetrates, a dense understory of brush and small plants develops on the forest floor. Some old trees die and remain standing as gray, weather-bleached snags. Others fall and decay slowly, releasing nutrients for centuries. Literally hundreds of plant and animal species, including the northern spotted owl and marbled murrelet, are found in such old-growth forests.

On US 101, just south of Forks at Bogachiel State Park, head east into the **Bogachiel Valley** rainforest. Past the Bogachiel River, North Hoh Road leads inland to the **Hoh Rainforest Visitor Center,** where the best-known rainforest trails begin. Farther south, US 101 leads east to **Lake Quinault,** where you will find trailheads, campgrounds, and outside the park, old **Lake Quinault Lodge.** This handsome retreat was built in 1926 and later restored with its high ceilings, wide French windows overlooking the lake, and a large lobby complete with a grand fireplace.

■ SOUTHERN COAST SETTING

Between Grays Harbor and the Columbia River, the mountains recede from the coast and are replaced by long, sandy beaches and dunes. The sand comes from the rivers and is moved by tidal currents. In some places, the beaches have been growing; in others, they have receded. On the Long Beach Peninsula, houses that were built close to the ocean in the 19th century are now far inland; at the northern end of Willapa Bay, severe erosion has cut into the shoreline. At Toke Point, near Tokeland, the sea eats into the coastline at a rate of 12 feet per year; farther out on the coast, at Cape Shoalwater, the erosion rate is 150 feet per year—Willapa Bay and its main channel have moved north about two miles since records were first kept in 1887.

You don't the see the sand in many places, because it is covered with grass, trees, and undergrowth. Cape Disappointment and North Head at the mouth of the

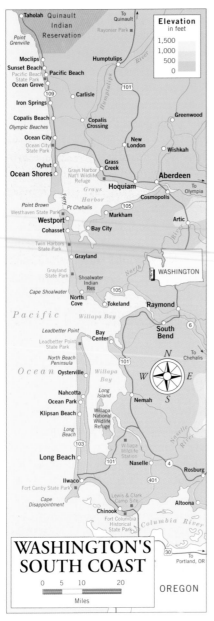

WASHINGTON'S SOUTH COAST

0   5   10   20

Miles

Columbia are rocky. They were once islands but are now connected to the mainland by low, sandy flats. Near Ilwaco the land is very low and was used as a portage during the days when canoes were the main form of transportation. In June of 1876, during an unusually high flood, the Columbia broke through and poured into Willapa Bay, diluting the salt water of the bay to such an extent that the native oysters died. (They recovered by 1884.) Willapa Bay was originally named "Shoalwater Bay," because it is very shallow. Its shores are lined by vast marshes which make for great wildlife habitat. The rivers, creeks, and tidal channels are perfect for watching birds from canoe or kayak—if it does not rain. Which it does much of the time. The beaches are very windy and attract kite-fliers from all over the Northwest. Because the sand of the beaches is packed down hard, locals and visitors like driving on the beach, which is, unfortunately, legal.

Two hundred years ago, this region was occupied by Chehalis and Chinook Indians, expert canoe builders who braved the coastal waters and rivers in all sorts of weather and impressed American explorers Lewis and Clark with their seamanship: ". . . they ride with perfect safety in the highest waves,

Hall of Mosses Trail in the rainforest of Olympic National Park.

and venture without the least concern in seas where other boats or seamen could not live an instant."

The Chinooks were the greatest traders on the coast, middlemen between the people of the coast and the interior. Their language became the basis for the "Chinook jargon," a trade language composed of Indian and European words that served as the Northwest Coast's lingua franca for more than 100 years.

By the time the exploration party of Lewis and Clark reached the mouth of the Columbia River in November of 1805, the Chinook had become experts in trading with American mariners. The first to come had been Yankee fur trader Robert Gray, who "discovered" the river in May 1792 by sailing his ship *Columbia* across the treacherous bar at the river's mouth. (British naval lieutenant William Broughton soon followed in Gray's wake, claiming the river for Britain.)

During Lewis and Clark's stay, they almost drowned on the Washington side of the river, when waves pinned them against a cliff. They found a more congenial campsite near the present-day town of Chinook, but decided to winter south of the river because they had to rely for subsistence on their arms "and be guided in the choice of our residence by the abundance of game which any particular spot may offer." Following the advice of the Indians, they wintered on what is now the Oregon side of the river (in a cluster of cabins they built and dubbed "Fort Clatsop"), because "the opposite side of the bay is better equipped with elk, an animal much larger and more easily killed than deer, with a skin better fitted for clothing and the meat of which is more nutritive during the winter…"

❖

The first settlers on the Washington coast were attracted by the plentiful oysters, which they shipped to San Francisco from Oysterville and from the now vanished town of Bruceport. Pioneer settler James Swan left an interesting account of his sojourn during the 1850s in *The Northwest Coast; or Three Year's Residence In Washington Territory.* Willapa Bay has remained a backwater, and oyster-growing along with fishing, crabbing, and logging are still the region's main industries.

During sailing-ship days, the heavy breakers and unpredictable currents at the bars of the Columbia River, Willapa Bay, and Grays Harbor, and the beaches to the north and south took a heavy toll of ships. Even now, a boat occasionally comes to grief on the bars.

■ GRAYS HARBOR

Curving inland around the Quinault Indian Reservation, US 101 connects the estuary and mill towns of Grays Harbor. The ocean beaches to the west have razor clams and are a favorite resort area of urban Washingtonians.

Grays Harbor has one of the largest estuaries on the Pacific Coast north of San Francisco. The towns of **Aberdeen** and **Hoquiam,** which stand beside the estuary, have always been forest-product centers, and old pilings driven into the seabed to hold log booms still rise from the water's edge. Though the two towns are so close you can hardly tell when you leave one and enter the other, they have never gotten along. Once, when the Chehalis River was in flood, the city of Hoquiam even built a dike across the main street, to "keep the floodwaters in Aberdeen."

You may see a tall-masted ship sail across the bay—a replica of Capt. Robert Gray's *Lady Washington* was built for the Washington Centennial in 1889 and occasionally offers rides. Oysters grow in the shallow waters on the south side of the estuary. You can buy local oysters at **Brady's Oysters** on Highway 105 just before Westport and west of the Elk River Bridge; (260) 268-0077. *(Also see "Buying Northwest Seafood," page 223.)*

The **Grays Harbor National Wildlife Refuge,** at the northern edge of the estuary, accommodates up to one-half of the million or so shorebirds that visit Grays Harbor at peak times. It's a good place for birds because it's a good place for eelgrass and other seaweeds, which birds eat, and for algae, invertebrates, and small fish. The estuary serves as a nursery for young salmon not yet ready to venture into the open sea, and for young crustacea. The best months to visit the refuge are April and May, and best times of day are one hour before and one hour after high tide.

Westport, at the southern edge of the estuary's mouth, harbors a fishing and crabbing fleet, and charter boats for catching salmon and bottomfish, or for visiting the whales that migrate up the coast every spring. A drive south from Westport takes you past dunes and cranberry bogs. In spring, look for wild strawberries growing in the dunes; in fall, search for wild cranberries growing in moist, boggy depressions among the sand hills. In season, you may dig for razor clams on the beaches.

■ WILLAPA BAY

Washington's other great coastal estuary—Willapa Bay, lies just south of Grays Harbor. Willapa Bay is the cleanest estuary anywhere in the United States outside Alaska. A quick drive south from Grays Harbor takes you to the old riverside logging town of **Raymond**, where a tall wooden statue of a logger stands in a pleasant little park. Take a short detour along the Palix River to the small oyster town of **Bay Center**. In summer, you can spot brown pelicans on the river (this is about as far north as these big birds migrate). The **Ekone Oyster Company** at 192 Bay Center Road southwest of town has delectable smoked oysters. Farther south, US 101 runs along the waterfront of **South Bend**, "the oyster capital of the world." Willapa Bay produces more oysters than any other place in the United States and ranks among the top five oyster-producing spots in the world. You can't miss the place: huge piles of oyster shells rise beside metal-sided packing houses at the water's edge.

In the early 1850s, men gathered the native oysters for sale to Gold Rush San Francisco. Explorer and writer James Swan arrived here at the end of 1852 to find 14 settlers and shoals "covered with shell-fish." Schooners from San Francisco

The Pacific coastline of Washington is foggy, wild, windy, and beautiful.

pulled into the shallow bay, and the captains would pay for oysters with gold. The oysters sold for a dollar a basket, and a schooner often took 1,200 to 2,000 baskets. Local growers have been selling Willapa Bay oysters ever since. The species has changed—today the Pacific oyster is cultivated here rather than the tiny native mollusk. Production is still measured in millions of pounds, and the industry provides a powerful incentive for local communities to keep the water clean.

On the residential hill above South Bend, the 1910 Pacific County courthouse, with its dark, spreading dome, looks out over the shallow bay. Parts of Willapa Bay have been protected since 1937 as a national wildlife refuge, providing winter habitat for black brant and a stopping place for up to 150,000 northbound shorebirds every spring, and for up to 100,000 southbound waterfowl every fall. Near the refuge headquarters, south of South Bend, **Long Island** supports a 4,000-year-old grove of western red cedar. The rest of the refuge is across the bay, at the northern tip of the **Long Beach Peninsula,** which separates Willapa Bay from the ocean. This is a low, fenny land of slowly meandering rivers, of reedy marshes and damp forests, of old docks and piles of oyster shells on the shore.

As you drive north on the peninsula, you can buy oysters at the **Jolly Roger Oyster Company** at the foot of the **Nahcotta** dock. **Oysterville,** once the center of the local oyster industry, has houses from the 1860s and 1870s and boasts a church with a small, ornately shingled steeple, a 1906 schoolhouse, and a sign that marks the site of the first Pacific County courthouse—the seat of local government until South Bend boosters stole the records and built a courthouse of their own. ("Stealing the courthouse" happened surprisingly often in the early Northwest.)

❖

Leadbetter Point State Park, beyond Oysterville but before the refuge land at the extreme tip of the peninsula, gives you the chance to walk along a bay that remains much as it was a century ago. Rafts of shorebirds rise, skim the water, flash white undersides as they turn, and settle up the beach. The air is filled with their twittering.

BUYING NORTHWEST SEAFOOD

You are driving down the coast, blissfully gazing out the window—salt water as far as the eye can see—and since the coast is where seafood comes from, you might as well stock up and send some of that good, fresh stuff home.

That's the idea, at least. Reality can be a bit different. Just a few years ago, it was pretty difficult to find fresh seafood on the coast, unless you caught, dug, or gathered it yourself. That's not because there weren't any fresh fish, clams, crabs, or oysters. There were. But they went from the boat to the packing house, from the packing house to the big-city distributor, and then from the distributor back to coastal fish markets and supermarkets. Which means that you might find fresher seafood in Vancouver or Seattle than you could hope for in fishing harbors like Bellingham or Astoria.

The locals didn't care. Not because they didn't know fresh from stale, but because they didn't have to buy seafood at a market. They'd catch it themselves or get it free from friends. Even today, they rarely order seafood when they eat out. They have enough of that at home. When the locals go out to eat, they order steak. Which is why, more often than not, the steak served in restaurants up and down the coast is better than the seafood.

But all that's been changing for at least a decade. Fewer people have time to go fishing or dig for clams, which means that even many of the locals now have to buy their seafood at a market. And that means that the quality is up, since seashore residents know what fresh seafood is supposed to taste like.

■ BRITISH COLUMBIA

Some of the freshest seafood in British Columbia is sold in **Chinatown fish markets in Vancouver and Richmond.** In **Steveston,** at the mouth of the Fraser River, you can buy fish, shrimp, and crab directly from the fishermen. In summer, this is the best place for buying freshly caught **Fraser River** sockeye salmon. Just look for boats with an awning stretched over their main deck. That's the sign that they have seafood for sale. But beware. Unfortunately not all fishermen are honest. Some will try to pawn off old fish which they may or may not have caught themselves. Others sell farm-raised salmon. Look the fish in the eye. Is it clear? Are the gills red, not brown? Does the flesh bounce back when you press the skin? Or does it leave a dimple? Does the fish smell fresh? Fresh fish has clear eyes, red gills, and resilient flesh, and it does *not* smell fishy. These rules apply to U.S. fishmongers as well.

(continues)

■ WASHINGTON

BOW / BELLINGHAM

Chuckanut Drive is a narrow road that winds south from Bellingham between steep sandstone cliffs and the tideflats of Samish Bay. **Taylor Shellfish Farm** has the most scenic of all oyster farm locations in Washington, sprawling at the foot of a densely forested bluff, where wild roses bloom in spring. To the west, the mountainous San Juan Islands rise from the sea. The farm's small store has been spiffed up recently and sells not only different types of oysters (if you're lucky, they'll have Kumamotos, Olympias, and European flats), but also fresh crab (live and cooked), pink scallops in the shell, clams, and mussels. 188 Chuckanut Dr., Bow; (360) 766-6002.

A bit off the beaten path, on Samish Island, is the **Blau Oyster Company.**

You can buy fish, crab and other seasonal seafood here as well. If you order a day ahead, you get a ten percent discount. 919 Blue Heron Rd., Bow; (360) 766-6171.

ANACORTES

On your way to the outer coast, if you're going by way of Fidalgo and Whidbey islands, is the small roadside shack of **Strom's Shrimp**. The locally caught shrimp are very tasty and make for a great snack while you're waiting for the Keystone ferry to take you to Port Townsend. 1481 State Route 20, Anacortes; (360) 293-2531.

HOOD CANAL

Driving south along the Hood Canal, look for the processing shacks and oyster shell piles of the **Hama Hama Oyster Company.** Here shellfish are kept fresh

Staked salmon is barbecued during the Makah Days festival held every August on the Makah Indian Reservation in Washington.

Piles of oyster shells discarded after shucking are recycled as fertilizer.

in live tanks. Besides the oysters, which here have an uncommonly delicate flavor, there are excellent clams for sale, as well as geoduck (pronounced "gooey-duck), the uncouth-looking giant clam of the Northwest. But never mind the way it looks. Its meat is delicious!

The Puget Sound inlets south of the Hood Canal have oyster farms, but these are difficult to find and prefer to sell wholesale. Just south of the Hamma Hamma River; (360) 877-6938.

WESTPORT

As you head down the coast, stop in Westport for shellfish. Northwesterners consider it a great pleasure to sit on the beach, sheltered from the sea wind by huge driftwood logs, and eat oysters on the halfshell and freshly cracked crab. Two good places to try are: **Brady's Oysters,** 3714 Oyster Place E.; (360) 268-0077; and **Nelson Crab,** 3088 Kindred Ave., Tokeland; (360) 267-2911.

WILLAPA BAY

On the east shore you can buy absolutely delicious smoked oysters. Try **Ekone Oyster Company,** 192 Bay Center Rd., Bay Center; (360) 875-5494.

LONG BEACH PENINSULA

Look for Jolly Roger Oyster Company at the Nahcotta dock; (360) 665-4111; and Oysterville Sea Farms at the Oysterville dock; (360) 665-6585. East Point Seafood Company in Nahcotta sells oysters and a variety of smoked and canned fish; (206) 284-7571.

■ OREGON

ASTORIA

South of the Columbia River, in Oregon, you have to stop at **Josephson's Smokehouse**, a local favorite for its smoked fish. Best of all, they ship, if you don't want to carry all that seafood around with you. If you're lucky, they'll have Columbia River sturgeon caviar, which is as good as the best imported roe. 106 Marine Dr.; (503) 325-2190.

TILLAMOOK BAY

Look for **Norm's Fish & Crab**, which sells smoked fish and fresh Dungeness crab, 8425 Hwy. 101 N, Bay City; (503) 377-2799; and try **Bay Ocean Oyster**, 603 Garibaldi Ave., Garibaldi; (503) 322-0040; **Tillamook Oyster Company**, 1985 Bay Ocean Rd. NW, Tillamook; (503) 842-6921.

You'll have to drive out to the fishing harbor docks to visit **Smith Pacific Shrimp**. The shrimp are great and so is the smoked fish. 608 Commercial Dr., Garibaldi; (503) 322-3316.

You can't miss the **Tillamook cheese factory**. It's just north of Tillamook, and a two-masted schooner sits out front. The large store sells not just cheese but a variety of Oregon food products. 4175 Hwy. 101 N., Tillamook; (503) 842-4481.

South of Tillamook Bay, US 101 leaves the coast and runs inland. Take Three Capes Loop if you want to drive along the scenic cliffs.

PACIFIC CITY

At Pacific City, fishermen go down to the sea in dories launched through the surf. You can watch them launch and bring in the boats, but beware the four-by-fours pulling the boat trailers—they really move. Sometimes there's just a split second between a safe launch and a swamped boat. Buy some of the fishermen's catch at **Doryman Fish Company Market**, 33315 Cape Kiwanda Rd.; (503) 965-6412.

LINCOLN CITY

Barnacle Bill's Seafood Market is a good place to stock up on the local catch. 2174 NE Hwy. 101; (541) 994-3022. Few people know that southern Oregon grows oysters, perhaps because the farms are off the beaten path. Look for **Umpqua Aquaculture** at the far end of the harbor on Ork Rock Rd. in Winchester Bay; (541) 271-5684. **Qualman Oyster Farms** is across the slough from Charleston harbor at 4898 Crown Point Rd.; (541) 888-3145.

BANDON

The best place for fresh fish in southern Oregon is **Bandon Fish Market**, 250 First SW St.; (541) 347-2851. Stock up on cheese and other local foods at **Bandon Cheese**, 680 E Second St. (US 101); (541) 347-2456.

■ THE COLUMBIA

Below the steep cliffs of Cape Disappointment, the Columbia River and the Pacific Ocean growl at each other across a barrier of sand where tall breakers pound the beach, crushing any ship caught by them. Many ships have come to grief in the last 200 years, though a lighthouse clinging to the sheer rock has warned of the danger since 1856. This was the beach on which Lewis and Clark first walked beside the Pacific in 1805.

Fort Canby was built on a rocky headland during the Civil War to protect the coast from Confederate raiders. An interpretive center contains journal excerpts from the Lewis and Clark expedition and photo murals of places on the explorers' route. Despite the construction of a couple of lighthouses, a few military bunkers almost invisible under dense foliage of trees and shrubs, and the interpretive center, these wild headlands have changed surprisingly little since Clark "accompanied by 11 men" stood here almost 200 years ago on November 18, 1805:

> This spot, which was called Cape Disappointment, is an elevated circular knob, rising with a steep ascent 150 or 160 feet above the water, formed like the whole shore of the bay, as well as the seacoast, and covered with thick timber on the inner side but open and grassy in the exposure next to the sea.

The woods are still as tangled as they were when Clark traversed them. You can walk through the crumbling concrete gun emplacements or hike out onto the north jetty, which guards the mouth of the river. Waves smash against the black boulders, throwing spray to the uppermost rocks, as gulls screech overhead.

Lewis and Clark Interpretive Center at Fort Canby State Park, is located 2.5 miles west of Ilwaco; (360) 642-3029.

■ EAST UP THE COLUMBIA

If you drive from Fort Canby up the Columbia (follow US 101 to WA 401, then to WA 4), you'll notice dark rock—a basalt flow older than the mountains—pushing through the soggy ground along the river bank. From the abandoned gun batteries at **Fort Columbia State Park** you can look straight down the river to the ocean. This is a delightfully rustic backwater. You pass willow-lined sloughs, old churches, and the green superstructure of the bridge to Astoria. Cattle graze in wet pastures. Abandoned houses and barns dot the land. A sign marks the site at

which Lewis and Clark camped for ten days in November 1805. A covered bridge dating from 1905 spans Grays River.

Abandoned cannery towns like Altoona, with tall pilings rising from the shore, are all that's left from the salmon traps and canneries that once lined the river. Across the Columbia, Cathlamet Bay is a maze of marshy islands and sloughs, where river folk live in floating homes, their boats tied up out front.

Be sure to wander through **Skamakowa,** a picturesque small town (just off WA 4) squeezed into a canyon so narrow that some of the houses are built on stilts over the water. You may also want to stop a bit further on in **Cathlamet,** a charming hamlet with white clapboard Victorians and storefronts, rising on a wooded bluff above low-lying pastures and fishermen's shacks of Puget Island. From here, if you are so inclined, you can take a ferry across the narrow channel separating the island from Oregon.

(above) Fishing boats in the harbor at Westport.
(opposite) The interior of the historic Pacific County Courthouse in South Bend.

■ TRAVEL AND CLIMATE

■ GETTING THERE

Even though the Olympic Peninsula is quite close to Washington's metropolitan centers, it is separated from the more settled part of the state by saltwater channels and thus remains sparsely settled. In recent years a rise in tourism has led to a corresponding increase in good lodging facilities and restaurants.

By Ferry. Car ferries depart from Seattle, Anacortes, and Victoria.

By Car. From the south you can drive to this region via US 101, which here is a narrow, winding two-lane highway skirting eerie bogs, moss-festooned forests, and clear-cuts overrun with alder and ferns. Even narrower roads lead from this parameter highway into the mountains and to quiet beaches. WA 8/US 12 links the coast at Grays Harbor to Olympia on Puget Sound. The road between Chehalis and Raymond is slow, winding, forest-lined WA 6.

■ CLIMATE

The coast is wetter but also warmer than the lowlands of western Washington; the northeastern part of the peninsula lies in the rain shadow of the Olympic Mountains and some years receives little precipitation. But the Olympic rainforest has one of the highest annual rainfalls in the US. Snow falls in the mountains every winter but rarely reaches the shore—even when Puget Sound is shrouded in white. Storms rolling in from the Pacific can be very fierce, with huge waves slamming into the shore and shooting logs of driftwood high into the air. Calm, balmy winter days are fine times for walking the deserted beaches.

■ ACCOMMODATIONS AND RESTAURANTS

☎   For chain lodgings see toll free numbers on page 352.

$$ For room and restaurant price designations see page 352.

✭   Means highly recommended.

ABERDEEN (PACIFIC COAST)

✗ **Parma.**
116 W Heron St.; (360) 532-3166
Great pasta dishes and freshly baked bread. Amazingly good restaurant for such a small town. **$$**

CHINOOK (PACIFIC COAST)

✗ **The Sanctuary.** ✭
US 101 and Hazel; (360) 777-8380
A comfy place in a converted church. Best steaks on the coast. Fishermen eat here. Open Thurs-Sun. **$$-$$$**

FORKS
(OLYMPIC PENINSULA)
⊤ **Kalaloch Lodge.**
US 101; (360) 962-2271
The old lodge and the rustic cabins on a bluff above the Pacific have made this place a lot of people's favorite. Newer accommodations are also available.
$$-$$$

GRAYLAND
(PACIFIC COAST)
✕ **The Dunes.** ✷
723 Dunes Rd. (off State Hwy. 105 at the sign of the giant razor clam); (360) 267-1441.
Literally in the dunes. Best razor clam fritters on the coast. $$-$$$

LAKE QUINAULT
(OLYMPIC PENINSULA)
⊤ **Lake Quinault Lodge.**
345 S. Shore Rd.; (360) 288-2900
The old lodge, built in 1926, sits right on the shore of Lake Quinault, on the western side of the Olympic Peninsula. Guests can take boats out on the lake, walk or run on nearby nature trails, or drive relatively short distances to serious hikes in the Olympics. $$$

LONG BEACH PENINSULA
(PACIFIC COAST)
⊤ **Sandpiper Beach Resort.**
4159 Rte. 109 (1.5 mi. south of Pacific Beach); (360) 276-4580
A modern resort near the beach. Suites, cottages, no TV or telephones. $$

⊤ **Shelburne Inn.**
4415 Pacific Way, Seaview; (360) 642-2442
The 1896 building is on the National Register of Historic Places. The interior is bright and stuffed with antiques. The older rooms tend to be a bit cramped. The highway right out front can be annoyingly loud. $$$

⊤ **Sou'wester.**
Beach Access Rd., Seaview; (360) 642-2542
The old lodge was built in 1892 by Sen. Henry Winslow Corbett, a Portland plutocrat, and later converted into a quirky, delightful bed-and-breakfast by a South African couple. $-$$

✕ **The Ark.**
273 Sandridge Rd., Nahcotta; (360) 665-4133
Right next to an oyster dock on Willapa Bay, the Ark has earned a reputation that goes far beyond southwestern Washington. Seafood is the big attraction but not the only one. $$$

✕ **Forty-Second Street.** ✷✷✷
Pacific Hwy. 103 and 42nd Pl., Seaview; (360) 642-2323
Cheri Walker and her husband Blaine put the Shoalwater Restaurant up the street on the national culinary map. A few years ago, they broke away and bought a place of their own, a small chicken-and-dumplings cafe known for its homespun fare. We hear rave reports about her pot roast. Yes, pot roast! Food for the gods. $$-$$$

✕ **The Lightship Restaurant** ☆
and Columbia Bar.
410 SW 10th St. SW (in the Edgewater
Inn), Long Beach; (360) 642-3252
Yes, it's in a motel, but it has a view of
the beach (much harder to come by on
the Washington coast than you might
guess), and the food is very good, especially the fish 'n' chips. $$-$$$

✕ **The Shoalwater Restaurant.** ☆ ☆ ☆
Shelburne Inn, Pacific Way 103 and
45th St., Seaview; (360) 642-4142
The Shoalwater has long been the best
restaurant on the Long Beach peninsula
Across the entryway from the restaurant
is the **Heron and Beaver Pub** (under the
same management), the snuggest place
on the coast. $$-$$$

PORT ANGELES
(OLYMPIC PENINSULA)

⊤ **Lake Crescent Lodge.**
416 Lake Crescent Rd.; (360) 928-3211
This old lodge stands on the shore of
deep, scenic Lake Crescent, west of Port
Angeles and just north of Olympic National Park. People come for the scenery
and the proximity to the mountains and
beach. $

✕ **C'est Si Bon.**
23 Cedar Park Dr.; (360) 452-8888
A French couple runs this French restaurant four miles east of Port Angeles.
Seattle diners who have stumbled into it
more or less by mistake remember it
fondly. Fine views of the Olympics, a
good wine list, and a menu that includes
local seafood and chocolate mousse. $$$

Lake Quinault Lodge in Olympic National Park.

PORT TOWNSEND (OLYMPIC PENINSULA)

James House.
1238 Washington St.; (360) 385-1238
Virtually everyone's favorite Port
Townsend bed-and-breakfast. Stuffed
with antiques, the house is listed in the
National Register of Historic Places. All
the rooms have character and some have
views. The house stands in the Victorian
residential neighborhood up on the
bluff. $$-$$$

Palace Hotel.
1004 Water St.; (360) 385-0773
Housed in an 1889 brick building that
was once a bordello. Near the heart of
Port Townsend's historic downtown. $$

Fountain Cafe.
920 Washington St.; (360) 385-1364
Nothing fancy, but the Fountain's
seafood, pasta, and other cafe dinners
served on linen tablecloths have given it
a reputation as one of Port Townsend's
best. Waiting lines are common, so it's
best to make reservations. $$

Salal Cafe. ⚥
634 Water St.;(360) 385-6532
The Salal offers large and tasty breakfasts. Lunch and dinner menus feature
pasta and seafood. $-$$

SEQUIM

**Granny Sandy's Orchard Bed-and-
Breakfast.** 405 W Spruce;
(360) 683-5748
Guests praise the gourmet breakfasts
here—crepes with fresh nectarines, for
example—and the close proximity (30
miles) to Olympic National Park. $$$

Sol Duc Hot Springs Resort in Olympic National Park.

SOUTHERN LOWLANDS
W A S H I N G T O N S T A T E

■ HIGHLIGHTS

Southern Puget Sound
Tacoma
Olympia
Mount Rainier
Mount St. Helens
Fort Vancouver

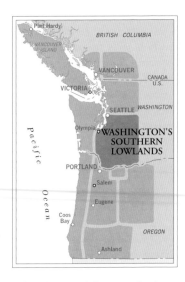

■ LANDSCAPE

SOUTH OF SEATTLE, THE LOWLANDS become
much divided by saltwater inlets of Puget
Sound cutting peninsulas into convoluted
puzzle shapes and separating islands from
the mainland. For this reason, this is a region of bridges and ferries. The latter
connect Vashon Island to Seattle and Tacoma, and the Kitsap Peninsula to Seattle.

South of Olympia, the lowlands continue as a wide trough, between the Cascades and the Coast Range, all the way to the Columbia River. To the southeast
rise the stately Mount Rainier and the broken-off top of Mount St. Helens, once
the most beautifully symmetrical of all Cascade volcanoes.

■ SOUTHERN PUGET SOUND

Traveling through the southern Puget Sound country is a delight. In much of the
southern lowlands, roads shaded by trees alternate with green pastures where cattle
graze contentedly; in southern Puget Sound, you never know when the trees lining
your road will drop away to reveal views of idyllic saltwater inlets. Peninsular roads
are quiet enough to allow for enjoyable exploration by bicycle. Because few ferries

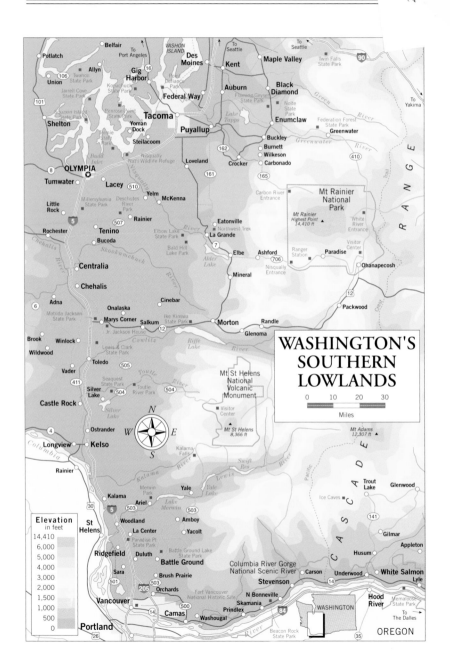

WASHINGTON'S
SOUTHERN
LOWLANDS

0   10   20   30
Miles

travel on the southern inlets, you'll have to bring (or charter) a boat to explore the intricate waterways. Many local mariners do that in the same canoes they use on lowland rivers. But be aware that tidal differences are greater the farther south you travel. At Olympia, they can be more than 16 feet—and high tides create strong currents at ebb and flood.

When Capt. George Vancouver named Puget Sound in 1792, he made it clear he was referring only to its southern end: "...to commemorate Mr. Puget's exertions, the south extremity of it I named Puget's Sound." The name has since become applied to a much greater region, encompassing Admiralty Inlet to the north and even Washington Sound (Bellingham Bay and the San Juan Islands).

The bay Vancouver named after Mr. Puget was most likely Commencement Bay, where the city of Tacoma is now located. Puget's party made note of the people living along the water's edge:

> They seemed not wanting in offers of friendship and hospitality; as on our joining their party, we were presented with such things as they had to dispose of: and they immediately prepared a few of the roots, with some shell fish for our refreshment, which were very palatable. (Journal, May 20th, 1792)

Which is just what might happen to a modern-day visitor coming upon a clambake on the beach.

■ TACOMA

Tacoma, draped dramatically over a waterbound headland between Commencement Bay and Puget Sound, offers great views of Mount Rainier, excellent parks, and a downtown with some very interesting and very ornate late-19th-century buildings.

Visitors will find much beauty in Tacoma, and many things to admire. To see the city from its best angle, visitors should arrive by ferry from Vashon Island to the north (take the ferry from Fauntleroy Cove in Seattle to Vashon; drive down the island, and take the ferry from Vashon to Tacoma). You'll be facing the tree-clad slopes of Point Defiance as you arrive, with the port stretching to the east.

But most visitors arrive in town via Interstate 5 and take Interstate 705 downtown, a spur that ends on A Street. **Old City Hall** and **Northern Pacific Railroad**

headquarters stand as portals at the north end of downtown. Just up the hill, the restored 1918 **Pantages Theater** and the restored **Rialto Theater** draw people to plays, concerts, and films. At the south end of downtown, the old, domed Union Station has been restored as part of a new federal courthouse. The **Washington State History Museum** here has historical artifacts, displays, and a research library, as well as high-tech video displays, talking figures, and interactive computers. You can pinpoint the history of each region on a huge wall-sized relief map. Computers provide access to historical information about each region. Located at 1911 Pacific Avenue; (888) 238-4373. The **Tacoma Art Museum** at the corner of 12th and Pacific houses a small permanent collection of European and American art plus interesting temporary shows; (206/253) 272-4258.

Point Defiance Park, one of the most spectacular city parks anywhere in the United States, can be reached from Interstate 5 via WA Highway 16 and WA Highway 163 (N. Pearl Street), and Five Mile Road (which circles the park). From downtown Tacoma, you can drive to Point Defiance Park by taking Ruston Way north along the waterfront (follow signs). Or you can travel to Point Defiance Park (and Tacoma) by ferry from Vashon Island. The park, on a wooded peninsula which juts into the sound, has miles of tree-shaded roads winding through idyllic glens, a beach running along the saltwater shore for miles, a fine aquarium and zoo, rose gardens, picnic tables, big trees, grassy slopes, and brushy ravines echoing with the song of birds. There's an outdoor museum of old logging equipment here, and the (original) granary from the Hudson Bay's old Fort Nisqually stands here among several reconstructed buildings.

On the shore of Puget Sound between Tacoma and Olympia, the fields and marshes of the spreading Nisqually Delta are preserved as the **Nisqually National Wildlife Refuge.** Walk through the refuge (reached from I-5 at exit 114) to the water's edge. To the north, beyond the sprays of purple daisies and the brown marsh grass beaten flat by high water, the gray-green Nisqually River, lined by dense stands of trees, flows toward Puget Sound.

■ OLYMPIA

An hour's drive south of Seattle, Olympia sits at the junction of I-5 and US 101, at the narrow extremity of Budd Inlet—a fat finger of Puget Sound. Founded in

The state capitol in Olympia.

1850 and named for the majestic mountains that loom northwest of the city on clear days, Olympia has been Washington's capital since Washington Territory was severed from Oregon in 1853.

You can see the tall **capitol dome,** which wasn't completed until 1928, from the freeway, rising above **Capitol Lake.** Up close, it's an unusually handsome building set in nicely landscaped gardens.

Olympia's **downtown** (along Fourth, Fifth, and State Avenues West and along the lower reaches of Capitol Avenue) is low-key but interesting, replete with used book shops, cafes, and interesting old brick buildings.

❖

Because the small, nationally respected, aggressively non-traditional **Evergreen State College** stands nearby, Olympia is something of an "alternative" culture center. The town hosts independent film festivals and supports a vigorous music scene —locals claim that Nirvana, the quintessential "Seattle band," got its start here.

■ MOUNT RAINIER

Mount Rainier National Park lies 92 miles (two hours) south of Seattle, and 143 miles (three hours) north of Portland. Embracing the slopes of the 14,410-foot volcano, the park contains broad tracts of old-growth forest, waterfalls, glaciers, and meadows carpeted in summertime by wildflowers. Roads lead to vantage points on all sides of the mountain, each with its own celebrated views (when the clouds lift), lodges and campgrounds, and hiking and cross-country ski trails. You don't have to walk far from any road here to enjoy Rainier's wild beauty: even near a much-traveled entrance road a brief uphill walk from the pavement can leave you standing all alone, contemplating the sharp outline of a bear's fresh paw print.

❖

Mount Rainier can be approached by road from the west, the northwest, and the east. That said, keep in mind that the southwestern and one of the eastern approaches actually take you to the southern slopes of the mountain.

Park headquarters, including a visitors center and an inn, are located in the southwestern corner of the park at Longmire, 2,761 feet above sea level; (360) 569-2275. From there, the road climbs 13 miles to **Paradise,** at 5,400 feet. You

Paradise Inn in Mount Rainier National Park. The ranger station here records more snow annually than any other place on earth—over 100 feet in a recent year.

can drive through a forest of huge trees to the old **Paradise Lodge** at any time of the year—in summer to enjoy the hiking, in winter for the cross-country skiing. From Paradise, which offers spectacular views of the mountain, you can follow paved trails, explore rough, open country sliced by ravines, or start up toward the climbers' 10,000-foot base camp at Camp Muir. The summit that you see from Paradise stays white all year long. The mountain's 35 square miles of glaciers trap 156 billion cubic feet of water and make up the largest single-peak glacier system in the nation. Five thousand years ago, an eruption melted the glacier, creating a huge mud flow that swept all the way to Puget Sound.

Ambitious backpackers can launch out on the 93-mile circumnavigation of the mountain on the Wonderland Trail.

■ MOUNT ST. HELENS

A trip to Mount St. Helens is, even today, almost two decades after the volcanic eruption that destroyed the mountain's top, a bit like a visit to a war zone, albeit to one whose wounds are healing. But the scars are still prominent on this rather impressive manifestation of nature's awesome power. Before making the long drive to the mountain along State Highway 504, stop at the **Mount St. Helens Visitors Center at Silver Lake,** where you learn about the eruption of Mount St. Helens; (360) 274-2100. At the center you can walk through a giant model of the volcano and pick up maps and information for touring. It is also possible to hire guides to lead you into the blast zone for overnight camping

Until 1980, Mount St. Helens was a serene-looking 9,677-foot volcano, younger, slightly smaller, and easier to climb than the Cascades' other landmark peaks. Visitors to nearby Spirit Lake enjoyed the reflection of the perfectly symmetrical cone in the lake's blue water. Then, in the spring of 1980, geologists noticed some ominous rumblings and warned that St. Helens was about to erupt.

No one was really prepared for what happened. On the morning of May 18, the mountain exploded. More than 1,300 feet of its top simply disappeared. Instead of going straight up, the blast went north, destroying everything in its path. Old-growth forests were vaporized. Big trees a little farther from the blast were scattered across the hillsides like straw or simply killed where they stood. Soil was incinerated, too, and nearby slopes were scoured down to bedrock. Volcanic ash fell on 22,000 square miles of land, including much of eastern Washington. The

Alta Vista Trail winds through fields of wildflowers in the Paradise area.

sky in many eastern Washington communities darkened at midday, and ash piled up like drifted snow on the streets and sidewalks. Snow and glacial ice melted by the blast poured down the mountain, creating rivers of mud that swelled the Toutle River, which rose 66 feet above its normal level, sweeping away homes and bridges. Mud flowed down to the Cowlitz and the Columbia, where millions of tons had to be dredged from the shipping channel. Fifty-seven people died. The devastation appeared complete.

But pocket gophers living underground survived the blast, and fireweed and other plants started recolonizing some of the blast area within a year. Soon herds of huge brown elk wandered comfortably across the mud and the ridges above. Much of the area remains a moonscape, but life is returning—as it has after volcanic eruptions in the Cascades for millions of years. Weyerhaeuser, which owned most of the land in the path of the blast, traded some to the federal government, which included it in a new Mount St. Helens Volcano National Monument.

From a helicopter at the crater's rim, you can look into an amphitheater of sheer gray cliffs and see a lava dome steaming in the shadows.

Mount St. Helens smolders above Coldwater Lake (left). The 1980 eruption leveled everything for miles around. Above is what remains of a forest that once thrived on the shores of Spirit Lake.

■ FORT VANCOUVER

Some 104 miles south of Olympia, the Columbia River's main channel divides the states of Oregon and Washington—which is why the stateline is closer to the Washington bank, because that's where the main channel runs. Today it is crossed by a modern Interstate 5 bridge with an unusual feature: it has a draw span that opens for big ships and for sailboats with tall masts. Whenever the bridge opens for one of these vessels, it causes miles-long backups on southbound and northbound Interstate 5.

Just before the bridge, on the north side of the freeway, is the site where the Hudson's Bay Company established a fort on the bluff above the north shore of the Columbia. The first European settlement in what is now Washington State, the fort was moved closer to the river in 1828, to the site of the modern reconstruction. Northwest historian Carlos Schwantes writes that within the 20-foot stockade, "Fort Vancouver constituted a small, almost self-sufficient European community that included…30 to 50 small houses where employees (*engages*) lived with their Indian wives." The fort also had a hospital, storehouses, workshops, mills, a shipyard, a dairy, orchards, and a farm of several hundred acres. The governor of the fort was John McLoughlin, the Hudson's Bay Company's chief factor for the Columbia District, who ran the fort in a truly imperial manner. He generously gave supplies on credit to American settlers who came over the Oregon Trail—despite company policy against helping Americans and despite the fact that few settlers paid him or the company back.

The last of the original fort burned to the ground in 1866, but since the mid-1960s, most of its buildings have been reconstructed of heavy, rough-milled timbers inside a stockade of pointed logs, on the fort's original site. Outside the stockade stands an apple orchard and a large, orderly garden full of flower and vegetable species—everything from Japanese lanterns to artichokes—that were cultivated by the fort's inhabitants 150 years ago. Inside the stockade, park rangers dressed in period costume offer demonstrations in the bakery and the smithy.

The **Fort Vancouver National Historic Site** is located at E Evergreen Boulevard and E Fifth Street (just east of I-5, exit 1-C). State Highway 14 runs between the reconstructed fort and the river; (360) 696-7655.

Present-day Vancouver, Washington, developed on the river bench-land above the Hudson's Bay Company fort, and its downtown boasts a handful of beautiful art deco buildings built during the 1930s. The elaborate brick and terra-cotta styling of the Telephone Exchange building is one of the city's architectural highlights, along with the beautiful Elks Building—a three-story brick masterpiece with wrought-iron balconies and marble inlays. Every Fourth of July Vancouver is known for putting on the biggest fireworks show west of the Mississippi.

■ TRAVEL AND CLIMATE

■ GETTING THERE

By Car. This region lies between southern Puget Sound and the Columbia River (which divides Oregon and Washington). Interstate 5, its main north-south route, connects Seattle to Portland. Off the freeway, this is a very pastoral region of quiet farms and forests. Narrow two-lane highways connect the lowlands to the coast and to the high country of the southern Cascades. Mount St. Helens and Mount Rainier rise above the deeply green foothills to the east. US 12 skirts the lower slopes of Mount Rainier before crossing White Pass and descending into the fertile Yakima Valley to the east. (*See "Yakima Valley Food and Wine Tour," page 248.*)

■ CLIMATE

Weather in this area can be highly variable: the Coast Range intercepts much of the rain coming in from the ocean. Skies are often sunny or covered with broken clouds. Summer temperatures range from 65 to 80 degrees F. Winters can be quite cold and the lowlands can be covered with snow for weeks at a time.

■ ACCOMMODATIONS AND RESTAURANTS

  ☎   For chain lodgings see toll-free numbers on page 352.

  $$ For room and restaurant price designations see page 352.

  ✶   Means highly recommended.

GLENOMA

☎ **St. Helens Manorhouse.**
On State Hwy. 12; (360) 498-5243
Less than one hour from I-5, this unique bed-and-breakfast is a converted farmhouse, filled with antiques and good books. A pleasant base for trips to Mount Rainier or Mount St. Helens. $$

MOUNT RAINIER

� Paradise Inn.

State Hwy. 706; (360) 569-2413
This is exactly what a big mountain
lodge should look like. The large lobby
belies the small rooms. The location is
spectacular: a mile up the southern slope
of Rainier—with wildflower meadows,
hiking trails, and the main climbing
route to the top. (Closed in winter) $$-
$$$

OLYMPIA

☖ Harbinger Inn.

1136 East Bay Dr. NE; (360) 754-0389
This renovated 1910 mansion is now a
bed-and-breakfast overlooking Puget
Sound and the Capitol. $$

✕ La Petite Maison. ✭✭

2005 Ascension St. NW; (360) 943-8812
More formal than most Olympia restau-
rants—and better, too. $$-$$

✕ The Spar.

114 E. Fourth Ave.; (360) 357-6444
The interior of the Spar conjures an old-
time workingman's cafe, with wonderful
old logging photographs on the walls.
Milkshakes and traditional American
food. $

✕ Urban Onion.

116 Legion Way; (360) 943-9242
Located downstairs in the old Olympian
Hotel, once the center of Olympia polit-
ical and social life, the Urban Onion
serves good soups and sandwiches, as
well as more ambitious dishes. $-$$

TACOMA

✕ Antique Sandwich Company.

5102 N. Pearl St.; (206/253) 752-4069
Just up the street from Point Defiance
Park, this neighborhood sandwich shop
serves three meals a day among comfortable, eclectic furnishings. $

✕ Fujiya.

1125 Court C (between Broadway and Market); (206/253) 627-5319
A very good Japanese restaurant in a
pleasant second-floor space near down-
town. $$

✕ Harbor Lights.

2761 Ruston Way; (206/253) 752-8600
Fresh seafood on the tables, stuffed
seafood on the walls, and a view over
Commencement Bay have made Harbor
Lights a standard for decades. $$

✕ Katie Downs. ✭

3211 Ruston Way; (206/253) 756-0771
One of many restaurants along the Ruston Way waterfront, Katie Downs serves
good pizza and an array of Northwestern microbrews. This is not a place to
come for quiet or solitude. $

VANCOUVER, WA

✕ Pinot Ganache. ✭

1004 Washington St.; (360) 695-7786
A fun, bright place with fresh flowers, an
international menu, and great desserts.
$$

Mountain man Bob "Badger" Twyman at the annual Brigade Encampment in Fort Vancouver.

YAKIMA VALLEY FOOD AND WINE TOUR

The Yakima Valley is Washington's food basket and wine vat. Most people either travel here via Portland and the Columbia Gorge, coming up US 97, or they begin their trip in Seattle, crossing the Cascades on Interstate 90. Interstate 82, which starts in Ellensburg runs the length of the Yakima Valley. Or you can reach the valley on US 12, which skirts the southern flanks of Mount Rainier.

■ COUNTRYSIDE

The Yakima River flows southeast from its source in the Cascade Mountains, cutting steep canyons through serried basalt ridges. After merging with the Naches River it crosses the Ahtanum Valley as it passes the city of Yakima. At Union Gap, the river breaks through Ahtanum Ridge and enters the long valley bearing its name. Throughout its course, the Yakima is a rocky river, with many rapids. It was once a major salmon stream. A few salmon, undefeated by dams, still ascend the river to spawn.

Grass-covered hills, dun at harvest time, where the Yakama people freely roamed little more than a century ago with their vast herds of horses, rise above green fields, orchards, and vineyards. Horses still run wild in the Horse Heaven Hills on the Yakama Indian Reservation.

Apples and other fruits came to the valley in the 1890s, with the first irrigation schemes. Grapes came much later. Concord grapes were planted first (during the 1960s the valley supplied Gallo and other California wineries with Concord

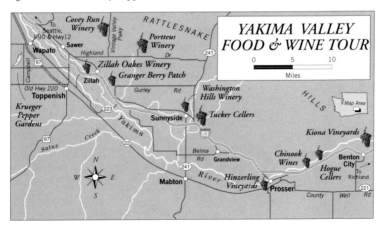

there were virtually no *vinifera* vineyards in the valley; today they dominate the local wine industry.

But this is more than just another wine valley. Other agricultural products are as important. The Yakima Valley grows most of the nation's hops, and some of its best asparagus—which is so tender, you can eat it raw, straight from the field. Tomatoes and chiles ripen to perfection in the long, hot summer days, and melons take on extra sweetness.

There are apricot, cherry, peach, and apple orchards as well. Their quality is good, though not as outstanding as that of the fruit grown in the east-facing valleys of the North Cascades. Yakima Valley apples get better the farther west you go, into the foothills of the Cascade Mountains. Which is why Selah, west of Yakima, is the apple capital of south-central Washington.

Conversely, the grape quality improves the closer you get to the mitigating influence of the Columbia River. Which is why Prosser and Benton City are the heart of the Yakima Valley wine country.

Because the vegetables of this valley are as important as the wines, we'll stop at a farm before we visit our first vineyard. But this is no ordinary farm.

■ TOURING THE VALLEY

Krueger Pepper Gardens

This exceptional farm, located in Wapato, is regionally renowned for the high quality of the more than 60 varieties of peppers they grow (bring your own container—it's strictly u-pick). The peppers are at their peak when the grape harvest starts, as are the tomatoes, eggplant, squash, and melon. Be sure to pick up a free recipe booklet at the farm office. 3491 Branch Rd., Wapato; (509) 877-3677.

Zillah Oakes Winery

As you drive west, the first vineyards of note are in Zillah. Zillah Oakes Winery is just off the Interstate 82 freeway. Like the town, the winery takes its name from a daughter of the chief engineer of the Northern Pacific Railroad. The wines are made in an easily quaffable style, and include an aligote and a grenache. The winery has recently been sold, and wine styles may change. Exit 52 at 1001 Vintage Valley Parkway; (509) 829-6990.

Covey Run

Harder to find, but worth the trouble. In downtown Zillah, turn left on Roza Drive, right on Highland Drive, then left again on Vintage. Covey Run sits high on a slope with a great view of the valley from several large decks and patios. This is one of the best picnic sites in the area. In the past, the wines have included a light, nouveau-style lemberger, complex merlots, cabernet sauvignons, and chardonnays, as well as elegant rieslings. The winery has been sold, and wine styles may change. 1500 Vintage Rd.; (509) 829-6235.

Portteus

The next winery is just a short jaunt down the road. Portteus gained fame as a grape grower—its grapes went into some of Washington's best reds—before making its own wine. Taste the cabernet and merlot as well as the spicy zinfandel. Yes, zinfandel. Portteus was the first Washington winery to vinify this noble California grape. 5201 Highland Dr., five miles north of Zillah; (509) 829-6970.

Granger Berry Patch

Located in nearby Granger, this farm sells many different varieties of berries, including such uncommon ones as tayberries, blackcaps, and yellow raspberries. The farm also grows raspberries that ripen in fall, just as the grape harvest gets under way. 1731 Beam Rd.; (509) 854-1413.

A picture-perfect vineyard of Yakima Valley near the town of Zillah.

Hyatt Vineyards in Zillah.

Washington Hills Cellars

There's nothing pretty about these cellars, which occupy an old dairy plant in Sunnyside, except the quality of the wines. Over the past decade winemaker Brian Carter has established a reputation second to none. His reds are particularly fine. Washington Hills divides its wines into three brands: Apex for the top of the line, Washington Hills for varietals and blends, and W. B. Bridgman for easily drinkable quaffing wines. Every respectable Northwest wine cellar should have some Apex wines, especially cabernet. merlot, and chardonnay. 111 E Lincoln Ave.; (509) 839-9463.

Tucker Cellars

East of Sunnyside, and as much a produce stand as a winery, everything here is home-grown and of the highest quality. In spring, there's beautiful asparagus; in summer, sweet onions, perfect melons and vegetables; in fall there's some incredibly sweet corn. At all times, you may sample the Tuckers' white popcorn, pickled vegetables, and wines. The winery produces refreshingly fruity riesling and chenin blanc. Red varietals and reserve chardonnay are sold only at the winery. 70 Ray Rd. (on US 12, just east of exit 69/WA 24; (509) 837-8701.

Hinzerling Winery

The small building housing this Prosser winery represents industrial chic of a different kind. It is in a converted garage that has seen little architectural change since this family winery was established here in 1976. Winemaker Mike Wallace is one of the pioneers of Washington's wine industry and has, over the years, made some truly incredible wine. Wallace's reds and his port-style wines are particularly impressive. He also seems to possess a special knack for bringing out the complex flavors of gewurztraminer. 1520 Sheridan Ave.; (509) 786-2163.

Chinook Wines

Located in a small white Prosser farmhouse is the kind of small winery enophiles dream about. The happy marriage of viticulturist Clay Mackey and winemaker Kay Simon has created some truly exceptional wines, particularly merlot, cabernet sauvignon, and sauvignon blanc. Unfortunately, these wines are always in short supply. But chances are you'll find some at the winery when they're unavailable anywhere else. Just off I-82, exit 82, on Wine Country Rd.; (509) 786-2725.

The Hogue Cellars

Located just down Wine Country Road, Hogue represents a successful marriage of a different sort—that of farmers and vintners. Besides grapes, the Hogues also grow hops and vegetables, and they produce excellent pickled asparagus and beans (all for sale at the winery). The Hogue fume blanc has gained a regional reputation; the dry chenin blanc is everyone's favorite summer afternoon wine; the reds go very well with food. You'll want to taste them all. Just off I-82 on exit 82 at Wine Country Rd.; (509) 786-4557.

Kiona Vineyards Winery

When John Williams and Jim Holmes planted a vineyard on the lower slopes of Red Mountain back in the 1970s, they seemed to move into the outback, where sand devils and curlews ruled. Today, the winery is one of Washington's most respected red wine producers. The cabernet sauvignon and merlot are rich and have deeply complex flavors; the late harvest wines made from riesling, chenin blanc, and gewurztraminer grapes rank among the best of their kind. Kiona is a great place to visit. Bring the fixings for a picnic, and spend a relaxing afternoon at the winery. 44612 North Sunset Rd., NE, Benton City; (509) 588-6716.

Other Wines of Note

Be sure to taste the merlots made by Gordon Brothers from their Snake River vineyards and by L'Ecole No. 41 from Walla Walla Valley grapes, as well as the Walla Walla cabernet sauvignons made by Leonetti Cellar and Woodward Canyon. And by no means neglect the lovely cabernets of Quilceda Creek.

Some of these wines are not easy to find. Look for them in wine shops or ask for them in restaurants (Yakima's Birchfield Manor has an excellent selection of rare local bottlings).

Note: Keep in mind that summer days in the Yakima Valley can get very hot. Don't leave wine or fresh produce in your car. The produce will cook; the wine bottles may pop their corks.

Rodeo mural in Toppenish.

(following pages) Mount Adams rises above the Lincoln Plateau in south-central Washington. This region is just to the southwest of the Yakima Valley along the road to Portland.

PORTLAND

■ HIGHLIGHTS

Portland Art Museum
Oregon History Center
Washington Park Rose Garden
Forest Park
Willamette River
Tom McCall Waterfront Park
Fine Northwest Cuisine
Brewpubs

■ SETTING

PORTLAND IS ONE OF the most beautiful cities in the West, its downtown snuggled between the Willamette River and tree-clad hills. Mount Hood, rising up majestically in Portland's backyard, adds to the city's ambiance and seems to anchor it in its lush green home.

Between springtime showers, Portland sparkles. The entire city greens up in an instant, and there's a heady burst of cherry trees, dogwoods, and daffodils, all damp from the last shower and pulsing with growth.

Metropolitan green spaces, access to rivers, and lively neighborhoods are important to Portland's sense of place. The touches of old-fashioned statuary and what's now called public art, from the elk at SW Third and Main to the umbrella man on Pioneer Courthouse Square or the Electronic Poet near 10th and Morrison, show that this is a city with a civic spirit. Among the best-loved graceful touches are the "Benson bubblers," non-stop water fountains on downtown streets. Simon Benson, an early timber king, reputedly donated the four-pronged fountains to divert employees from the evils of whiskey.

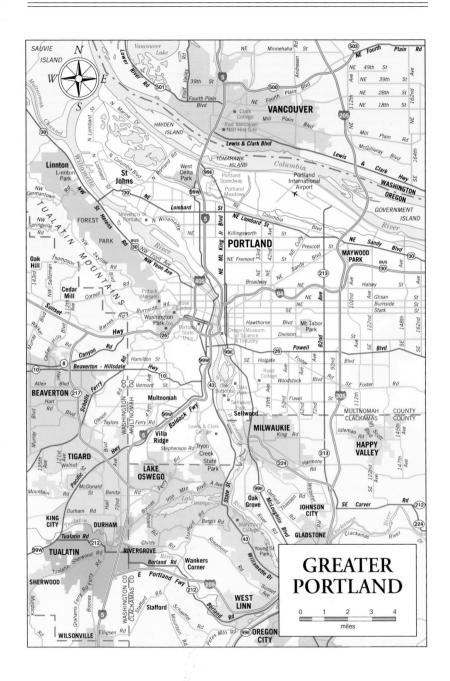

GREATER PORTLAND

0   1   2   3   4
miles

■ HISTORY AND CULTURE

The west bank of the Willamette River was a canoe stop for Indians traveling between the Willamette Valley and the Columbia River trading markets well before Portland's first settlers took a shine to it in 1843. Portland rose to become an important river and seaport, supplying the mines of Idaho and Montana and shipping out wheat from eastern Oregon and Washington farms.

As Portland grew, the north end of First Street was chockablock with sailors boarding in rooming houses, drinking in bars, and sleeping with the pros. When a ship needed more crew members, drunk or drugged men sometimes woke up below deck, shanghaied to serve as sailors.

Even as tree stumps were being pulled from the muddy streets, civic leaders were thinking about preserving corridors of trees and grass in the fast-growing city. In 1852, the stately **Park Blocks** were laid out through downtown, and with the exception of a seven-block stretch, they remain intact today. Park Blocks are a strip of city blocks set aside as a park, an oasis of tree-shaded lawns, walkways, and benches (with an occasional statue and fountain) one block west of Broadway.

The reclamation of the west bank of the Willamette River between 1974 and 1982 gave the city the **Tom McCall Waterfront Park,** a three-mile swatch of green shared by visitors, transients, joggers, and bicyclists, and, from late spring through the summer, a different festival nearly every weekend.

The elm-shaded South Park Blocks, a few blocks south and west of the square, are flanked by the **Portland Art Museum** and the **Oregon History Center.** The art museum draws raves for its Northwest Coast Indian collection and for its Wednesday evening "Museum After Hours" concerts. Exhibits change seasonally at the History Center's museum, and the bookstore, facing onto Broadway, is a fine place to step in from the rain and browse. Located at 1219 SW Park Avenue; (503) 226-2811.

The fancy new brick building just north of the History Center is the **Performing Arts Center,** the city's premier spot for live theater. Next door is the "Schnitz" (the Arlene Schnitzer Concert Hall), a grand Portland vaudeville house, host to the Oregon Symphony and the popular Portland Arts and Lecture Series. Watching plays performed by the Tygres Heart Shakespeare Co. alone is worth a special visit to Portland.

Vineyards grow up to Portland's suburbs, and the downtown is only a short half-hour's drive from the wineries of the northern Willamette Valley. Portland has more microbreweries and brewpubs than any other city in the U.S. Thirty-seven breweries and brewpubs at last count. Portlanders claim that no part of their thirsty city is more than 15 minutes from a brewpub or brewery outlet. Best of all, you don't have to mix drinking and driving but can explore the breweries on the **Portland Brewbus,** which takes visitors on a five-hour guided tour. For information and reservations, call (888) 244-2739.

■ WALK THROUGH DOWNTOWN

Office workers and street kids carve out their territories on the inscribed bricks of Pioneer Courthouse Square, and it's a rare summer afternoon when "downtown's living room," as it's called, doesn't feature a concert or rally. **Pioneer Courthouse Square,** reclaimed from a parking lot in 1983, is a good place to start a walking tour of downtown. **Powell's Travel Store** (near the Sixth and Yamhill corner of the square) produces a good free downtown map; the flip side details an afternoon-long stroll through Portland.

Before its tenure as a parking lot, Pioneer Courthouse Square was the site of the Portland Hotel, an elegant building that, were it still standing, would turn heads today. The eponymous courthouse, across Sixth Avenue from the square, was Portland's earliest sign of civilization. When it was built in 1869, it was considered too distant from the city's waterfront hub. Traffic patterns changed, and for a century, the Pioneer Courthouse has marked downtown's center.

Niketown, at SW Sixth and Salmon, offers up a more pedestrian culture. The vault-like shoe store is a celebration of professional sports. It's a reliquary for Bo Jackson's baseball jerseys, Andre Agassi's tennis racquets, and Michael Jordan's humungous basketball shoes. Don't be tempted to think of this as an actual store—locals cross the Willamette and shop at the Nike outlet at 3044 NE Martin Luther King Boulevard.

At the postmodern **Portland Building** at SW Fifth and Main, city bureaucrats complain about the tiny windows in architect Michael Graves's "birthday cake" of a building. This was Graves's first big public commission and the nation's first postmodern public building—a triumph of theory over the shapes and spaces that comfort human beings. Wander into the lobby, visit the balcony gallery, or sit in on a public meeting, and see whether you're pleased or appalled.

Portlandia, the 37-foot-tall, six-and-a-quarter-ton copper statue of a woman kneeling over the front door of the Portland Building gets as much attention as the building itself. The elk statue in the middle of SW Main between Third and Fourth is a whimsical favorite. The plaza next to the statue was once a meadow where elk grazed. Today pigeons and courthouse workers feed here. (All manner of people use the benches here; the bathrooms are not a safe bet.)

The waterfront, once lined by wharfs, then overrun by a freeway, is now a pleasant park. Salmon Street Springs, a fountain whose flow is timed to be highest when the city is bustling, is a great place to pause and watch it all happen.

Stroll north past men fishing for sturgeon with giant hooks (occasionally one is pulled onto the seawall) to the Japanese-American memorial, just north of the Burnside Bridge. It's a quiet spot, where stone-carved words recall the lives and contributions of Portland's Issei, Japanese immigrants who were forced into eastern Oregon internment camps during World War II.

In **Old Town,** near Burnside Bridge, cast-iron facades on old brick buildings hint of a grand past. The pilaster-fronted New Market Theatre (SW First and Ankeny) was the reputable place to spend an evening in the 1880s, though second-floor theatergoers had to put up with the din and muddle of first-floor green-

A view of Mount Hood and downtown Portland from Washington Park.

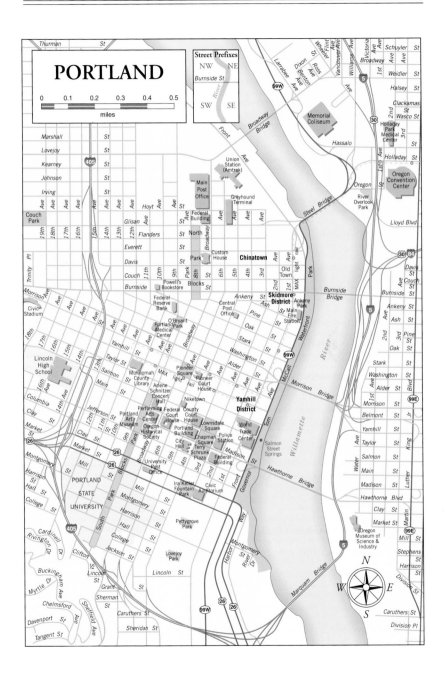

PORTLAND

0   0.1   0.2   0.3   0.4   0.5

miles

Street Prefixes

NW   NE

Burnside St

SW   SE

grocers and butchers. Outside, the four graceful bronze women of Skidmore Fountain hold an overflowing basin aloft. The fountain was built in 1888 for "men, horses, and dogs," and remains a lovely rendezvous for men, women, children, and dogs (well, the occasional horse, bearing a cop, still comes by).

On Saturdays and Sundays, Portland's justly famous **Saturday Market** is held in several adjacent parking lots between First and Front streets near the Skidmore Fountain. It's the nation's largest crafts fair, with more booths than you can possibly stop and shop at in one weekend. Ethnic food booths serve a great variety of different cuisines from American barbecue to Latin American, African, and Southeast Asian specialties. It's the perfect place for a quick and very inexpensive luncheon or snack. A tent protects diners from sun, rain, or snow.

Nightlife and comparatively wild times still thrive around Burnside. Local pundits like to say Portland has three genuine tourist attractions: Darcelle's drag shows, Powell's Books, and the Church of Elvis. Even if all of Portland doesn't turn out for **Darcelle's drag shows,** it's certainly not a seedy venue, and it's a five-block walk from the SW Pine Street coin-operated **Church of Elvis,** where 25 cents will get you an interesting fortune. If drag shows and Elvis lose their thrill, try **Powell's Books,** crammed with new and used books. It is open till 11:00 P.M. most nights at 10th and W. Burnside, and it's Portland nightlife at its most typical.

Powell's is on the southern edge of the Pearl District, a post-industrial neighborhood of lofts, galleries, and brewpubs. If it's the first Thursday evening of the month, check out the gallery openings. Wind up at the Bridgeport Brewpub and sit on the loading dock for some of Portland's best pizza and microbrewed beer. For a young, hip scene try **La Luna** at Ninth and SE Pine off Burnside. The bar offers microbrews and the music is usually alternative rock at least three times a week with big names and local artists playing regularly.

■ WEST OF DOWNTOWN

Though some contend that Portlanders are, by nature, a little distant from their neighbors, this modern malady may be at least partly ameliorated by the local coffee culture. **Northwest 23rd Avenue,** between Burnside and Thurman, is perhaps the best place to dip into the scene and stroll through trendy shops.

Northwest Portland took off in 1905, with the Lewis and Clark Exposition, an orgy of boosterism. John Olmstead, son of Frederick Law Olmstead, who designed

New York's Central Park, came to town and designed a fairground with most of the buildings in Spanish Renaissance style. The building everybody talked about for years to come was decidedly different—a gigantic log "cabin" housing a forestry exhibit.

Portland must have gotten the hang of putting on a fair back then because it wasn't long before the city decided to celebrate its gardeners' penchant for roses by staging a Rose Festival in 1907. It's been going strong ever since, the crowning event of a quirky, old-fashioned Oregon subculture. High schools elect Rose Princesses and one becomes the city's Rose Queen—even if queens are a bit out of fashion these days. Business people aspire to become Royal Rosarians who dress up in white suits and wave straw boaters during parades. Military vessels line the Willamette, and sailors flood the town, taking advantage of the (for real, and officially sponsored) date-a-sailor hotline.

A short uphill walk from Northwest Portland or an easy bus ride from downtown leads to well-manicured **Washington Park,** home of the **Rose Test Garden.** Here, Portland's mania for the Rose Festival begins to make sense. From the Rose Gardens' hillside perch (where the names of Rose Festival queens are enshrined in a cement path), downtown is framed by shiny green leaves and deep rich blooms.

Uphill from the Rose Gardens are the peaceful **Japanese Gardens,** where water trickles through bamboo chutes. A shuttle bus and hiking trail climb the steep grade.

Washington Park Zoo, Vietnam Memorial, and **Hoyt Arboretum** are about a mile west of the gardens. Hoyt Arboretum trails join the **Wildwood Trail,** and continue north to Forest Park, which on a drizzly Sunday afternoon proves itself the lifeblood of Portlanders. The 50-some miles of trails are well-used, but rarely clogged. Before the park was established in 1947, the 1,100-foot hills rising straight from the Willamette had been heavily logged; most of the trees are second growth, with hardy red alder eclipsing the young Douglas fir and western hemlock. Spring comes to Portland when Forest Park trilliums bloom. August means it's time to wade deep into thorny vines while dreaming of blackberry pie.

Forest Park, in the city's northwest corner—seven and a half miles long and a mile and a half wide—is one of the country's largest city parks. There are no manicured gardens or swing sets in Forest Park and even though it abuts the state's most densely populated neighborhood, it's remarkably wild. Wildlife, including deer, coyotes, and warblers use it as a corridor to the Coast Range to the west.

Determined berry-pickers skip the trailside thickets and drive out US 30 to **Sauvie Island,** a flat agricultural island known for pick-it-yourself berry patches, bird-watching, and Columbia River beaches (including a nude beach). A highly productive bottomland since well before Lewis and Clark stopped here in 1805, this was a favorite trading spot of the Chinook Indians. They swapped tuberous wapato lily, which women pulled from marsh bottoms with their toes, and fished with huge cedar-bark nets that they sunk to the bottom of the river with rocks.

■ EASTSIDE

For a breath of air, and a different view of the city, walk over one of the nine bridges spanning the Willamette—the Hawthorne and the Broadway are best for strolls from downtown. The Willamette River bisects Portland, with most of the wealth falling out on the hilly west side and a funky charm and rapid gentrification surrounding the shopping streets of **SE Hawthorne** (used-book stores are the neighborhood specialty) and **NE Broadway.** Because Portland's sports stadiums and convention center are also on this side of the river, the area around Burnside is attracting a slew of new restaurants.

Washington Park Rose Garden.

The Portlandia *statue outside the Portland Building on Fifth Avenue.*

Sellwood, at the city's southern edge, has had an antique row for years. Its riverside park is worth a picnic or a swim in the outdoor pool. Oaks Park, an old-fashioned, slightly down-at-the-heels amusement park, abuts Sellwood Park and is adjacent to Oaks Bottom, a wetland crisscrossed by trails that's ideal for bird-watching.

From the west side of the Sellwood Bridge, a greenway for cyclers and hikers runs three miles along the Willamette to downtown's Waterfront Park. Early in the morning, great blue herons can often be seen flying above racing sculls.

The Eastside has another distinction: Mount Tabor makes Portland the only U.S. city with a dormant volcano within city limits. If you thought the eruption of Mount St. Helens was exciting, wait until Mount Tabor blows its top.

■ TRAVEL AND CLIMATE

■ GETTING THERE AND GETTING AROUND

Portland is easy to reach, located at the junction of major freeways (I-5 and I-84) and railways. Portland International Airport has numerous daily national and international flights, as well as flights to other Oregon towns, like Bend or Eugene. At the airport it's easy to rent cars or get vans into town.

Portland's downtown is very compact—a walker's delight. Within prescribed downtown borders, public transportation is free. A transit mall was built on Fifth and Sixth avenues and crossed by light rail (MAX) trains in 1987. Stop by TriMet Customer Service in Pioneer Courthouse Square for bus and MAX (suburban light rail transit) information. In general, you'll find this a convenient and affable city, with good restaurants and hotels.

■ CLIMATE

Portland's weather can be wet (pioneers called themselves "webfeet"), but the weather is often sunny and balmy in spring and fall and can be quite warm in summer. In winter, icy storms blowing down the Columbia River Gorge can chill down things in a hurry. Like other metropolitan areas of the Pacific Northwest, Portland is paralyzed by snow—which, luckily, does not fall very often or stay long.

■ ACCOMMODATIONS AND RESTAURANTS

⌑   For chain lodgings see toll free numbers on page 352.
$$ For room and restaurant price designations see page 352.
✮   Means highly recommended.

⌑ **Benson Hotel.**
309 SW Broadway at Oak; (503) 228-9611
Portland's longtime favorite fancy hotel, built by timber king Simon Benson in 1913. $$$

⌑ **Fifth Avenue Suites Hotel.** 506 SW Washington St.; (503) 222-0001 or (800) 711-2971
A grand new hotel in an old—believe it or not—department store shell. The rooms are luxurious and quiet. Best of all you're right in the heart of Portland, within walking distance of museums and theaters.

⌑ **Governor Hotel.**
611 SW 10th at Alder; (503) 224-3400
Nicely renovated, classy hotel. Check out the robots on the outside trim. $$$

⌑ **Heathman Hotel.**
1001 SW Broadway at Salmon; (503) 241-4100 or (800) 551-0011
Most people think this is Portland's finest hotel. Service is as good as it gets anywhere. $$$

⌑ **Hotel Vintage Plaza.**
422 SW Broadway; (800) 243-0555
A perfect, intimate boutique hotel with large, comfortable rooms. The staff is friendly and very helpful. There's wine

in the lobby in the afternoon—a great spot for getting to know your fellow guests. $$$

✕ **Berbati.**
19 SW Second Ave.; (503) 226-2122
Traditional Greek cuisine. Hip bar, belly dancing, pool room, and eclectic music venue. $$

✕ **Caprial's Bistro & Wines.** ✲
7015 SE Milwaukee Ave.;
(503) 236-6457
TV-fame and other forms of public attention have not turned Caprial Pence into a snob. Her cooking is as good and as inspired as always. Dinner reservations advised. $$

✕ **Common Grounds.**
4321 SE Hawthorne; (503) 236-4835
Charming neighborhood coffee house. Enjoy a latte, sprawled out on a cozy couch with your favorite periodical. $

✕ **Couch Street Fish House.**
105 NW Third Ave.; (503) 223-6173
An elegant, somewhat stuffy place with well-prepared, traditional seafood accompanied by beautiful sauces. (Pronounce the name "Cooch" not "Couwch.") $$$

✕ **Couvron.** ✲✲
1126 SW 18th Ave.; (503) 225-1844
Chef Anthony Demes captured the hearts of Portlanders right from the start with the inspired cooking in this new restaurant. A highly critical friend called it "fabulous." The wine list is as good as the food. $$$

✕ **Dan & Louis Oyster Bar**
208 SW Ankeny; (503) 227-5906

This old-time place is a favorite visitors' hangout near the Willamette waterfront, but locals come here too, for the old-fashioned oyster stew and the fresh seafood salads. This is one place where you can taste fresh Oregon oysters. $$

✕ **L'Etoile.**
4627 NE Fremont St.; (503) 281-4869
Very French fine dining. Sip a cocktail by the fire in the dark, romantic bar. Best escargot around. $$$

✕ **Genoa.** ✲✲
2832 SE Belmont St.; (503) 238-1464
Splendid seven-course Italian meals, impressive wine list, and knowledgeable staff add up to a delightful dining experience. Escape the formal dining room, and sip your aperitif on the overstuffed furniture in the smoking lounge. $$$

✕ **Heathman Bakery and Pub.**
901 SW Salmon; (503) 227-5700
A noisy lunch and dinner spot with great microbrew convenient to downtown. $$$

✕ **The Heathman Restaurant & Bar.** ✲✲✲
SW Broadway and Salmon;
(503) 241-4100
Some of the best food you'll find anywhere. French-trained chef Philippe Boulot applies an artist's creative touch to fresh Northwest ingredients. His wife Susan, a native of Portland, does incredible desserts. The wine list has an outstanding selection of Oregon's best. Service is fabulous. $$$

✕ **Indigne.**
3723 SE Division; (503) 238-1470
Small, eclectic restaurant with a devoted

clientele in an unassuming neighborhood. $$-$$$

✕ **Jake's Famous Crawfish.**
SW 12th and Stark; (503) 226-1419
Old-time Portlanders go here; traditional American cooking with flair. $$-$$$

✕ **Jo Bar and Rotisserie.** ✭
715 NW 23rd Ave.; (503) 222-0048
This always-busy restaurant has two wood-burning ovens where meats are roasted to perfection. Soups and salads are also very good. No wonder the place is so popular. $$

✕ **McCormick & Schmick's Seafood Restaurant.**
235 SW First Ave.; (503) 244-7522
The seafood is always fresh, cooked to perfection, and seasoned with just the right touch. A cavernous, popular restaurant; make reservations well in advance. $$

✕ **Paley's Place.** ✭✭✭
1204 NW 21st Ave.; (503) 243-2403
A small dining room in an old house, a chef trained in New York and France turning out light but exquisitely flavorful dishes, great service, and an exceptional wine list. No wonder the place is always packed. $$

✕ **Pazzo Ristorante.** ✭
627 SW Washington; (503) 228-1515
This comfortable restaurant in the Vintage Plaza Hotel has all the ingredients for a perfect night out: great Italianate food, a well-selected cellar of Northwest wines, attentive service, and a comfortable atmosphere. $$

✕ **Red Star Tavern and Roast House.** ✭
503 SW Alder; (503) 222-0005
This bright, boisterous place became one of Portland's favorite restaurants right from the start—and deservedly so. $-$$

✕ **Wildwood.** ✭✭✭
NW 21st and Overton; (503) 248-9663
Named for Forest Park's Wildwood Trail, this northwest Portland restaurant is setting trends with its food and ambiance. Try Portland's best dish of mussels here. $$$

✕ **Zefiro.** ✭
500 NW 21st; (503) 226-3394
Mediterranean and Pacific Rim cuisine prepared with fresh local ingredients. Consistently original, sophisticated, and delicious. Located in trendy Northwest Portland, this is the place to see and be seen. $$$

■ BREWPUBS

Bridgeport.

1313 NW Marshall (between 13th and 14th); (503) 241-7179

Portland's most atmospheric brewpub is near old warehouses and railroad tracks. Sit out on the loading dock, where hop vines trail off the sides of brick buildings, and sip Blue Heron or Coho Pacific ales. The McMenamin brothers started out with a neighborhood tavern featuring a Deadhead ambiance. Then they began making wild microbrew beers, tinted with raspberries or chocolate. Terminator Stout is their hallmark brew.

Heathman Bakery and Pub.

901 SW Salmon St.; (503) 227-5700

A mix of suits and slackers, sipping lemon-tinted wheat beer, or trying the coffee and pastries.

Portland Brewing Company's Brewhouse Taproom & Grill.

2730 NW 31st St.; (503) 228-5269

One of Portland's best brewpubs is located off the beaten track in industrial NW Portland.

Widmer Gasthaus.

955 N Russell; (503) 281-3333

An excellent pub across the river in North Portland.

The Heathman Bakery and Pub, also known as B. Molloch's.

COLUMBIA GORGE
AND MOUNT HOOD

■ HIGHLIGHTS

Old Columbia Highway
Waterfalls and Scenery
Windsurfing
Hood River Valley
Mount Hood
Hiking
Skiing

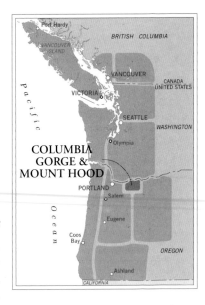

■ OVERVIEW

THE COLUMBIA RIVER GORGE east of
Portland is not only the most beautiful
stretch of a very scenic river, it is beautiful whether you traverse it on the north
or the south bank of the river. Even hur-
ried drivers rushing through the gorge on the I-84 freeway can't escape the almost
overpowering beauty of the scenery, since the freeway runs close to the level of the
river.

The entire river is 1,245 miles long. It springs from the Columbia Glacier, an
ice field in the Canadian Rockies, and at first runs north, through the Rocky
Mountain Trench, then turns south to northeastern Washington. Here it first
flows south, then swings west to the eastern foothills of the North Cascades, turns
east at the Rattlesnake Mountains and, after being joined by the Snake River
flowing in from the east (the Snake rises in Yellowstone Park), it breaks through
the Wallula Gap and flows west towards the Pacific Ocean. The fact that the river
runs through its gorge at almost sea level attests to the fact that the Columbia is
older than the Cascade Mountains and cut its way through the range as it slowly
rose from the earth's crust. As the river forces its way west, through a fairly level,

RIVER THROUGH TIME

As a river cutting through the Cascades at almost sea level, the Columbia at the gorge has been an important trading route since ancient time. Resident tribes controlled trade on the river between inland and coastal tribes.

When American explorers Lewis and Clark floated down the Columbia in 1805, cedar plank longhouses up to 200 feet in length dotted the riverbanks. Cedars were also crafted into long canoes, and Chinook Indians (including Cascades, Wascos, and, on the Washington side, Wishrams) took the rapids in canoes.

Oregon Trail immigrants portaged their belongings past the river's roughest section on an 1842 wagon road built around the five-mile-long Cascade rapids, followed by a mule-drawn tramway along the north bank of the river. Soon the south shore also had a portage railroad. Since the Columbia River tightly squeezes through basalt cliffs at several points along the gorge, it leaves little room for a roadway. In 1872, the Oregon legislature called for a wagon road between Troutdale and The Dalles, and a few stretches of the narrow road are still visible at Shellrock Mountain near milepost 52. Portage railroads around rapids were spliced together, often using the wagon road as a railbed, and in 1883, formed part of a transcontinental line.

Sternwheelers that could "float on mist," made it through some dodgy rapids and shoals, but railroad portages around the Cascades were essential until 1896, when the Cascade Locks, a 3,000-foot-long canal, cleared a path for boats. It's still possible to ride a sternwheeler along the Willamette and Columbia rivers, but it's strictly a party boat now. Barges and tugs took over most of the river work in the 1940s, when being a tug captain was as glamorous a job as any Oregonian could hope for.

Sam Hill, son-in-law of the Great Northern Railway's James J. Hill, began scheming to build a road through the Columbia Gorge in the early 1900s. He hired Samuel Lancaster to build a riverside highway, and together they went on a European tour to study ancient road patterns. They traveled through the Alps, drove on Roman roads, and thought of the rustic natural designs of the American Craftsman movement. When construction started, Lancaster worked with Italian-American stonemasons, whose arched guardrails gracefully line the road. The road was finished in 1916, and its remaining stretches are nearly as popular now as they were then.

(following pages) The view from Women's Forum Park looking east up the Columbia River Gorge to Crown Point.

narrow passage, its deep waters are hemmed in by the steep rock walls of the Cascade Mountains, densely covered by Douglas fir and larch forest to the west, and by grasslands and ponderosa pine and oak woods to the east on the "dry" side of the Cascades. Much of the narrow sliver of land at the foot of the cliffs is taken up by road and railroad beds. Here and there is enough arable land for a farm or two, though there are orchards on the benchlands of the Washington side and in the fertile Hood River Valley, which branches off to the south near the eastern end of the gorge. It is towered over to the south by Mount Hood, one of the most beautiful and symmetrical of Cascade volcanos, and to the north by broad-shouldered Mount Adams. If you look closely, you may even spot a vineyard or two.

The scenery of the gorge is truly spectacular, with its views of dark basalt cliffs, and the winding river sparkling in the sun (or half hidden by mists—depending on the weather). Mists may envelop the river, but rainbows stretch across almost every shoulder along the Columbia Gorge. That's because of the difference in the climate at the east and west ends of the gorge. Even if it's rainy on the west side, the east side generally has blue skies. The dark layers of basalt dominating the rock walls of the gorge are ancient lava flows (some of which cover the plateaus to the east to a depth of more than 3,500 feet). About 10,000 years ago, an ice dam in northern Idaho backed up a huge lake stretching over much of what is now western Montana. Periodically, the dam would pop up, like an ice cube in a drink, releasing torrents of water across eastern Washington and through the Columbia River channels. The flood waters scraped the basalt so clean that even today, no topsoil has established itself on many of the steep walls, leaving them bare of vegetation.

Explorers Lewis and Clark took this route as they traveled west to the mouth of the Columbia and back, and they were the first explorers to note that the river runs almost at sea level. Pioneers followed in their wake, braving fierce rapids now submerged by the waters of Bonneville and other dams.

Interstate 84, a major east-west freeway, passes through the canyon following the route taken by the old Oregon Trail. Portlanders love to take visitors on "the loop," a long day's drive up the Columbia to Hood River, then south for a sunset at Mount Hood's Timberline Lodge, and back to Portland in the dark. Or you can make it a shorter loop trip by driving up the Washington side of the river in the morning and returning via the Oregon side in the afternoon.

■ OREGON SIDE OF THE COLUMBIA

Begin a Columbia Gorge drive from Portland at exit 17 off Interstate 84. For the **Columbia Gorge Scenic Highway,** turn left at the first light past the outlet mall, where the sign says "Corbett." (A right turn here leads to the Edgefield complex, the former county "poor farm," now the most expansive of the McMenamin's brewpubs.) The scenic highway follows the Sandy River, known as "Quicksand R." to Lewis and Clark. Stop at **Dabney State Park,** with riverside trails, fishing, and boat launches. When the water warms up, the Sandy's swimming holes fill up with local kids, and its modest rapids host floaters in inner tubes. Past Dabney, the scenic highway cuts away from the Sandy and heads through upland orchards to Corbett. The Columbia first becomes visible at the **Portland Women's Forum Park;** roundish, green hills give way to blocky, dark basalt upstream. The **Crown Point Vista House** is on the next bluff upstream, and the Women's Forum Park is a great vantage point for photographers. The Vista House, built in 1918, offers great views up the gorge. The stocky stone octagonal house has picture windows topped by stained glass and a copper-green dome.

Between Crown Point and Multnomah Falls, the old highway is at its best. The arched stone guardrails are softened by moss, and ferns grow in every interstitial niche.

Everybody stops at **Multnomah Falls,** for good reason. The falls drop 620 feet, and they are unfailingly impressive. It takes an hour to hike to the top of the falls, and the trail continues on to Larch Mountain (another five miles uphill). Little exertion is required to see naturalist John Muir's favorite bird here. Even in the iciest weather, American dippers plunge their faces into the stream at the base of the falls.

If you don't have time for more than a two-hour hike, try the **Horsetail Falls/Oneonta Trail loop,** which has a nice mix of waterfalls and river views. From the tall spray-spitting plume at the scenic highway, it's half a mile uphill to the step-behind Upper Horsetail Falls. In spring the trail is lined with springtime trilliums and lavender bleeding heart. False Solomon's seal reaches long lily-leaved, flower-tipped arms towards shafts of light. The trail then follows a sun-struck ridge above the Columbia, where pikas squeal from their rockslide homes. The short descent into the next drainage offers a look down through the narrow

Oneonta Gorge and a return to the highway. On the roadside walk back to the car, it's tempting to wander back into the Oneonta Gorge. If it's warm enough for wet feet, go with the urge; there's no place quite like this dark chasm, home to rare shade-loving plants.

❖

Bonneville Dam, a few miles upriver and just off I-84, was one of the great Depression-era public works projects and has been a source of pride for decades. Bonneville and the other Columbia River dams generated huge amounts of electricity and spawned the region's aluminum industry, a notoriously power-thirsty business. Head to the sub-basement fish-viewing window in the dam's visitor center. Official fish-counters sit in their own darkened cubicle, counting each fish swimming past their window. **Eagle Creek** trailhead is about a mile east of Bonneville, and is, after Multnomah Falls, the gorge's most popular stop. In the spring, water streams down in dozens of makeshift falls, turning portions of the trail into a refreshing shower. Hikers measure the spring's wetness by the number of falls and the intensity of the wildflower display.

At **Cascade Locks**, just upriver from Bonneville Dam, the focus shifts back to the Columbia River. Cascade Locks Marine Park is a grassy, relaxing riverside spot. A footbridge spans the now-obsolete 1896 lock. Below it, Indian dipnet platforms hang from guy wires like a window-washer's rigging above rushing water. The sternwheeler *Columbia Gorge* departs from the Marine Park several times daily from mid-June until early October (during the winter, it's based at Portland's Waterfront Park).

The **Bridge of the Gods** spans the Columbia at Cascade Locks. Even when the west end of the gorge is clouded over, the sun often breaks through at Hood River. The climate here is nearly perfect for fruit trees, and the steep gorge walls funnel winds into a fury near Hood River, making it the **windsurfing capital** of the Northwest, if not the nation. The sport really does permeate the local culture. Wind reports are regular features on every radio station, and it's a great place to shop for a sailboard or wetsuit.

■ MOUNT HOOD LOOP

From Hood River, Highway 35 heads south up Mount Hood, and the freeway, Interstate 84, continues east. A surviving stretch of the old highway splits off the freeway at Mosier (17 miles east of Hood River) and climbs past cherry orchards, through scattered oak and pine trees, to the Rowena Plateau, where the transition from a wet west-slope habitat to a drier east-side environment is manifest. From the wildflower-fringed high plateau, it's all mounds and swales down to the river. Yellow daisy-like balsamroot and deep blue-violet lupine grow on meadows spread out on top of basalt flows.

OR 35 heads south and uphill from Hood River's laid-back trendiness into orchard country—the Hood River Valley is famed for its apples, pears, and cherries. The **Mount Hood Railroad** runs from Hood River south to Parkdale; it's a popular springtime trip, when snowy Mount Hood is the backdrop for pink and white blossoms. For information call (541) 386-3556. The road wastes no time before beginning the long pull up Mount Hood. Stop at a fruit stand for a trunkload of apples and pears. **River Bend Organic Farm** has tours and a store at 2363 Tucker Road, near Odell. Turn off at **Parkdale** toward a perfect canoeist's view of the mountain from the middle of Lost Lake. The little lakeside resort has cabins, a restaurant, and canoe rentals.

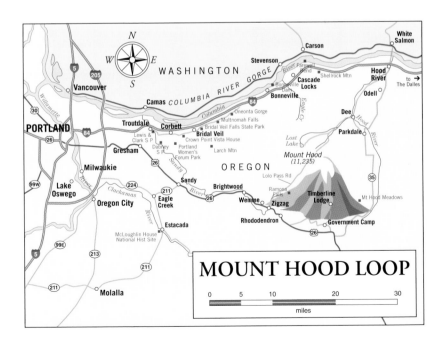

■ MOUNT HOOD

Mount Hood erupted sporadically through the 1800s but never with the devastating force of Mount St. Helens' 1980 blast.

Portlanders have long looked to Mount Hood when they needed to feel intrepid. Four Portlanders climbed 11,235-foot mountain in 1857, and it caught on. Two hundred people climbed through sleet and thunder in 1894, the inaugural climb of the Mazama Club. (This mountain club is restricted to those who have climbed a glaciated Cascade peak.) The Portland-based Mazamas still sponsor mountaineering classes and climbs.

Developers have long eyed Mount Hood; in the 1920s, the Mazamas fought against a tramline up to the peak. By 1937, there was nothing but applause for **Timberline Lodge,** built as a WPA project. Unemployed artisans were put to work fashioning beams from giant trees, carving newelposts into owls and bears, and weaving rugs and chair covers. There's now a separate, 1980s, concrete-bunker-style day lodge filled with contemporary crafts, ski-rental shops, and snack bars. But Mount Hood savants know the second-floor bar in the old lodge has comfortable sofas, great sunset views down the Cascades, and a happy blend of rusticity and comfort for weary hikers and skiers. It's safe to climb the mountain only from May through early July. Climbers start from Timberline Lodge around 2:00 A.M., aiming to reach the summit by mid-morning and be off the mountain when the afternoon sun increases the chance of an avalanche. Silcox Hut, a sturdy stone bivouac cabin just up the mountain from the lodge, houses climbers for that short pre-climb night. For details call (503) 231-7979.

For those who prefer to see the horizon a little bit at a time, a 40-mile trail circles the mountain at timberline; pick up the trail at Timberline Lodge and walk the loop (allow a few days). Or light out west to Paradise Park, an exuberant alpine meadow five miles from the lodge. Continue another five and a half miles past a deep V of a chasm holding the cascading headwaters of the Sandy River to Ramona Falls, where basalt terraces split the creek into a multitude of thin falls, then funnel them back together at the bottom of the 100-foot drop.

❖

Downhill skiing runs through the summer on above-timberline Palmer Glacier snowfield. During the winter, Mount Hood Meadows overtakes Timberline in popularity—it's just east of the pass (on Hwy 35), which frequently means good weather in Oregon's westside-eastside precipitation sweepstakes. Cross-country

CENTRAL OREGON

■ HIGHLIGHTS

Mount Bachelor
Bend
Cascade Lakes
Deschutes River
Newberry Volcano
Smith Rock
Warm Springs Reservation

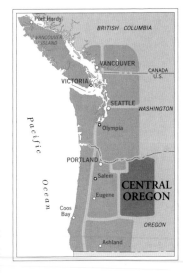

■ LANDSCAPE

CENTRAL OREGON IS A TAPESTRY of volcanic rocks, edged with towering peaks and basalt cliffs, and textured with perfect cinder cones. Forests, mountain lakes, and rivers dab the landscape with blues and greens. Skiers, floaters, and anglers skid and cast across the rugged quilt. The lava underfoot may not even have a dusting of soil covering it, though most of it was laid down 14 to 16 million years ago during a burst of volcanism so intense that volcanic flows covered all but the tips of the Blue and Wallowa mountains.

The volcanic spine of the Cascades rose when the oceanic plate dove beneath the North American continental plate. Friction generated heat and lava poured forth. Mount Hood, Mount Jefferson, Three Fingered Jack, Mount Washington, the Three Sisters, Broken Top, Mount Bachelor, Mount Thielson, Mount Mazama (now Crater Lake), and Mount McLoughlin are the volcanic high Cascade peaks. They are ages younger than the low western Cascades, worn-down piles of ash and lava, just off their western shoulders.

Central Oregon's Cascades form the backdrop of quintessential Western scenery right out of a movie. On clear days, the Metolius headwaters or the Crooked River Canyon at Smith Rock are as mesmerizing as any place on earth. Summers are hot, winters are cold, and flash floods can follow drought on the east side of the Cascades. Tourist bureaus say the sun shines 310 days a year, but plenty of snow falls from these supposedly cloudless skies, especially at higher elevations. There are more resorts here than in any other part of the state, and they run the gamut from funky little log cabins on a mountain lake to upscale Sunriver condos.

■ HISTORY

At central Oregon's northern edge, the Columbia River divides Oregon from Washington as it cuts a low—almost sea-level—path through the Cascade mountains. Back before French-Canadians named the Columbia's basalt-walled narrows after giant Gallic flagstone gutters ("Les Dalles"), The Dalles was called Winquatt, a "Place Encircled by Rock Cliffs." For Indians, this was a prized fishing area. Salmon resting in eddies and pools were easy dipnet or spear targets, and traders were drawn from all over Oregon, bringing items from afar: Minnesota pipestone, Southwestern turquoise, Vancouver Island dentalium, Alaskan copper, and Puget Sound dried clams. Two main groups lived on the Columbia's south shore, Sahaptin-speakers and Chinook-speakers. To supplement their salmon diet, they hunted, and they gathered roots and berries.

The tribes of north-central Oregon stayed on good terms with early white settlers and Indians did a brisk business ferrying Oregon Trail pioneers through the Columbia River rapids. But as settlers from the east wanted even more land, the Indians were moved to the Warm Springs Reservation in 1855. The lands given up by the Indians were occupied by cattle ranchers, sheepherders, and wheat farmers. You can spot their homesteads by the tall black locust trees the pioneers planted to provide shade. Look for hawk nests atop tall trees just off the highway.

■ THE DALLES

When steamboats plied the Columbia, during the late 1800s, The Dalles was a bustling port where wheat from eastern Oregon was transferred onto Portland-bound boats. Rudyard Kipling, in high tourist mode, rode a steamer up the Columbia to The Dalles in 1898 and reported that "all the inhabitants seemed to own a little villa and one church apiece."

The Dalles has escaped the gentrification creeping up the gorge—it's a no-nonsense place, stuck tight to the basalt. Cherry canneries, quiet most of the year, whir into action in early summer, and The Dalles hums with migrant pickers.

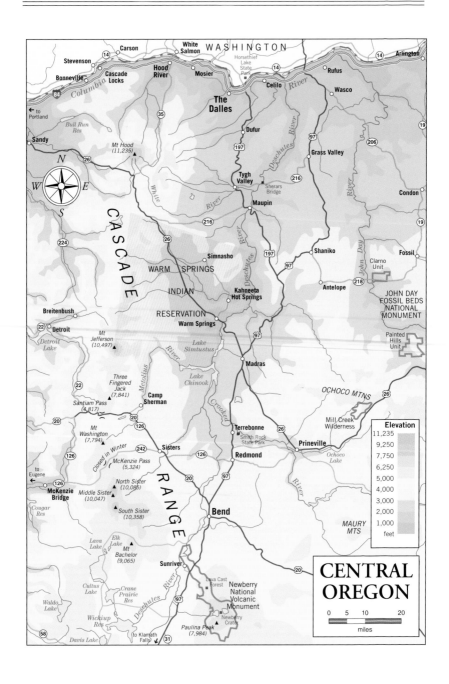

WASHINGTON

Carson
Stevenson
Bonneville
Cascade Locks
Hood River
White Salmon
Mosier
Horsethief Lake State Park
Celilo
Rufus
Wasco
Arlington

Columbia River

to Portland
Sandy
Bull Run Res
Mt Hood (11,235)
The Dalles
Dufur
Grass Valley

CASCADE

White River
Tygh Valley
Sherars Bridge
Maupin
Condon

Simnasho
WARM SPRINGS
INDIAN
RESERVATION
Kahneeta Hot Springs
Warm Springs
Shaniko
Antelope
Fossil
Clarno Unit
JOHN DAY FOSSIL BEDS NATIONAL MONUMENT
Painted Hills Unit

Breitenbush
Detroit
Detroit Lake
Mt Jefferson (10,497)
Metolius River
Lake Simtustus
Lake Billy Chinook

Three Fingered Jack (7,841)
Santiam Pass (4,817)
Camp Sherman
Madras
OCHOCO MTNS
Mill Creek Wilderness

Mt Washington (7,794)
Closed in Winter
McKenzie Pass (5,324)
Sisters
Terrebonne
Smith Rock State Park
Prineville
Ochoco Lake
Redmond

to Eugene
McKenzie Bridge
Cougar Res
North Sister (10,085)
Middle Sister (10,047)
South Sister (10,358)

RANGE

Bend
MAURY MTS

Lava Lake
Elk Lake
Mt Bachelor (9,065)
Sunriver
Cultus Lake
Crane Prairie Res
Waldo Lake
Wickiup Res
Davis Lake
Lava Cast Forest
Newberry National Volcanic Monument
Newberry Crater
Paulina Peak (7,984)
to Klamath Falls

Elevation

11,235	
9,250	
7,750	
6,250	
5,000	
4,000	
3,000	
2,000	
1,000	
feet	

CENTRAL OREGON

0   5   10   20
miles

Across the river, on the Washington side, at **Horsethief Lake State Park,** a trail leads to **petroglyphs** that escaped the floodwaters of The Dalles Dam (many rock carvings are now displayed at the dam's visitor center). Here, the petroglyph called *Tsagigla'lal,* or "She Who Watches," forever watches over the waters.

■ COLUMBIA PLATEAU

From The Dalles, US 197 climbs south to the Columbia plateau, where the sun bounces off wheat fields with a high bright glow, and the spaces get big in a hurry. Drive south as far as the crossroads town of **Tygh Valley,** overlooked by rimrock and home of the mid-May all-Indian rodeo. To the east is the Tygh Valley State Wayside. A triple-tiered White River waterfall splashes down to the stony bones of a hydroelectric power plant—it's lovely in an eerie, ruined way, as though a river finally won a round in its match with technology. The road descends through dry canyons to the Deschutes River to Sherar's Bridge, and crosses the frothing waters at the bottom of high canyon walls at one of the few remaining Indian dipnet

A bull rider hangs on during the All Indian Rodeo Days Celebration at Warm Springs Reservation.

fishing spots, where rickety-looking platforms reach out over rapids. In season, tribal fishers snare salmon with long-handled nets.

Maupin, built on a mesa-like bench above the river, is a close-to-perfect place to fish, float, or sit and watch the play of light on the Deschutes. Steelhead, wild trout, and salmon keep anglers busy year-round. In the summer, Maupin's river outfitters run whitewater trips down the Deschutes.

■ WARM SPRINGS AND VICINITY

In 1855, the Warm Springs Reservation was allotted to the Tenino, Tygh, John Day, and Wyam people. These tribes are now, together, called "Warm Springs." The Confederation of Warm Springs Indians includes the Warm Springs, Wasco, and Paiute tribes. They have bought out all the private holdings within the reservation, including the hot springs that now form the core of the Kah-Nee-Ta resort.

Traditional activities, both spiritual and economic, still go on. Fishing platforms at The Dalles and Sherar's Bridge are used, though they yield fewer salmon every year. The season's first salmon are feted, blessed, then eaten at a ritual dinner. The First Salmon Feast is supplemented by a Root Festival. Honored tribal members dig the tuberous *piyaxi* (bitterroot). After several days' preparation, the roots are cooked, as dances are performed. When the meal is presented, initial sips of water and bites of food are taken as the name of each food is called out. After these first ritual bites, everybody chows down.

In June, *Pi-Ume-Sha* celebrates the 1855 treaty with a pow-wow and rodeo. Non-tribal members are welcome at these events.

Kah-Nee-Ta (root-digger), an upscale resort, was named after a woman who once lived in the Warm Springs Valley. It has an enormous swimming pool with natural, 168-degree water. Even a golf course cannot hide the raw beauty of the land, towered over by Mount Hood and Mount Jefferson, and awash with pungent scents of pine and juniper. **Warm Springs Museum,** on US 26 in the town of Warm Springs, has an unparalleled collection of beadwork and basketry.

❖

East of **Antelope,** off US 97 and OR 218, are the **John Day Fossil Beds**—beautifully sculpted, very colorful rocks with red, tan, and green striations—where many unusual fossils have been found, including those of sabertooth cats and hornless rhinos.

■ SMITH ROCK

West of the town of Prineville, the Crooked River cuts through Smith Rock State Park. (From US 97, turn east at Terrebone and follow the signs.) Dramatic red-orange rock faces and pinnacles are traced against deep blue sky. The cliffs are speckled with rock climbers, inching upward through prisms of pure color.

There's a good network of trails and some easy rock scrambles for non-climbers. Hike the riverbank trail to the base of Monkey Face and scramble up just until the Cascade peaks come into view.

A railroad bridge over the 320-foot-deep Crooked River Gorge near Terrebone was a tough bit of engineering when it was built in 1911. Crews from both the Great Northern and the Union Pacific railroads worked from opposite sides of the river to control the way to central Oregon markets. Sabotage was common. A truce called for the Great Northern crew to finish the span but for the two lines to share the use of the bridge. Today, a rest stop at the US 97 offers a spectacular peer over the dizzying gorge.

■ SISTERS AND VICINITY

Sisters feels Western, with its namesake trio of snow-capped peaks, once called Faith, Hope, and Charity, now North, Middle, and South Sister, in the town's backyard. Real ranchers and cowboys stick out pretty easily from the tourists flocking to false-front shops. But they may raise llamas instead of cattle on the 30-some (and counting) llama ranches of the area. The Patterson Ranch, west of Sisters on Highway 242, is the biggest llama outfit; the herd is usually visible from the road. The animals pack gear on wilderness trips. Some sheepherders keep llamas close to their flocks because they protect the herds from coyotes.

From Sisters, Highway 242 climbs southwesterly to McKenzie Pass, intersecting the **Pacific Crest Trail.** In the summer you can follow it southbound along a ridge running the west slopes of the lava-strewn, wildflower-lit, and glaciated Three Sisters peaks. North Sister is the oldest. The Middle and South Sisters are younger and less sculpted. South Sister, at 10,358 feet, is the highest peak; there's a crater with a small lake at the top. (The best trail to the peak starts from the Cascade Lakes Highway.)

US 20, the Santiam Pass road, heads northwest through pine forests. A few

(following pages) A winter sunset over Smith Rock State Park.

miles from town, the **Metolius River** springs in a big rush from rocks at the base of Black Butte. With clear, piney air and Mount Jefferson in the background, this area is idyllically beautiful. The Metolius runs 30 miles through a glacier-scoured basin before it's swallowed up by Lake Chinook. Fish thrive in the clear, 46-degree water. Wild bull (Dolly Varden) and rainbow trout share the stream with brown and brook trout, whitefish, and kokanee salmon.

Stop for a snack at the Camp Sherman store and linger at the riverside deck, or venture downstream to the **Wizard Fish Hatchery,** renowned for its spectacular setting and tank of oddball fish.

■ BEND AND MOUNT BACHELOR

Bend is an ordinary town that's the tourist hub of central Oregon. Since the turn of the century, people have moved here to be near the mountains and out of the rain. Scandinavian timber workers started skiing around town in the early 1920s, and the sport caught on. Outdoorsy Californians and western Oregonians began moving here in the 1970s and the boom continues. Bend's **High Desert Museum,** 3.6 miles south of Bend at 9800 S. US 97, is one of the best history and ecology museums in the West. Sophisticated dioramas reproducing the birdsongs and the scent of sage envelop a marsh-side Paiute wickiup, and the trapper's tent smells like dirt. Outdoor exhibits include river otters and porcupines; (541) 382-4754.

Mount Bachelor, 20 minutes from town on Century Drive (a.k.a. the Cascade Lakes Highway), and 9,065 feet high, has alpine slopes and cross-country ski trails. Separate day lodges for downhill and cross-country skiers offer food and warmth, but no overnight accommodations are available. (Most skiers stay in Bend; the Inn at Seventh Mountain, a condo-cum-motel, is closest to Bachelor's slopes.) The ski season is long and powdery. Bachelor usually opens around Thanksgiving and has snow well through the spring. Call (800) 829-2442 for general information; (541) 382-7888 for a ski report.

■ CASCADES LAKES

The Cascade Lakes Highway starts in downtown Bend near Drake Park, passes a thicket of condos and resorts, and begins climbing. During the winter, the road is plowed only as far as Mount Bachelor. After Bachelor, the mountain lakes, many formed by lava dams, really start in, and a new Cascade peak springs into view at every break in the lodgepole pines. Trails into the Three Sisters Wilderness Area sprout from the road; virtually every lake has a few campsites on its shores, and resorts at Elk Lake, Cultus Lake, and South Twin Lake have lakeside cabins. The Deschutes' headwaters spurt up from springs beneath Little Lava Lake. Crane Prairie Reservoir, which impounds the fledgling Deschutes, is home to a fascinating osprey colony. They nest on snags in the reservoir and dive for rainbows, brookies, kokanee, and largemouth bass.

■ LAVA LANDSCAPES

The slopes of bulky **Newberry Volcano,** 23 miles south of Bend, are riven with fissures. Vents and over 400 cinder cones have lined up along these weak spots. Most of the effluent from Newberry flowed from these vents. As lava oozed out, the volcano's top collapsed, leaving a five-mile-wide caldera, Newberry Crater. The glassy, obsidian flow in the caldera is from Newberry's most recent eruption, some 1,300 years ago.

Newberry's really staggering view is from **Paulina Peak,** the high point on the volcano's rim. Visitors descending to the caldera with its two perfect lakes learn that one of them, East Lake, comes complete with a stinky, milk-of magnesia-textured, dig-it-yourself hot springs. Non-native trout and kokanee, the Big Obsidian Flow, down-home resorts, and a handful of campgrounds are there too.

A trail leads from the **Lava Lands Visitor Center** (16 miles north of the Newberry Volcano turnoff on US 97) to the base of Lava Butte over jagged 'a'a lava. A narrow, spiraled road leads careful, non-acrophobic drivers to a butte-top viewpoint. You should stop by the visitor center before a scramble through the nearby Lava River Cave, where hot lava moved beneath the crusted-over surface, leaving caves and tubes. It's a rough ride to the stony tree-trunk molds in the Lava Cast Forest (nine miles east of US 97), where basalt flowed into, then out of, a forest, leaving tree trunks coated with molten rock. The trees slowly burned from the hot lava, but the hollow black lava casts remain.

(following pages) Fields of wildflowers form the foreground to a view of Iron Mountain.

■ TRAVEL AND CLIMATE

■ GETTING THERE

US 97, a two-lane highway (that often runs straight as an arrow through the pines), is the main north-south route; US 20, a twisting, two-lane road, is the main route across the Cascade passes. **Horizon Air** flies to Bend from Portland and Seattle.

■ CLIMATE

Central Oregon gets a lot of snow in winter, though the region lies in the rain shadow of the Cascades. It's the best kind of snow: dry and powdery, making for ideal skiing. Spring, summer, and autumn are warm to hot—which is when local rivers and the numerous lakes seem particularly inviting.

■ ACCOMMODATIONS AND RESTAURANTS

☎   For chain lodgings see toll-free numbers on page 352.

$$ For room and restaurant price designations see page 352.

✶   Means highly recommended.

BEND

☎ **Bend Cascade Hostel.**
19 SW Century Dr.; (541) 389-3813
Spiffy new hostel on the road to Mount Bachelor. $

☎ **Inn of the Seventh Mountain.** Five miles west of Bend on Century Dr.; (541) 382-8711 or (800) 542-6810 in Oregon
A full-scale resort, with any activity you could want; close to Mount Bachelor. $$ (summer)-$$$ (winter)

☎ **Mill Inn Bed and Breakfast.**
642 NW Colorado; (541) 389-9198
Ten standard bed-and-breakfast rooms or, for the frugal, a bunk room and breakfast in the renovated boarding house of an old lumber mill. $-$$

☎ **Rock Springs Guest Ranch.**
64201 Tyler Rd.; (541) 382-1957
Lovely, well-run spot just outside Bend, with horseback riding, fishing, tennis, swimming pool. $$$

✕ **Baja Norte.**
801 NW Wall; (541) 358-0611
Astoundingly good, inexpensive, and fresh California-style Mexican food. $

✕ **Cafe Paradiso.**
945 NW Bond; (541) 385-5931
Overstuffed chairs, board games, and music on the weekend nights make this a comfortable spot for coffee and dessert. $

X Deschutes Brewery
1044 NW Bond; (541) 382-9242
A microbrewery and restaurant with a
trendy après ski atmosphere; pasta to eat
with your Black Butte Porter. $$

X Pine Tavern Restaurant. ☆
967 NW Brooks; (541) 382-5581
The locals' favorite "fancy restaurant"
(remember, this is Oregon, so you don't
have to dress up). Great wood-hewn
building at the foot of Oregon Ave.
Make reservations. $$

X Westside Bakery.
1005 NW Galveston; (541) 382-3426
A big family spot—Star Trek and Disney murals, an electric train running
round the wainscotting, and giant pan-
cakes with Mickey Mouse ears. The
food is good, and it's a prime spot to
carbo-load before skiing or hiking. $

CAMP SHERMAN

☥ Metolius River Lodges.
Off Hwy. 20; (541) 595-6290
Beautiful riverside site, well-kept but
rustic cabins. $$

☥ Metolius River Resort. 2551 SW Forest
Service Rd. 1419; (541) 595-6281
A fancier place to stay in Camp Sher-
man. $$-$$$

REDMOND

☥ Eagle Crest Resort.
(541) 923-2453 or (800) 682-4786
Full-on golf and equestrian resort five
miles west of town. $$-$$$

☥ Quality New Redmond Hotel.
521 SW 6th St.; (541) 923-7378
1930s brick downtown hotel on the Na-
tional Register of Historic Places. $$

SHANIKO

☥ Shaniko Hotel.
Hwy 218/Hwy 97; (541) 489-3441
Brick hotel left over from Shaniko's hey-
day as a rail hub, now a bed-and-breakfast inn. $-$$

SISTERS

☥ Black Butte Ranch.
13653 Hawksbeard off Hwy. 20; (541)
595-6211 or (800) 452-7455
Luxury resort, hotel rooms, condominiums, and houses; horseback riding, golf,
tennis, outside Sisters. $$$

X Hotel Sisters Restaurant.
Fir and Cascade; (541) 549-7427
No hotel, just food and drink. $$

X Papandrea's Pizza.
325 E Cascade; (541) 549-6081
Small, family-owned operation serving
Sicilian-style pizzas.$

SUNRIVER

☥ Sunriver Lodge.
US 97, 15 miles south of Bend;
(541) 593-1221 or (800) 547-3922
Sunriver Resort was planned to blend in
with the natural surroundings, and it
does a credible job. Golf courses, tennis
courts, and bikeways. Sunriver main-
tains its own nature center. $$-$$$

☥ Sunriver Lodging Information. General
lodging reservation is available at this
number; (800) 800-8334

WARM SPRINGS RESERVATION

☥ Kah-Nee-Ta.
Off Hwy. 26; (800) 831-0100
Stay in a room or teepee; hot-springs
swimming pool, golf, tennis, fishing,
and salmon bakes. $-$$$

WILLAMETTE VALLEY
AND WESTERN CASCADES

■ HIGHLIGHTS

Wine and Hazelnuts
Covered Bridges
Corvallis
Eugene
North Santiam
Oregon City
Salem
Willamette River

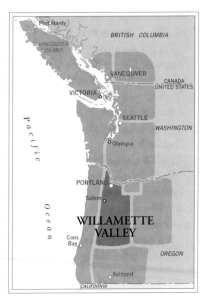

■ LANDSCAPE AND HISTORY

MUCH OF THE WILLAMETTE Valley is a
serene, rustic place of meandering rivers,
small farms and ranches, fields and
meadows. Vineyards climb gentle, south-facing slopes, and fields of multicolored
irises spread across the valley floor. Ancient groves of oaks border orchards and
berry patches. Cattle and sheep graze in lushly green meadows. Side roads follow
whitewater rivers east into the Cascade Mountains and west into the Coast
Ranges, past ancient barns and over covered bridges, and through small towns little changed for a hundred years, with names like Sublimity and Sweet Home.

Bustling cinderblock malls and used-car lots blight their urban fringes, but the
old quarters of the valley's cities—Salem, the state capital, and the college towns of
Corvallis and Eugene—have also preserved a special charm. As you drive the valley's byways and relax by a river, you'll understand why 19th-century pioneers considered this the Eden at the end of the Oregon Trail.

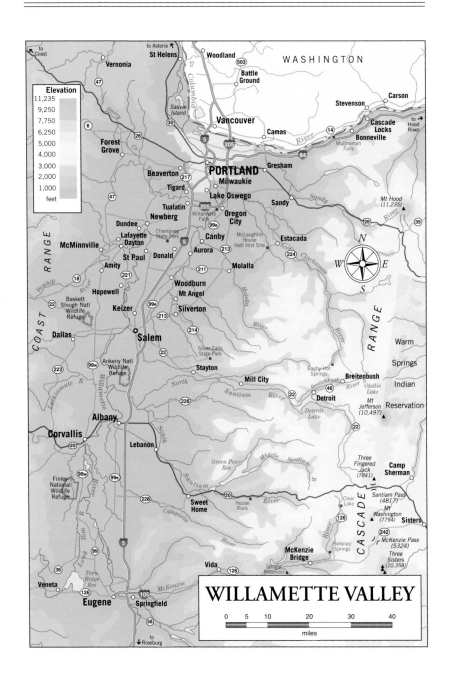

WILLAMETTE VALLEY

0	5	10	20	30	40

miles

■ NORTH WILLAMETTE VALLEY

Oregon City, 20 miles up the Willamette from the Columbia River and near a splendid falls, was the site of an 1829 Hudson's Bay Company settlement. Etienne Lucier was posted here, and he built three cabins and a store. Today, Oregon City is a suburb of Portland, a testament to urban sprawl, and there's something poignant in the idea that this spot was the end of the "rainbow."

The Oregon Trail's "official" end of a 2,000-mile trek from Independence, Missouri, was at Abernethy Green, now the site of the **Oregon Trail Interpretive Center** (Washington Street and Abernethy Road). At Oregon City, emigrants picked up land deeds from the federal office, where all the West Coast plats were held (see San Francisco's original plat at the Clark County Museum overlooking Willamette Falls). In 1845, British citizen and well-known director of the Hudson's Bay Company, John McLoughlin, joined the Willamette Valley settlers. His house is now a museum at 713 Center Street.

At Willamette Falls, a dam generates power, and locks ease boat travel. For a good view of the dam and the scene around it, ride the city's pink elevator 90 feet up the basalt cliffs from the riverside business district to a roadway built on a bench above the river. The Seventh and Railroad elevator, which has operated since 1913, was hydro-powered until it was converted to electric power in 1954.

❖

South of Oregon City, Highway 99E winds past small farms and orchards in all hues of green. **Aurora,** a community of cherry orchards and endless fields of tulips and irises, was a utopian community in the mid 1800s.

In Aurora, a turn right (west) on First Street and a turn right (north) on Main will take you on a pretty country drive across the valley. Turn right (north) onto Butteville Road (after crossing Interstate 5), then left (west) onto Champoeg Road. After a few miles, you'll see a sign on the right directing you to **Champoeg State Park,** a beautiful area that looks much like the Willamette Valley the pioneers saw, with its wildflower meadows, streamside woods, and marshes filled with bird song.

Champoeg Park marks the place where Joe Meek called Oregon's first political convention in 1843, to establish an American provisional government. At the time, Champoeg was an open prairie at the river's edge, used by fur-traders and farmers as a landing for trans-shipping furs, grain, and produce. Today the bank is densely overgrown by tall trees and dense brush. The world's largest black cottonwood tree towers above the riparian trees along one of the sloughs. Shaded trails invite visitors to take a walk or bike ride through walnut orchards or groves of native oak trees. The Willamette River is big and fast here, running between steep wooded banks. Raccoons and deer leave tracks beside streams, and harmless snakes slither away from sunny spots when they're disturbed (rattlesnakes are rare north of Eugene; none have been found north of Salem). Blue-flowered camas dots wet meadows.

St. Paul to the southwest was the site of the first church (a log building) within Oregon's present boundaries, and also of the state's first vineyard where Jesuit padres planted Oregon's first grapevines. Now St. Paul is best known for its Fourth of July rodeo, a lively scene, and one of western Oregon's few big rodeos.

If you have the time, be sure to take the rustic **Wheatland Ferry** across the Willamette, near the town of **Hopewell.** The six-car ferryboat runs on an underwater cable. On the river's east side, there's a transition from vineyards to hop fields where more than 14 different varieties of the bitter, aromatic herb are grown. Hop vines grow up trellised strings like giant pole beans, and by late summer form a green canopy. These hops go into some of America's best microbrews.

For a tour of the wineries in this area, see page 312.

■ SALEM AND VICINITY

Salem, the capital city, is a study in contrast between old, tree-shaded residential neighborhoods (traversed by tree-shaded Mill Creek, which opens to unexpectedly idyllic vistas right in the center of town), and the greensward of the government office campus. As modern buildings were erected, old trees were spared, unifying the old and the new. Built in 1938, after the original capitol burned, the statehouse is an art deco marvel with a golden pioneer perched on top. The interior is decorated with striking WPA murals—a gargantuan, muscled logger and fisherman, and scenes from Oregon's history. The venerable buildings and tall trees of Willamette University, the oldest college in the West, rise just across the road from the capitol. The Willamette River flows by just west of downtown. The vineyards of the Eola Hills lie beyond. Salem has started to turn the parking lots at the river's edge into a park, to reunite the city with its river.

Salem has some truly execrable malls along Lancaster Drive and along the Interstate 5 corridor, as well as ticky-tacky housing developments, but it also has a bustling downtown where old buildings, like Reed's Opera House, have been turned into modern shops and restaurants. Of all the state capitals in the West, Salem has the best restaurants.

While Salem is a city of trees, rhododendrons, and roses, nearby fields are planted to irises, one of the area's important floral products. East of town, the valley rises in a series of hills, which rivers descend in whitewater rapids. Driftboat fishing for steelhead can be very rewarding, in season. At **Silver Falls State Park,** about 25 miles east of Salem, a seven-mile trail passes 10 waterfalls. This is a great place to visit. One trail even leads behind a waterfall, where the air is refreshingly cool on a hot summer day.

Mount Angel, north of Silverton on Highway 214, is one of the Willamette Valley's most interesting towns. A hilltop Benedictine abbey dominates Mount Angel, and the museum there is a fascinating mishmash, even for heathens. (Where else can you find a Coke bottle collection, or a giant hairball under glass?) The state-of-the-art library, designed by Finnish architect Alvar Aalto, houses a surprisingly good collection of ancient manuscripts. Mount Angel celebrates Oktoberfest every September (try that timing on for size), and tries to maintain a Bavarian theme year round.

Albany, upriver from Salem, is a treasure trove of historic homes. These Victorian and Craftsman houses are reminders of Albany's late 19th- and early 20th-century prosperity, when produce and flour were shipped out by riverboat. (To experience the flavor of the old town, you might want to pick up a map of historic homes from the kiosk in the Market Place, 300 SW Second Avenue.) Numerous covered bridges—the greatest number in the West—cross creeks and rivers east of Albany, off OR 26. Look for them on Crabtree and Thomas Creek. The **Shimanek Bridge** over Thomas Creek near Scio is unique for Oregon: it is painted barn red, instead of the usual white. Tiny **Scio** is a town frozen in time, with false-front buildings on its main street and a very rustic museum. And also see the essay in this chapter, "The Bridges of Linn County."

A road leads to the top of 4,097-foot-high **Mary's Peak** west of the pleasant university town of **Corvallis.** The highest point in the Oregon Coast ranges, the peak has a gorgeous display of unusual wildflowers in late spring and early summer.

South Falls in Silver Falls State Park.

BRIDGES OF LINN COUNTY

Oregon has more covered bridges than any other state on the West Coast—some 59 at last count. And that's not only because Oregonians are more conservative than Californians, Washingtonians, or British Columbians. It's because they're penny pinchers. Covered bridges, built with locally abundant logs, can be built at a lower cost than steel or concrete spans.

Why do these bridges have roofs? A wagster once said it was because their builders were farmers who knew how to build barns but knew nothing about building bridges.

That's not true, of course. As old-fashioned as they look, these bridges are actually marvels of modern engineering. But that doesn't make them any less pretty to look at. These bridges are covered over because it rains a lot in western Oregon. Rainwater collecting in exposed joints of wooden bridges makes them rot, and pretty soon an uncovered bridge falls down. On a covered bridge, the roofs protects the joints—giving it a life expectancy five times that of an open bridge. Ounce by ounce, they're at least as strong as steel bridges. Perhaps that's because steel goes into their construction, too, in the form of vertical steel rods strengthening compression joints. But the wood of these bridges actually gets stronger with age, as it seasons under the protective covering of a bridge's roof. One engineer estimated that, after proper seasoning, the trusses were more than half again as strong as when they were first put into place. These bridges have to be built strong, to accommodate logging trucks heavily loaded with green timber.

Covered bridges span creeks and rivers throughout western Oregon, from Josephine County north to Portland, and from the coast to the Cascades. But the easiest ones to visit on a day trip (or half a day, if you're in a hurry), are south and east

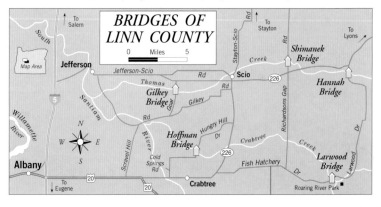

of Scio, in Linn County, just a few miles east of the Interstate 5 freeway near Albany. Leave I-5 at exit 233 in Albany and drive east on US 20 to OR 226 and continue towards Crabtree. Take Cold Springs Road to Crabtree Road and turn immediately left into Hungry Hill Road. You'll get to the first of the bridges in about a mile.

Hoffman Bridge

The Hoffman Bridge, a 90-foot covered span, crosses Crabtree Creek. This pastoral creek did not get its name from the Oregon crabapple trees common in the area, but was named after pioneer settler John Crabtree, who obtained a Donation Land Claim in 1845 (a year before Oregon became officially an American territory), and settled on the banks of the creek in 1846. The whitewashed bridge is lit by Gothic-style windows, a departure from the more commonly open sides of Linn County covered bridges. Look for adze marks on the trusses (diagonal timbers) and chords (horizontal timbers), indicating they were shaped by hand. The portals were originally rounded, but were enlarged and squared to allow larger loads to pass. Despite its old-fashioned look, this bridge was built in 1936.

Gilkey Bridge

To reach the next bridge, return to Crabtree Road, turn west (left) and then turn right on Gilkey Road. After about three miles, turn left into Goar Road (just before the railroad crossing). You'll see the bridge after another half mile. The 120-foot long Gilkey Bridge, across Thomas Creek, was built in 1939. It is painted white, like most of Linn County's covered bridges, but its sides are open, exposing the thick, square timber trusses. The roof fully protects the bridge deck and trusses from rain, despite the open sides. Until 1960, a covered railroad bridge spanned Thomas Creek just to the east.

The Gilkey Bridge spans a popular local swimming hole (look for the swimming rope tied to the bridge frame).

Shimanek Bridge

Return to Gilkey Road, turn left and left again onto OR 226. Follow this state highway through the small farm country town of Scio to Richardson Gap Road. A left turn will bring you to the Shimanek Bridge, the longest and most unusual of Linn County covered bridges: the 130-foot-long bridge is painted a bright barn-red and has white, louvered, Gothic-style windows. The inside is painted white to improve visibility. Be careful where you park: there's too much traffic to park on the highway,

Shimanek covered bridge.

and roadsides are quite soft. This bridge was built in 1966, mostly by volunteer helpers from nearby Scio, to replace a covered bridge destroyed in the 1962 Columbus Day Storm. This is a very popular and photogenic bridge.

Larwood Bridge

Make a u-turn on Richardson Gap Road and drive south. Cross OR 226 and continue for three miles south to Larwood Drive. Turning east brings you in four miles to the Larwood Bridge. This 105-foot-long, whitewashed bridge with rounded portals and open sides, has the prettiest location of all Linn County covered bridges, spanning Crabtree Creek near its confluence with the Roaring River in a rustic woodsy setting. The unusual thing here is that the Roaring River flows into Crabtree Creek. A river flowing into a creek is so unusual in U.S. geography, that it was featured in *Ripley's Believe It Or Not*. Adjacent Crabtree Park, a tree-shaded oasis, is very popular with fishermen and swimmers.

The park has picnic tables and is a great place for a picnic, especially in midsummer when this shady nook offers a respite from the Willamette Valley heat.

Hannah Bridge

To visit the last of the bridges, return to OR 226 via Larwood and Richardson Gap. Turn right on OR 226 and drive east for about four and a half miles. The bridge is just off the highway at Burmester Creek Road. Or if you're adventurous, drive south on Larwood Drive to Fish Hatchery Road, and the site of the town of Larwood. Turn left and follow this road around Rogers Mountain. After the state fish hatchery, the name of the road changes to Tree Farm Road, but chances are you will not see any road signs. North of Rogers Mountain, turn left on Burmester Creek Road. That will bring you to the Hannah Bridge just before you return to OR 226.

The Hannah Bridge looks much like the Larwood Bridge but crosses Thomas Creek in a more exposed place, with no picnic site nearby. It is, however, easier to photograph, because it is not quite as hidden by trees.

The drive back to Scio leads through some of the Willamette Valley's prettiest farm land. As you look around, you can easily understand why the pioneers who braved the hardships of the Oregon Trail, felt they had rediscovered the Garden of Eden when they reached the Valley.

Note: A fine book on the subject is *Roofs Over Rivers* by Bill and Nick Cockrell.

Hannah covered bridge.

■ WESTERN CASCADES

East of the valley's broad agricultural floor rise the western, or old, **Cascade Mountains.** This tree-covered range is home to some of the last old-growth forest of the Cascades.

Several scenic highways lead from the Willamette Valley into the Cascades and across passes to Central Oregon. From Salem, OR 22 follows the North Santiam into the mountains. This river is dammed to form **Detroit Lake.** Just north of the Forest Service's Breitenbush campground, turn east to the **South Breitenbush Gorge** trail. The trailhead is not far from the main road, and it's as splendid an example of a old-growth forest as you'll find. Leggy rhododendrons and Oregon grape break through the mossy floor; cedars and Douglas firs rise to the sky or lie fallen on the ground, nourishing young trees as "nurse logs." Keep an eye out for black bears scrambling up and down tree trunks. Consider it a special treat to come across a bear, but do keep your distance.

Turn off Highway 46 about 27 miles north of Detroit for an 18-mile trip to **Olallie Lake** with its no-frills resort and campground. It's worth the long, slow drive. In the Chinook jargon (19th-century trader's pidgin) "olallie" means huckleberry, and huckleberry bushes dominate the understory beneath the lodgepole pine and mountain hemlocks. Olallie is the largest of the many lakes in the area, most of which are small, shallow basins scooped out by glacial ice. From **Olallie Butte** there's a fine view of the lakes and of Mount Jefferson.

Past the Olallie turnoff, Highway 46 follows the Clackamas River. Pullouts and trailheads dot the road, and steam plumes rise from hot spots in the river.

From Albany, US 20 follows the track of the **Santiam Wagon Road** which once crossed the Cascades. Traces of it remain near the House Rock Campground, 24 miles east of Sweet Home, where a huge boulder sheltered early travelers. Old-growth trees now form a broad canopy; a short trail leads to a waterfall on the South Santiam River.

■ EUGENE AND THE MCKENZIE RIVER

Eugene revolves around the University of Oregon in a loose, elliptical orbit. This is one of the few towns in America where tie-dyed T-shirts have been fashionable

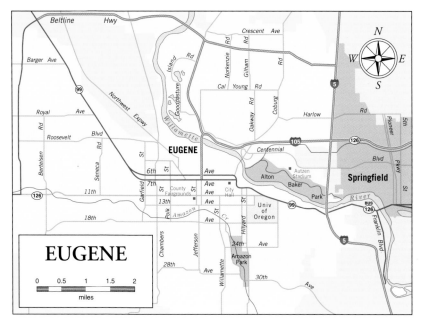

for 25 solid years. It's certainly one of the few places in the state where the corner grocery stocks soy milk and nitrite-free sausage. But a culinary tour of Eugene won't disappoint those with more sophisticated and carnivorous tastes—the local restaurants are quite good.

There's as much partying here as in any college town—*Animal House* was filmed in Eugene. But what sets the town apart is the laid-back atmosphere at its fairs and markets: the weekly **Saturday Market** downtown; the **Oregon Country Fair** in Veneta in early July; and the **Eugene Celebration** in late September. The Saturday Market offers the expected mix of beads and dried herbs; the Eugene Celebration is lively, but not too giddily foreign for the unprepared visitor. The University itself is set on a gracious campus and is highly thought of. If you stop by the **University of Oregon Museum of Natural History at** 1680 E 15th Avenue, you can see the 13,000-year-old Fort Rock sagebrush sandals—one of the oldest Paleo-Indian artifacts ever to be found.

A paved foot/bike path runs through town along the **Willamette River** (past riffles named Pietro's Pizza Rapids, after a local hangout above the shore). The river here was the head of navigation for daring riverboat captains; today, locals run the rapids in rubber rafts. Bike paths line many streets and run to the hinterlands. A pleasant drive or bicycle trip takes you south to Spencer Butte, bounded by Willamette Boulevard and Fox Hollow, for good views of the Cascades and the Three Sisters.

OR 126 winds east into the Cascade foothills along the **McKenzie River** past hazelnut orchards into the mountains. On a sunny day you might want to pack a picnic basket and dawdle up the highway to the **Goodpasture Bridge** for a picnic.

❖

Tokatee Golf Course, near Cougar Reservoir and McKenzie Bridge, is one of Oregon's loveliest and most celebrated. The nearer you get to the headwaters of the McKenzie (at Clear Lake, on Highway 126), the more mysterious the river becomes. Clear Lake, formed by a lava dam, flooded a forest still visible underwater.

The scenery along winding **McKenzie Pass Highway**, OR 242, undergoes a startling transition, as it crosses from the ferns and trees near McKenzie Bridge to a moonscape of crusty, brown-black lava flow. Parts of the flow are only 400 years old. Just 30 years ago, these lava fields stood in for the moon, when astronauts practiced landing and walking on the lunar-like surface here. (Apollo astronauts left a Central Oregon lava rock on the moon, in exchange for the moon rocks they ferried back to Earth.) This road is not plowed in winter.

■ TRAVEL AND CLIMATE

■ GETTING THERE

The Willamette Valley is a long, green river valley dividing the southern Cascades from the Coast Range. Even though urban sprawl gnaws at its edges, it is still mostly agricultural, its rivers hidden behind dense stands of cottonwood, ash, and willow, its fields and meadows dotted with copses of ancient oaks. Corn, berries, plums, pears, apples, and nuts grow here; the wines made from local pinot noir, chardonnay, and muscat grapes are justly famous.

By Car. Only one freeway, Interstate 5, runs the entire length of the valley, and because it's so easy to breeze along, going faster and faster, it's also easy to get a speeding ticket—highway patrol cars have a way of materializing out of blackberry bushes. There are two rustic and scenic alternatives to the freeway—99 W, which connects Portland to the Yamhill County Wine Country, Corvallis, and Junction City; and 99E, which connects Salem and Albany to Portland.

■ CLIMATE

Willamette Valley weather is mild, with abundant rain in winter and sunny summer weather, but it varies considerably through the 110 miles of the valley. Because of the mitigating influence of the Columbia River, which channels cool marine air inland, Salem, near the northern end of the valley, is often cooler in summer and warmer in winter than Eugene, near the southern end. It's also more likely to snow in Eugene. But even in the coldest of winters and wettest of summers, the inclement weather never lasts long, and in a pinch you can always find a spreading oak or maple tree under which to hold your picnic.

■ ACCOMMODATIONS AND RESTAURANTS

   ☖   For chain lodgings see toll-free numbers on page 352.

   $$ For room and restaurant price designations see page 352.

   ✳   Means highly recommended.

CORVALLIS

✕ **Bombs Away Cafe.**
2527 Monroe; (541) 757-7221
Who'da thunk it? Duck confit chimichangas on a bed of citrus rice? In Corvallis? It's hip and hopping. **$**

✕ **Nearly Normal's.**
15th and Monroe; (541) 753-0791
Classic post-hippie joint with big wholesome meals. **$**

DETROIT

☖ **Breitenbush Hot Springs Retreat.**
10 miles northeast of Detroit on Rd. 46; (503) 854-3314
Ex-hippies and New-Agers will feel at home. Others will want to hide in their rustic cabins. **$**

DUNDEE

✕ **The Red Hills Provincial Dining & Fine Wines.** ✳✳

276 Hwy. 99 West; (503) 538-8224
When you come into town from the north, slow down or you'll miss this restaurant occupying an old house just above the road. Every wine-country town should have a comfortable restaurant like this where the food is excellent and enhances the local wines. **$$**

EUGENE

☖ **Atherton Place Bed and Breakfast.**
690 West B Rd.; (541) 683-2674
It's an easy bike ride to campus, a pleasant walk to downtown from this comfortable, quiet spot. **$$**

☖ **Best Western New Oregon Motel.**
1655 Franklin Blvd.; (541) 683-3663
Close to the university and the Willamette River, with a good indoor pool. **$$**

☷ **Black Bart B&B.**
14 miles north of Eugene in Junction City on Love Lake Rd.; (541) 998-1904
Two rooms with baths on 13 acres. $$

☷ **Valley River Inn.**
1000 Valley River Way; (541) 687-0123
A beautiful, modern resort right on the Willamette River. $$$

✗ **Ambrosia.**
Broadway at Pearl; (541) 342-4141
Italian, with new-wave pizza. $$

✗ **Anatolia.**
992 Willamette St., downtown on the mall; (541) 343-9661
Greek and Indian cuisine; lunch and dinner, different curries, spanakopita, kotta psiti, and salads. $-$$

✗ **Cafe Navarro.**
454 Willamette; (541) 344-0943
Latin American and Caribbean cuisine. $

✗ **Cafe Soriah.** ✶
384 W 13th Ave.; (541) 342-4410
A favorite—food with a Mediterranean flair and an appealing wine bar. $$

✗ **Cafe Zenon .** ✶✶
898 Pearl St.; (541) 343-3005
There's always something tempting on the ever-changing eclectic menu in this bustling bistro. $$

✗ **Chanterelle.** ✶
Fifth and Pearl; (541) 484-4065.
A small restaurant whose chef serves accomplished dishes made from the freshest of local ingredients in a dining room comfortably suited to such exquisite fare. Don't miss the desserts. $$-$$$

✗ **Excelsior.** ✶✶
754 E 13th; (541) 485-1206
One of Eugene's first restaurants with Northwest sophistication. $$-$$$

✗ **Gazebo.**
19th and Agate near the University; (541) 683-6661
Healthy Middle-Eastern cuisine. College students take their parents here. $$

✗ **High Street Cafe.**
1243 High St.; (541) 345-4905
Pub fare, microbrewery. $

✗ **L & L Grocery.**
16th and Willamette; (541) 686-2985
Gourmet market with bakery, cafe, and coffee shop. Tables all around provide an all-day hangout for locals and visitors alike.

✗ **Steelhead Brewery and Cafe.**
199 E Fifth Ave.; (541) 686-2739
The faux-British pub decor doesn't detract from the good pizza and microbrew beer. $

McMINNVILLE

✗ **Cafe Azul.** ✶✶
313 Third St.; (503) 435-1234
Mexican food takes on new, unexpected nuances when prepared by a chef trained at Berkeley's Chez Panisse. Despite the spice, the dishes go very well with the local wines. $$

✗ **Nick's Italian Cafe.** ✶
521 E Third St.; (503) 434-4471
Take a homey Italian storefront cafe, add top-notch five-course meals and an impressive cellar of local wines, and you've got Nick's. It's one of the state's best restaurants. $$$

McKENZIE BRIDGE

Log Cabin Inn.
Hwy. 126; (541) 822-3432
Classic resort cabins with back porches
on the river. The restaurant is in a 1906
log lodge. An angling hotspot three miles
from Oregon's prettiest golf course. **$$**

SALEM

Marquee House.
333 Wyatt Court NE; (503) 391-0837
A colonial house surrounded by trees
overlooking quiet Mill Creek—you'll be
hard pressed to find a more serene coun-
try-style manor in the heart of the city—
within walking distance of the Capitol
Mall. The rooms are very comfortable;
the breakfast is sumptuous. **$$**

Allesandro's Park Plaza. ✶
325 High St. SE; (503) 370-9951

Good Italian food in quiet, elegant surroundings, just a few blocks from the
heart of the city. **$$**

Boone's Treasury.
888 Liberty NE; (503) 399-9062
Salem's equivalent of the counterculture
hangs out here, drinking microbrews in
the old brick treasury building. **$**

La Margarita. ✶
545 Ferry St. SE; (503) 362-8861
Good margaritas, fajitas, and mesquite-
grilled meats in a laid-back restaurant
with very good service. **$**

Off Center Cafe.
17th and Center; (503) 363-9245.
If you're not in a hurry, you can enjoy a
good meal here. They also provide food
to the cafeteria in the basement of the
capitol building. **$**

Black Bart Bed and Breakfast in Junction City.

WINE AND HAZELNUT TOUR

■ THE HAZELNUT-FILBERT CONNECTION

The orchards of low, somewhat bushy trees you see on gentle hillsides are hazelnuts. Oregon grows more than 90 percent of the U.S. harvest of these compact, flavorful nuts. They're known locally as "filberts," even though the Oregon Hazelnut Commission renamed them (and itself) a decade ago. Not more than a couple of decades before that, there were even more hazelnut orchards in Yamhill County—and no vineyards. In fact, the first winery you'll encounter on this trip, Rex Hill Vineyards, began its working life as a nut drier.

■ PIONEER VINTNERS

While winemaking in Oregon predates Prohibition, it wasn't until Richard Sommer planted grapes in the Umpqua Valley in 1961 that wineries took off. *(See Southern Oregon, page 322.)* Following Sommer's pioneering efforts, Charles Coury planted European grape varietals in the northern Willamette Valley. He was soon followed by David Adelsheim, Dick Erath, and David Lett, who established the first Yamhill County vineyards and wineries. Their first wines proved them right: this was prime wine country indeed.

Today, the valley's wineries are booming, and Yamhill County is turning into the Napa Valley of the Northwest, because the soils and microclimates are perfect for growing grapes. Vintners are just not sure yet which grapes will do best here and produce great wines. Like the Napa Valley, these vineyards are close to a major city. Portland is only half an hour's drive away, assuring a steady stream of visitors.

Pinot noir was an early favorite among locally grown grapes and makes great wines in the hands of master vintners like Ken Wright, Myron Redford, Dick Ponzi, and Dick Erath. But some vintages have proved to be disappointing; others have not aged well. Recently there's been a boom in pinot gris plantings. This pink Alsatian grape does very well here —and may make a better wine in Oregon than it does in its native Europe. It is the perfect wine for accompanying fresh salmon, crab, and other seafoods. But Oregon chardonnays and rieslings have also shown well, as has another rare European grape, muscat ottonel.

Visit a few of the vineyards listed on the following pages to get a solid introduction to Oregon's burgeoning wine industry.

■ TOURING THE VINEYARDS

Rex Hill Vineyards

One and a half miles north of Newberg Highway 99W, the main road through Oregon's wine country, you have to look sharp for the blue sign directing you to Rex Hill. Tall evergreens shade the winery from the road. The winery sits in splendidly landscaped grounds beneath hillside vineyards. A grassy picnic area is framed by rose arbors and beds of flowers. The wines to taste here are pinot noir, pinot gris, and chardonnay. Be sure to call ahead. The beautiful picnic area is a popular place for weddings. 30835 N Hwy. 99W, Newberg; (503) 538-0666.

Argyle

The tasting room for Argyle—The Dundee Wine Company—is in a Victorian house surrounded by flowers. It's just off the highway and hard to miss, but the parking lot just to the north is. Look carefully. The traffic can be horrendous on weekends. Argyle makes very good sparkling wine and very drinkable chardonnay, pinot noir, and dry riesling. 691 Hwy. 99W, Dundee; (503) 538-8520.

(continues)

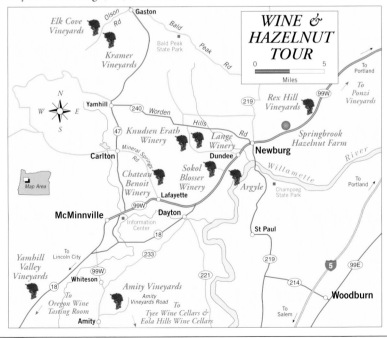

Chateau Benoit Winery

The winery sits high above the valley on a hilltop, and the staff is friendly. Among the wines made here, you should taste the brut sparkling wine, the sauvignon blanc, and the easily drinkable muller-thurgau, which is just right for a picnic on a warm Willamette Valley afternoon. As you look across the landscape, you'll realize how rural and unspoiled Yamhill County still is, thanks to its land use ordinance restricting non-agricultural developments. 6580 NE Mineral Springs Rd., Carlton—off Hwy. 99W just west of Lafayette; (503) 864-2991.

Take Worden Hill Road from Dundee into the hills to reach the next two wineries. Follow signs (the lane leading to Lange angles off to the right).

Lange Winery

Hidden under trees at the end of a long, winding road through an idyllic farm landscape. Call ahead to make sure someone is home. The pinot noir, pinot gris, and chardonnay are wines you'll want to take home. 18380 NE Buena Vista Dr.; in Dundee turn right on Ninth; (503) 538-6476.

Knudsen Erath Winery

A bit farther up the road, on an oak- and vineyard-covered slope, rises Knudsen Erath. This is one of Oregon's first wineries, dating back to 1972. Winemaker Dick Erath makes excel-

Chateau Benoit.

lent pinot noir, dry riesling, and chardonnay. Be sure to taste the reserve wines. The winery has a picnic patio with some beautiful views. It's a great place to while away an afternoon sipping wine. Crabtree Park next to the winery is a great place for taking a walk before you head back onto the road. 17000 NE Knudsen Lane, Dundee; (503) 538-3318.

Sokol Blosser Winery

The winery sits on a hilltop with great views, but it's just off OR 99W south of Dundee. Sokol Blosser makes first-rate

The tasting room at Rex Hill Vineyards.

pinot noir and chardonnay. The tasting room is well stocked with local foods. A shady picnic area beckons you to linger over a bottle of wine. You might want to take the self-guided vineyard tour to learn about vines, viticultural practices like trellising. 5000 Sokol Blosser Lane, Dundee; (503) 864-2282.

Elk Cove Vineyards

Northwest of Newberg, near the small farm town of Gaston, Elk Cove Vineyards nestles into a vine-covered "cove." The wines are as beautiful as the setting. Elk Cove produces excellent pinot noir and pinot gris, highly enjoyable chardonnay, cabernet sauvignon, and—if the weather is right at harvest time—some beautifully balanced dessert whites. All of these are "food wines," designed to enhance Oregon meats, seafoods, fruits, and cheeses. 27751 NW Olson Rd., Gaston; (503) 985-7760.

Kramer Vineyards

A short drive up the road from Elk Cove Vineyards brings you to Kramer Vineyards, a winery known for its pinot gris, pinot noir, and—raspberry wine. 26830 NW Olson Rd., Gaston; (503) 662-4545.

Wine barrels.

Amity Vineyards

A bit south off McMinnville, on OR 99W, look for the sign directing you to Amity Vineyards. It's uphill all the way, both in elevation and wine quality. Amity's winemaker, Myron Redford, is one of the true artists of Willamette Valley winemaking. He makes lovely pinot noir that's excellent with food, as well as excellent riesling, dry gewurztraminer, and chardonnay. The big fig tree next to the winery, bedecked with ripe fruit in late summer, is a Seattle native transplanted by Redford when he started the winery some 20 years ago. SE Amity Vineyards Rd., Amity; (503) 835-2362.

Yamhill Valley Vineyards

Southwest of McMinnville, on the way to the Coast, just off OR 18, these vineyards are tucked into the foothills of the Willamette Valley. A full-bodied pinot noir and intense pinot gris are the high points, but you might want to sip the riesling while you're relaxing out on the deck. 16250 SW Oldsville Rd., McMinnville; (503) 843-3100.

Oregon Wine Tasting Room

A great place for tasting and buying hard-to-find local wines. It's on the way to the coast at a crossroads called Bellevue. At the Lawrence Art Gallery, 19706 SW Hwy. 18, McMinnville; (503) 843-3787.

Springbrook Hazelnut Farm

To learn more about local hazelnuts, you might want to stay at this bed-and-breakfast with a 60-acre hazelnut orchard. 30295 North Hwy. 99W, Newberg; (503) 538-4606.

Ponzi Vineyards

A winery you might want to visit as you head back to Portland, Ponzi is famous for pinot noir and pinot gris. 14665 Southwest Winery Lane, Beaverton; (503) 628-1227.

Eola Hills Wine Cellars

To the south of the Eola Hills, just west of Salem, Eola Hills Wine Cellars, has a local reputation for its Sunday brunch. Call to make a reservation. 501 S Pacific Hwy. W, Rickreall; (503) 623-2405.

Tyee Wine Cellars

If you have the time to explore other parts of the valley, you might want to visit Tyee Wine Cellars,. This is a "century farm" that has been run by the same family for over a hundred years. Once race horses were raised and raced here, but dairy cattle, sheep, and hazelnuts were the mainstay until grapes were planted in 1985. The tasting room is in an old dairy house. Tasting highlights include the pinot noir, pinot gris, chardonnay, and gewurztraminer. There's a picnic area in a pristine meadow, shaded by ancient Oregon oaks. This land has never felt the bite of a plow. Look for beavers in the marsh below. 26335 Greenberry Rd.; Corvallis; (541) 753-8754

■ GOOD WINES TO BUY

You may want to taste the products of these wineries not open to the public:

Adelsheim Vineyard, pinot noir, pinot gris.
Cameron Winery, pinot noir and chardonnay.
Chehalem, intense pinot noir, barrel-fermented pinot gris.
Domaine Serene Winery, beautifully complex pinot noir.
Ken Wright Cellars, pinot noir.
Panther Creek Cellars, pinot noir, chardonnay, melon.

An award-winning Oregon chardonnay.

SOUTHERN OREGON

■ HIGHLIGHTS

Umpqua River Valleys
Rogue River Valley
Oregon Caves
Jacksonville
Ashland
Oregon Shakespeare Festival
Crater Lake

■ LANDSCAPE AND HISTORY

BETWEEN EUGENE AND ASHLAND, 162 miles to the south, Interstate 5, the great north-south road, runs through some of the prettiest scenery in the Pacific Northwest. The road skirts cliffs, climbs mountain passes, and winds through wooded river canyons and pastoral valleys. In Sunny Valley a white, covered bridge just east of the freeway adds to the charm.

In spring, purple-tipped grasses grow taller in the meadows than the backs of grazing sheep. In summer, the meadows are dotted with white daisies, and the brushy edge of the woods glows bright blue with ceanothus blooms. Madronas, cedars, oaks, and manzanita line the road. In the southern corner, where US 199 runs to the coast, you'll even see a few redwoods.

Crater Lake and the Oregon Shakespeare Festival are among regional highlights. Old-timers keep cabins up their favorite rivers and fill them with fishing rods, trophy heads, and furniture hewn from gigantic logs.

■ UMPQUA RIVER

The Umpqua is a most unusual river. It is created by the lowland confluence of two main forks which rise high in the western Cascades—and which are so different from each other that it seems odd they share a last name.

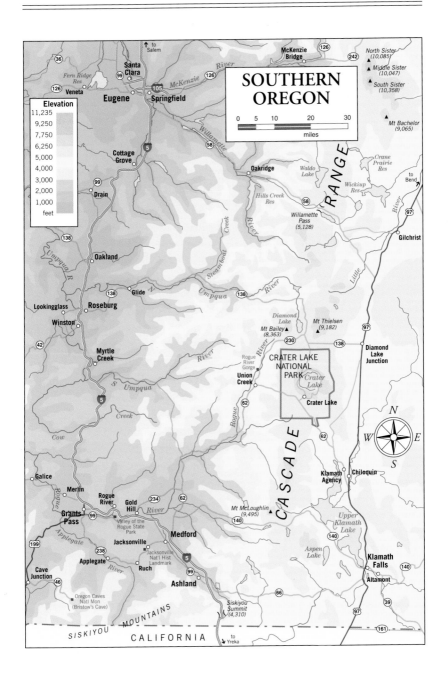

SOUTHERN OREGON

0   5   10   20   30
miles

Elevation
11,235
9,250
7,750
6,250
5,000
4,000
3,000
2,000
1,000
feet

The **North Umpqua** rises in the wilderness of the high western Cascades, in Maidu Lake (east of Diamond Lake), its waters fed by the snow fields of Fairview Peak, Elephant Mountain, Mount Bailey, and Mount Thielsen. Its course is swift, as it tumbles for some 50 miles through deep chasms of basalt pillars, past hillsides densely clad with stands of tall fir, cedar, and hemlock. Here the waters of the river are deep blue-green and magical. Trails, most leading to waterfalls, leave the road every few miles; riverside campsites are plentiful. **Steamboat Creek,** alive with trout, drains an area that was a major draw for placer miners in the 19th century. After rushing through the narrow defile of **Idleyld Park,** the silty Little River roils into the jade-colored waters of the North Umpqua near Glide, amidst a jumble of giant rocks, before sliding down in the eastern reaches of the Umpqua Valley.

The steep-walled gorge of the North Umpqua, gushing with waterfalls, is a popular place to fish for spring chinook and summer steelhead. Coho salmon travel upriver in fall to spawn; wild brown trout live in the river's upper reaches. To reach the best fishing holes, as well as the **Steamboat Inn,** a top-flight but unpretentious fishing lodge with a splendid riverfront location and great food, take OR 138, the North Umpqua Road east of Roseburg into the mountains. From Rock Creek (east of Idleyld Park) to Lemolo Lake (north of Diamond Lake, near the headwaters of the North Umpqua), the river is open to fly fishing only. Even so, you may have to fight for standing room near the shore, when the fish are biting.

The South Umpqua is a great place for dangling your feet in the water or for skinny-dipping in a cool pool on a hot summer day. The two forks of the South Umpqua (Castle Rock and Black Rock) rise in a landscape much drier than that of its northern sibling. Starting in the high country of the western Cascades, the river flows through subalpine meadows before gently dropping over a huge half-dome rock at **South Umpqua Falls** into a narrow valley which, unlike the valley of the North Umpqua, occasionally opens into fertile terraces and lush meadows. Near Canyonville, the South Umpqua heads north to Myrtle Creek and Roseburg. It is a shallow, sometimes placid stream, bordered by open forests of ponderosa pine and black oak, its wooded margins painted blue by ceanothus blossoms in spring. Its water level drops considerably in summer, while its main tributary, Cow Creek, may almost dry up. Cow Creek also rises in the high Cascades in a parallel valley but swings far to the west through oak-clad hills before joining the South Umpqua near Riddle.

Portions of southwestern Oregon are still blanketed by deep and wild forest.

The North and South Umpqua join west of Roseburg, in a flat, fertile valley. The united waters of the Umpqua flow smoothly through oak-studded meadows and hillsides of the Coast Range at a level of only 400 feet above the sea. The river is interrupted in its leisurely course by gentle rapids until it becomes a placid lowland stream at Scottsburg, a few miles above tidewater. Its lower course is a calm estuary, reaching deeply into the forested hills of the Coast Range. It flows into the Pacific at Winchester Bay.

Roseburg, the metropolis of the Umpqua Valley, is a good "base camp" for exploring the region. In easy driving distance of both forks of the Umpqua and of the main stream, with several wineries nearby (see below), the town has a number of inexpensive motels and restaurants. The smell of fresh-cut wood sharpens the air here. Mount Nebo—supposedly a resting place for the mythical giant logger Paul Bunyan and his blue ox Babe—rises above the river in a series of rocky cliffs.

A few miles west of Roseburg, in the lower part of the south fork valley, is Oregon's Umpqua Valley **wine country.** Two of the nine wineries in this area are pioneers of winemaking in the Northwest—and still produce premium wines.

■ HILLCREST VINEYARDS

Richard Sommer is the modern pioneer of Oregon winemaking. He first planted grapes on the western slopes of the valley in 1961 and made his first wines at Hillcrest Vineyards in 1963. Sommer believes the region is ideal for producing great rieslings—and so far he's been right. But he also makes long-lived cabernet sauvignon and pinot noir. The winery is open daily. To get there, take Garden Valley from Interstate 5 in Roseburg west to Melrose, turn left and follow Melrose to Doerner (a fork in the road) and keep right. Another right turn on Elgarose will bring you to the winery. Driving distance is about 10 miles from I-5 at 240 Vineyard Lane; (541) 673-3709.

■ HENRY ESTATE WINERY

Scott and Sylvia Henry's Henry Estate Winery, a few miles downriver, below the junctions of the two forks of the Umpqua, was established in 1978 (the first grapes were planted in 1972) on the old family ranch. Henry Estate's pinot noirs and chardonnays have been consistently excellent—and have just as consistently been under-rated and under-priced. To reach the winery, take OR 138 west from I-5 and bear left at Fort McKay Road/Sutherlin Umpqua Road, which turns into

Hubbard Creek Road in the hamlet of Umpqua. Winery address is 687 Hubbard Creek Road; (541) 459-5120.

Other wineries in the valley include **Callahan Ridge** (pinot noir), **La Garza** (cabernet sauvignon), **Lookingglass** (cabernet sauvignon and pinot noir), and **Umpqua River Vineyards** (cabernet sauvignon and merlot).

■ ROGUE RIVER

Grants Pass, a lumber town in the Siskiyou Mountains, caters to travelers lured to the Rogue River's whitewater. The town is scrappy and partly malled, but historic homes converted into bed-and-breakfasts and antique shops can be found in the venerable downtown. On Saturday mornings, downtown streets take on extra color, fragrance, and bustle at the **Farmers' Market.**

The main attraction here is the Rogue, described thus by Western writer Zane Grey:

> ... *D*eep and dark green, swift and clear, and as pure as the snows from which it springs. . . . It is a river at its birth, gliding away through the Oregon forest with hurrying momentum, as if eager to begin the long leap down through the Siskiyous. The river tumbles off the mountain in mellow thundering music, racing between its timbered banks down the miles to the sheltered valley. Twisting through Grants Pass, it enters the canyoned wilderness of the Coast Range.

Congress declared the Rogue "Wild and Scenic" in 1968, a classification that limits development. A permit is necessary to raft protected stretches of the Rogue. Permits are parceled out by lottery each February and are sometimes available throughout the summer at the Rand Visitor Center just downstream from the town of Galice. To enter the permit lottery, call (541) 479-3735.

Rafting outfitters in Grants Pass and neighboring communities get a good share of the permits. They offer everything from rides on guided rafts to inflatable kayak rentals.

Jet boats are a common way to see the river's unprotected stretches. They leave from Grants Pass and the nearby town of Rogue River, or from Gold Beach on the coast.

❖

The **highest stretches of the Rogue River** aren't far from Crater Lake *(consult map, page 319)*. Less well-known but no less lovely than the upper section of the river, this area is well worth exploring. Stop off at the **Rogue River Gorge,** on Highway 62 near Union Creek. Turn north to glacier-scoured **Diamond Lake,** popular year-round with southern Oregon families. In the winter it's possible to cross-country ski here and in the summer to boat and hike.

■ OREGON CAVES

From Grants Pass, Interstate 5 heads off east and south through Medford and Ashland on its way to California. A two-lane, forest-shaded road, US 199, runs to Crescent City, California. It crosses and runs up the valley of the Illinois River, a pleasant stream that flows north to the Rogue in convoluted meanders, before brushing the northern limit of redwood forests. En route, it passes a few wineries, and many old mining sites.

White-water rafting on the North Umpqua River.
(opposite) Oregon Caves Chateau is a National Historic Monument.

A 45-minute, winding drive climbs from Cave Junction to the 4,000-foot-high cave entrance to **Oregon Caves National Monument.** The cedar-shake **Cave Chateau,** a huge rustic inn, snugs in against the waterfall-streaked hillside. The caves are a subterranean wonderland of limestone formations. Three miles of trails are mapped, but the networks may be far more extensive. Tickets for cave tours are sold next to the gift shop. The tour is strenuous, and the air in the caves, cold. Dress warmly.

■ JACKSONVILLE

Jacksonville, five miles west of Medford, had a gold boom in 1852. After gold ran out, Jacksonville almost became a ghost town, but it is now a paean to historic preservation with antique shops, pear trees, and the Britt Festival, a summer-long outdoor music festival.

Peter Britt, Jacksonville's most revered pioneer, was a Swiss-born photographer and painter. Back in the days when photography meant heavy cameras and glass-plate negatives, Britt lugged his equipment all over the wilds of southern Oregon. (He was the first to photograph Crater Lake.) He was also an amateur horticultur-ist and his gardens are still a quiet, lovely grove. He was a pioneer Oregon vintner and is also remembered for introducing fruit trees. Like Ashland's Shakespeare Festival, the Britt Festival is hugely popular, and for good reason. The hillside setting lends itself to a relaxed, picnic-like atmosphere, and the good feeling rubs off on the performers, who run the gamut from bluegrass to classical musicians. For tickets and information call (541) 773-6077.

Also of interest is the town's **Museum of Southern Oregon History.** Exhibits tell the story of the Applegate Trail and Jacksonville's gold rush days. Next door, the old jail houses a Children's Museum. Located at 206 N Fifth Street; (541) 773-6536.

■ ASHLAND

A cultural hub, the charming theater town of Ashland is home to good bookstores and excellent restaurants. The half-timbered **Elizabethan Theatre** was being torn apart when Shakespeare aficionado Angus Bowmer noticed that, without the domed roof, the building bore an amazing resemblance to Shakespeare's Globe

Theatre. Ashland residents built a 16th-century-style stage, dug through attics for clothes to use as costumes, and put on a show. The first Shakespeare Festival was staged in 1935.

Since then, it's been unstoppable. Three theaters now run 11 plays in repertoire from mid-February through October. Shakespeare is always represented in the Oregon Shakespeare Festival's outdoor **Elizabethan Theatre,** but most of the plays staged in the large **Angus Bowmer Theatre** or the smaller **Black Swan** are by other playwrights. Backstage tours and lectures are all enjoyable. Book in advance, and call the box office for the schedule; (541) 482-4331.

Lithia Plaza, at the town's hub, has two fountains spewing alkaline lithia water. It probably takes a special palate to appreciate its odoriferous effervescence. Lithia Park is a 100-acre corridor of trees, tennis courts, playgrounds, and Japanese gardens overlooked by the theaters. Trails lead from here into the wild mountains west of town.

During the off season, room rates plummet, and locals head south to Mount Ashland's ski slopes. In summer, the top of Mount Ashland has one of the most beautiful displays of wildflowers in the region.

■ CRATER LAKE

Gold miners stumbled across Crater Lake in 1853. It was formed after the eruption of Mount Mazama 7,700 years ago. A violent explosion emptied the magma chamber of 10,000-foot-high Mount Mazama and blasted fiery ash beyond Bend. The mountain top collapsed into a 2,000-foot-deep pit. Lava continued to pulse up from the bottom of the basin, building smallish cones, including Wizard Island, which now breaks the surface of the lake.

A thousand years later, the caldera filled to within 1,000 feet of its rim with rainwater. No streams flow into or out of Crater Lake; it gains and loses water from precipitation and evaporation. Crater Lake is Oregon's only national park, and the country's deepest lake.

The road to the lake from Klamath Falls climbs past big ponderosa pines until it reaches the crater's rim. There you can park, walk across the road past historic **Crater Lake Lodge,** and look down into the lake, where blue sky is reflected in the lake. Its water is 1,932 feet deep, a constant 39 degrees, and so clear you can read the face of a (hopefully waterproof) watch six feet below the surface.

(following pages) On the rim of the crater surrounding Crater Lake. Wizard Island can be seen rising as a perfect cone from the middle of the lake.

From the north rim, you can take a steep trail down to the water and catch the lake tour boat. (A boat leaves every hour; tickets are available at the dock.) Winter is incredible at Crater Lake. The southern entrance is plowed year round, but the rim road is closed to all but cross-country skiers (the lakeside concession rents skis). Within yards of the rim parking lot, the only sounds beyond the chatter of Clark's nutcrackers and gray jays is the *whoosh* of snow falling from tree branches.

■ TRAVEL AND CLIMATE

■ GETTING THERE

This is a region of tall mountains, several broad and beautiful valleys, and deeply cut, swift-flowing rivers.

By Car. Interstate 5, the main north-south road, is quite curvy south of Eugene. Watch for ice in spring, fall, and winter. Carry chains because several of the mountain passes are above 1,500 feet, and 4,310-foot Siskiyou Summit, just north of the California state line, can be a nightmare to drive even in pleasant weather. In winter, snow can pile up in prodigious quantities. Several times each winter, snow falls in the valleys, too. US 199, a two-lane highway, is the main road to the coast. It too can be slick and icy and may be temporarily closed if winter snowfall is too heavy. Inquire in Grants Pass if you're in doubt about road conditions.

■ CLIMATE

The weather of this mountain wonderland can be very cold in winter and hot in summer. Spring and autumn are balmy and sunny, providing almost ideal conditions for hiking, fishing, or boating.

■ ACCOMMODATIONS AND RESTAURANTS

⌂　　For chain lodgings see toll-free numbers on page 352.

$$　　For room and restaurant price designations see page 352.

★　　Means highly recommended.

ASHLAND

⌂ **Chanticleer Inn.**
120 Gresham; (541) 482-1919
Only a few blocks from the Shakespeare Festival theaters, this bed-and-breakfast inn seems in its own peaceful world. $$$

⌂ ✕ **Winchester Country Inn.**
35 S Second St.; (541) 488-1113.
Attractive, uncluttered rooms; near to the theaters. Excellent restaurant. $$$

⊺ Columbia Hotel.
E Main between 1st and Second Sts.;
(541) 482-3726
A small, friendly, nicely renovated hotel,
downtown. $-$$

✗ **Ashland Bakery & Cafe.**
38 E Main St.; (541) 482-2117.
A good place to hear breakfast chatter
about last night's shows. $-$$

✗ **Chateaulin.** ✫✫✫
50 E Main; (541) 482-2264.
This delightful French cafe near the
Bowmer Theatre serves dinner only but
stays open for the after-theater crowd,
who appreciate the good bar menu. $$-
$$$

✗ **Macaroni's Ristorante.**
58 E Main St.; (541) 488-3359
Italian food, better than the name
would suggest. $$

AZALEA

✗ **Heaven on Earth.**
Exit 86 from Interstate 5, Quines Creek
Rd.; (541) 837-3596
The sugar rush from a gargantuan
cinnamon roll will fuel you clear to San
Francisco. $-$$

CAVE JUNCTION

⊺ **Oregon Caves Chateau.**
20000 Cave Hwy.; (541) 592-3400
The rustic wood chalet is open May
through October. It's built practically on
top of a waterfall, and the entrance to
the caves is just across the drive. At
Oregon Caves National Monument.
$$-$$$

✗ **Cave Junction Pizza Deli and Brewery;**
249 N Redwood Hwy.;
(541) 592-3556.
The setting is unlikely, with no more
charm than a doublewide trailer, but the
Nut Brown Ale is a prize winner. Most
of their beer-making is in the British
tradition. Their pizza is sliced into small
parallelograms. $

CRATER LAKE

⊺ **Crater Lake Lodge.**
At Crater Lake; (541) 830-8700
Newly renovated historic lodge at the
crater's rim. $$$

⊺ **Prospect Hotel.**
391 Mill Creek Rd.; Prospect;
(541) 560-3664 .
Tidy, renovated inn. $$

⊺ **Union Creek Resort.**
On Hwy. 62 north of Prospect; (541)
560-3339
Stay in the rustic creekside cabins. $

CRESCENT LAKE

⊺ **Odell Lake Lodge.**
East Odell Lake; (541) 433-2540
Just off Hwy. 58, near the southern end
of the Cascade Lakes Hwy. Lodge room,
cabins, a restaurant, a mountain lake
with boat rentals, mountain bike/cross
country ski trails, and friendly
proprietors. $$

GALICE

⊺ **Galice Resort.**
(541) 476-3818
Right on the Rogue, they offer raft rentals
and guided trips, cabins, and a lodge.
$-$$

GRANT'S PASS

▣ **Morrison's Rogue River Lodge.**
8500 Galice Rd.; (541) 476-3825
Full resort facilities on the Rogue. Very comfortable. $$$

▣ **Paradise Ranch Inn.**
700 W Monument Dr.; (541) 479-4333
Don't confuse this with the Paradise Bar Lodge. This is a guest ranch-turned-resort. $$-$$$

▣ **Rogue Valley Resort,**
7799 Rogue River Hwy.; (541) 582-3762. $-$$

✕ **Pongsri's.**
1571 NE 6th St.; (541) 479-1345
You wouldn't expect to find a good Thai restaurant in Grants Pass, but life is full of wonderful surprises. $

JACKSONVILLE

▣✕**Jacksonville Inn.**
175 E California St.; (541) 899-1900 or (800) 321-9344
An old eight-room hotel with tiny rooms and claustrophobic showers upstairs, and a dressy restaurant downstairs. $$$

MEDFORD

✕ **La Burrita.** West of town on Hwy. 238 (2715 Jacksonville Hwy.);
(541) 770-5770
It's cheap, authentic, and tasty. $
(541) 849-2570

STEAMBOAT

▣✕**Steamboat Inn and Restaurant.** ✭✭
38 miles east of Roseburg on Hwy. 138; (541) 498-2411
Cabins, cottages, and suites available; a fine, well-known establishment, well thought of by locals and tourists alike. Closed January and February. Gourmet fishermen's dinners served just after dark so fishermen can pull up that last catch; cafe-style breakfasts and lunches also available. Rustic, but reservations required for dinner. $$$

TALENT

✕ **New Sammy's Cowboy Bistro.** ✭✭
2210 South Pacific Hwy., between Talent and Ashland; (541) 535-2779
Great food served by the former chef of California's New Boonville Hotel in a tiny, very rustic cottage. Take the street address along; the place is unmarked. But be sure to make a reservation. $$

WOLF CREEK

✕ **Wolf Creek Tavern.** 100 Railroad Ave.; (541) 866-2474
Built in 1857 as a stagecoach stop, the tavern has hosted Jack London, Sinclair Lewis, and Rutherford B. Hayes. Between Roseburg and Grants Pass. $$

Crater Lake Lodge is a great, historic National Park lodge in the same league as other greats such as the Yellowstone and Glacier Park lodges.

OREGON COAST

■ HIGHLIGHTS

Astoria
Fort Clatsop
Seaside
Cannon Beach
Tillamook Bay
Cape Perpetua
Oregon Dunes
Bandon

■ LANDSCAPE

ON THE OREGON COAST cold green waves
thunder toward evergreen headlands and
craggy shorelines. Sea foam cold as shaved ice rolls up onto beachcombers' bare
feet and curls around the fantastic forms of gray driftwood. Offshore lie fog-
shrouded rocky islands filled with nesting seabirds. In winter, storms thunder in
off the Pacific; during the summer, fog hovers over the coast. The ocean spray is so
refreshing that even sedentary people seem game for long walks. Cliffside houses
range from the palatial to weathered shacks, and the generally uncrowded beaches
belong to the people.

Rocky headlands and cliffs alternate with sandy beaches which shelter estuaries
and marshes—home of birds and other wildlife—from the ocean's fury. Oregon's
beaches are public. In 1967, a bill was enacted that provided public access to the
dry sand areas above the high-tide mark.

State parks, many with campsites, stipple the Oregon coast. Even on summer
weekends, when Portlanders flock to Lincoln City and Cannon Beach, the long,
broad beaches don't seem crowded. For real solitude, head to the south coast, pick
a remote wayside, walk a hundred yards from the parking lot, and it'll be you and
the sandpipers, investigating wave-tossed logs and huge hanks of kelp.

❖

The high surf of the Columbia River bar long obscured the river from early navigators, but in May of 1792, Boston sea captain Robert Gray took a chance and sailed toward the bar and into the river he named after his ship. American explorers Lewis and Clark spent a wet winter at Fort Clatsop near the mouth of the Columbia in 1805, and half a dozen years later, John Jacob Astor set up a fur-trading post in what is now Astoria. (It was sold to the British during the war of 1812 to keep them from seizing it.)

■ ASTORIA AND THE LOWER COLUMBIA RIVER

Driving to the coast on US 30 from Portland, you'll be tracing the route Lewis and Clark took, recalling the rainy-day passages of the journals describing "wet, cold, and miserable" weather—which hasn't changed one bit.

The Columbia River ushers travelers into **Astoria**, a gritty fishing and lumber port with many Victorian houses. From a hillside vantage point, or from a seat on a wharf, it's easy to imagine days long gone by, when Scandinavian fishermen ran gill-

A view of Astoria and its harbor in the 1880s. (Columbia River Maritime Museum)

NORTH COAST

0   5   10   20
miles

Elevation

	feet
	11,235
	9,250
	7,750
	6,250
	5,000
	4,000
	3,000
	2,000
	1,000

net boats, and Chinese laborers skinned fish in the riverside salmon canneries. Mammoth logs from the coastal mountains were, and still are, hoisted onto ships. Now they're sent, uncut, to Asia.

You might want to set aside an hour or two for a visit to the first-rate Maritime Museum on the river. The museum is on the south side of US 30 as you drive into town from the east. You can't miss it because there's a lightship moored right outside. If you have time, you might also want to drive up the hill and climb the 125-foot-high Astoria Column, a monument with a spiral frieze depicting much of Astoria's early history. From the top of the tower, the topography of rivers, bays, and estuaries becomes clear, and the urge to climb down and explore the countryside becomes strong.

Fort Clatsop, where Lewis and Clark spent the winter of 1805 is located southwest of Astoria on the west bank of the Lewis and Clark River. The reconstructed quarters of Lewis and Clark's winter camp seem quite cramped for 33 people and a Newfoundland dog. In summer, park staff presents historical re-enactments, but a damp, chilly winter visit on a day when the sun never really shines, and then sets at 4:00 P.M., will etch the experience deeper.

❖

Before striking out southbound on US 101, drive west to **Fort Stevens State Park,** near the town of Hammond, where a road leads to the end of Clatsop Spit. It's here that the Columbia flows into the Pacific. Pilots from neon-orange boats guide freighters over the bar. Fishing boats take it on their own, sometimes with a few knocks.

■ RESORT COAST

Back on US 101, in **Seaside,** Oregon's northernmost full-fledged beach town, be prepared for high-camp tourism. Ben Holladay, a Portland transportation mogul, built a resort here in the 1870s, and it became a Victorian-era hotspot. It's the coast's only town with a boardwalk (called "The Prom"). There's also a cruising street (Broadway), with a beachside loop ("The Turnaround").

Cannon Beach, nine miles down US 101 from Seaside, has long been labeled "artsy." The streets are jammed on summer weekends as people shop and enjoy **Cannon Beach Book Company,** or **Bill's Tavern.** You can escape the crowds by

Sunset behind the sea stacks of Cannon Beach.

walking or flying a kite on the broad, sandy beach. Thousands of seabirds crowd onto **Haystack Rock**, and tidepools cradle anemones that look like peppermint candies. There's summer theater, but the social event of the year is the **Sandcastle Contest,** held in late May or early June, when teams build shell- and seaweed-trimmed fantasies.

Oswald West State Park rises above Short Sands Beach, a sheltered cove at the foot of Neahkanie Mountain 10 miles south of Cannon Beach with waves big enough to draw surfers and kayakers. The coast's best campground is in an old-growth grove nestling 36 walk-in campsites. A trail from the campground leads through big trees and a thick understory out to the tip of Cape Falcon, which affords views south to Manzanita. A second trail begins across the highway from the campground and winds up Neahkanie Mountain.

Some of the north coast's best views are from US 101 between the park and the town of **Manzanita.** Manzanita is small and unhurried, "what Cannon Beach used to be," people lament. For local sagas or surfing tips, stop by Manzanita News and Espresso, or enjoy a great meal at Jarboe's. Spring and fall storms bring good beachcombing.

Nehalem, just southeast of Manzanita, on the eastern edge of tiny Nehalem Bay, is even smaller and less rushed than its neighbor.

■ TILLAMOOK BAY AND VICINITY

Tillamook Bay's main fishing port is **Garibaldi,** near the bay's northern edge. Fish merchants line US 101. Travelers can make an easy picnic of Dungeness crab, which come cleaned, cooked, and ready to eat. Or drop by Smith's Pacific Shrimp Company, out on the docks, for freshly caught and cooked shrimp.

East of Garibaldi, the bay is often filled with sea birds: cormorants, oystercatchers, grebes, harlequin ducks, and an assortment of gulls.

Tillamook is known for its lushly green pasture land. Local dairy farmers co-operatively own the Tillamook County Creamery Association, which supplies the **Tillamook cheese factory.** More people stop at the cheese factory, on the northern edge of Tillamook, than at any other spot on the coast. There's a self-guided tour of the factory, an exhibit extolling the virtues of butterfat, and an excellent gift shop selling Oregon products.

■ Spit, a Cape, and Three Heads

Three storm-tossed Pacific capes south of Tillamook are worth a detour. To reach them follow US 101 to OR 6 then swing back west from US 101 (this "Three Cape Loop" is well marked), then continue south on US 101 near Pacific City. If you're coming up from the south, look for signs directing you to the Three Capes Loop where US 101 swings away from the coast east of Pacific City. From the Three Capes Loop Road west of Tillamook, Bayocean Road runs north along the edge of Tillamook Bay. Bird-watchers walk or bike out on the seven-mile-long spit coming up from the south end of the bay. In late summer, thousands of sandpipers run across the mudflats. (You can also reach the spit by way of the Cape Meares Loop road, which runs north from Netarts through Oceanside and connects with Bayocean Road at the junction with Bayocean Dike Road.)

At **Cape Meares State Park,** parrot-billed puffins nest in the cliff, and sea lions, harbor seals, and murres frequent the surf-washed rocks.

Cape Lookout, the next cape south, sticks out into the Pacific like a finger. A well-marked trail here twists from the campground through big old spruce, hemlock, and cedar trees to Cape Lookout, offering long views north to Cape Meares and south to **Cascade Head.** Whales migrate south to Baja from December to February; then they go into reverse and head north to Alaska from March to May, with April the peak of migration. **Depoe Bay,** south of here, is the best place to join a whale-watching charter boat.

Cape Kiwanda, the southernmost cape on the Three Cape Loop, is a fine place to pit your leg muscles against sand. The trail leads up the high sandy cape to its windy head and, from a sheltered spot, affords a view of waves crashing far below. This is a place to feel as big as king of the hill, or as small as a speck of blowing sand. Hang gliders take off from Kiwanda for circuitous trips to sea level. In the mid-1960s, the Nature Conservancy acquired **Cascade Head,** between Neskowin and Lincoln City, preserving the sitka spruce, hemlock, and alder forests and the native prairie on the headland. Access to the two-mile trail is from Three Rocks Road; the parking area is just beyond the Sitka Center.

Five small towns between Cascade Head and the Siletz River grew together in 1965 to become **Lincoln City.** From the north end of town, Highway 18 takes off toward McMinnville and Portland. Minutes from the coast, in the hamlet of **Otis,** is the Otis Cafe, known for its pie.

■ NEWPORT AND VICINITY

Newport is enlivened by its active bayfront fishing port. It's certainly given a boost by the bustle at Nye Beach, an old-time beach resort gone derelict until the Sylvia Beach Hotel launched a neighborhood renaissance in the mid-1980s. The Sylvia Beach, a "hotel for booklovers," is as good as they come.

Newport's big draw is the **Oregon Aquarium,** where jellyfish swim through a room-sized cylindrical aquarium that glows like a beautiful lava lamp, and a giant octopus lives outside in a rock crevice surrounded by an aviary, where puffins and other seabirds fly. Keiko, an orca, is the (somewhat spoiled) latest attraction. She's been given a color TV in the hopes of diverting her from the boredom she must feel. (Orcas, the largest members of the porpoise family, are highly intelligent, and move through the oceans in family groups, playing and hunting together.)

Newport's old-town bayfront fishing village is a good place to enjoy a bowl of clam chowder while watching boats sail in and out of the harbor, and sea lions bob in the waves.

Tidal pools rich with mussels, starfish, and sea anemones dot the shoreline of Oregon as do lighthouses on many of the headlands. Above is Heceta Head Lighthouse, located about 12 miles north of Florence.

■ YACHATS AND CAPE PERPETUA

South of Newport, the Coast Range presses closer to the sea, and commercial hustle gives way to tidepools, sea lions, and whales. **Yachats** [YAH-HOTS] may be the perfect coast town. It's close to the water, nearly buried in salal and huckleberry. From April until October, sea-run smelt hurl themselves up the Yachats River, aiming straight toward clever, triangular smelt nets. **Cape Perpetua,** the epitome of the rocky, wild Oregon coast, is just a few miles south of Yachats. The picture window at the Cape Perpetua Visitor Center is a good place to watch for whales. Even if it's raining, it's worth taking the short walk to the **Devil's Churn,** where the ocean cleaves a thick basalt flow into a narrow chasm. Starfish keep a stubborn suction-grip on the sides of the wave-battered basalt cliffs. Chartreuse rock-top slime grows a stone's throw from a damp, dark-green forest. An oceanside trail continues south from Devil's Churn, and it's easy to spend a morning staring at the waves and poking into tidepools.

If, along the beaches, you notice small sand dunes that seem to be made of shells, they're middens formed by the Alsea Indians, who used these beaches regularly, and left behind the refuse of their meals: clam, oyster, crab, and mussel shells.

The area around Yachats and Cape Perpetua has stretches of coastal temperate rainforest. Two small wilderness areas, Cummins Creek and Rock Creek, are enveloped in a canopy of sitka spruce, Douglas fir, western hemlock, and western red cedar. A trail up **Cummins Creek** leads to a rainforest with nine-foot-diameter spruce trees growing among downed and decomposing nurse logs. Almost all the ground is covered by a dense green mat of salal and ferns.

■ FLORENCE AND VICINITY

An elevator drops 208 feet to **Sea Lion Caves,** tucked under the cliffs between Cape Perpetua and Florence. At the bottom are great close-up views of the 800-pound behemoths lounging and playing in the cave. Sea lions are usually visible in the ocean near the cave's entrance from the clifftop parking lot. It's pretty easy to tell Oregon coast pinnipeds apart: sea lions tend to be larger than seals, and unlike their smaller brethren, they have ears and can get up onto all fours.

Darlingtonia Wayside, four miles north of Florence, is home to fragrant cedars, Oregon grape, salal, kinnickinnick, and delicate ferns surrounding a sphagnum bog filled with the coast's most fascinating plant, *Darlingtonia californica,* also known as cobra lily or pitcher plant. This is a flesh-eating plant, and while *Darlingtonias* rarely eat anything bigger than a bug, they grow a foot or two tall and they stand close together, and they look weird—as you look at them you feel like you're staring down into a snake pit. Trails and wooden boardwalks lead on through the bog.

All the original bridges on US 101 are distinctive, but the **bridge spanning the Siuslaw River** at Florence is particularly charming. It beckons one to leave the car and walk across, inspect the dark green river, and explore the old town beneath the bridge, a charming place to linger.

■ OREGON DUNES

The dense forests and seaside basalt cliffs of the northern coast are replaced by giant sand dunes from the mouth of the Siuslaw south to Coos Bay. Here ocean sands blow inland, forming vast shifting hills. In some places, these sand hills reach a couple of miles inland.

To get a sense of their scale, walk toward the ocean. There's an observation wayside halfway between Florence and Reedsport (10 miles from either town) where blue-topped posts guide hikers. On a sunny day, you can find warm spots in the lee of dunes—and enjoy spending an hour or two reading and napping in the sand.

European beach grass, introduced around 1900 to hold sand down and prevent it from blocking river channels, is forming a mat over the sand, and the dunes no longer blow and shift as they once did. Once dunes are held firmly in place, other vegetation takes hold, and grasses, shrubs, pines, and firs begin to cover the shifting sands.

■ SOUTH COAST

Coos Bay, with its Siamese twin **North Bend,** is the coast's largest city. It's the only place on the coast where buildings rise to five or six stories. Coos Bay ex-

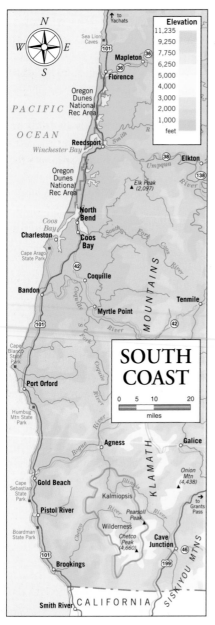

Elevation
11,235
9,250
7,750
6,250
5,000
4,000
3,000
2,000
1,000
feet

SOUTH
COAST

0   5   10   20
miles

ports more timber than any other port in the world, and it's the best natural harbor between San Francisco and Puget Sound. Local craftsmen are known for fashioning fragrant and durable myrtlewood into highly polished clocks, coffee tables, and salad bowls.

Charleston, eight miles southwest, is a fishing town, where you may wander around the docks. Seafood markets sell fresh local catch, and Qualman's Oyster Company, across the slough from town, (you guessed it) fresh oysters.

South on Seven Devils Road is **South Slough,** a broad estuary extending half a dozen miles inland. Hiking trails touch different habitats; the best trail takes two hours to hike and passes through coastal forest and 19th-century logging sites down to a boardwalk built across a swamp and a salt marsh (where sharp-edged grasses brush bare legs, and the humidity is broken by wisps of ocean breeze). Coos County was once strewn with such marshes (the city of Coos Bay was originally named Marshfield).

■ SMALL TOWNS OF THE
SOUTHERN COAST

Bandon has been livened up by artists and craftspeople. Across the mouth of the Coquille River from Bandon, a restored stucco lighthouse marks the bar. Though fishing boats tie up in downtown Bandon, summer winds make the bar crossing hazardous.

Some of the coast's most spectacular views are from the bluff at **Port Orford** when Humbug Mountain, south of town, is shrouded in misty clouds. To get a feel for the town, head down to the port. There are no boat slips or rampways—a hoist plucks boats from the water and lifts them onto the dock. Sport fishers go after rockfish, lingcod, and other bottomfish. Stacks of crab traps and mesh-net traps suspended inside chickenwire cubes crowd one end of the dock—the latter are used to catch sablefish ("black cod").

Port Orford is famous for its straight-grained and durable Port Orford cedar. Much of the harvest goes to Japan, where one tree may fetch up to $10,000. **Grassy Knob Wilderness Area,** seven miles east of the Cape Blanco turnoff, is a good place to see and smell these fragrant trees.

Gold Beach first attracted settlers in the 1850s when gold was found in its sands. After floods swept the beach clean of gold in 1861, the town survived on the timber harvest in the Coast Range and on the fishery in offshore waters. Mail boats started making the upstream trip to Agness in 1895, when it took several

Highway 101 snakes along the southern coastline between Cape Sebastian and Pistol River State Park.

days of rowing to travel the 32 miles from Gold Beach; now, jet boats shoot upriver in two hours.

Boardman State Park, north of Brookings, is a long strip with many waysides, where trails lead down steep cliffs to sheltered coves. These beaches are rarely crowded; a hundred yards past the parking lot your only companions will be birds and waves and rocks.

Brookings is, all winter long, the warmest spot in the state. The fishing port of **Harbor,** on the south side of the **Chetco River,** is a good place to hang out and chat with the locals. In season, fields are white with flowers, as Brookings grows most of the nation's Easter lilies.

The banks of the broad, shallow Chetco River are lined with myrtlewood trees. Their bay-like leaves are used to season food. **Loeb Park,** off North Bank Road, is flush with salmonberries and myrtlewood trees. From Quail Prairie on the edge of the Kalmiopsis Wilderness Area, it's a short 1.4-mile hike to **Vulcan Lake,** which nests in a glaciated red peridotite basin, a favorite swimming hole for Brookings residents. Here, you're far from coastal fog and into the hot, dry zone of the Kalmiopsis. To get to the trailhead for Vulcan Lake involves a bit of driving: You head east from Brookings on Northbank Chetco River Road/CR 784 (the last road north of the Chetco River Bridge, on the east side of the road). The road turns into a well-maintained gravel road after a few miles; and the trailhead is at mile 31.5.

■ TRAVEL AND CLIMATE

■ GETTING THERE
US 101, a slow, winding, two-lane road, is the one north-south highway. OR 126 runs inland from Florence to Eugene; US 20 takes you inland from Newport; OR 18 runs from north of Lincoln City to the Yamhill wine country and Portland.

■ CLIMATE
The Oregon Coast is a water wonderland in more ways than one. Summer and winter it is often cold and rainy—or foggy. Even sunny days tend to be cooled down by chill winds. Bring warm clothes.

■ ACCOMMODATIONS AND RESTAURANTS

☎ For chain lodgings see toll-free numbers on page 352.

$$ For room and restaurant price designations see page 352.

★ Means highly recommended.

AGNESS
(SOUTH COAST)

☎ **Lucas Lodge.**
Call for directions; (541) 247-7443
Get a myrtlewood-shaded cabin and explore the nearby Lower Rogue River Trail. $-$$

ASTORIA
(NORTH COAST)

☎ **Crest Motel.**
5366 Leif Erickson Dr.; (503) 325-3141 or (800) 421-3141
Basic rooms with fine river views. $$

☎ **Red Lion.**
400 Industry St.; (503) 325-7373 or (800) 547-8010.
Likewise, but right on the harbor, and you can feed the seagulls right from your balcony. $$$

✗ **Columbian Cafe.**
1114 W Marine Dr. at 11th St.; (503) 325-2233
Come with time on your hands and a willingness to be engaged in social and political commentary. Astoria's newspaper editor may have a challenger to his status as pundit-in-residence here — the waitress and cook are crackerjack analysts. (And the *huevos* are definitely worth the wait.) $

✗ **Ship's Inn Restaurant.**
1 Second St. at the river's edge; (503) 325-0033

View and good fish and chips (though the fish and chips at the Red Lion Coffee shop have been better, at times.) $-$$

BANDON
(SOUTH COAST)

☎ **Sea Star Hostel and Guest House.**
375 Second St.; (541) 347-9632
Budget travelers should stay in the hostel; for a little more privacy, go for a guest room. $-$$$

✗ **Andrea's.**
160 Baltimore Ave; (541) 347-3022
A Bandon hangout for well over a decade. The breakfast blintzes are as good as ever, and the whole-grain ambiance has aged as well as good wine. Good homegrown lamb. $$

BROOKINGS
(SOUTH COAST)

☎ **Best Western Beachfront Inn.**
16008 Boat Basin Rd.; (541) 469-7779
Modern hotel at the harbor. All 78 rooms have ocean views. $

☎ **Chetco River Inn.**
21202 High Prairie Rd. off North Bank Rd.; (800) 327-2688
Seventeen miles up the Chetco from town (the last few miles on a gravel road), but you won't regret the drive. Fishing's a big attraction, and it's a good place to just relax by the river. $$-$$$

X **Rubio's.**
1136 Chetco Ave.; (541) 469-4919
Back before anybody in Oregon had
given half a thought to tomatillos, the
Rubio brothers started this tiny Mexican
restaurant. Chile rellenos have a light
touch, and seafood dishes are quite
good. $-$$

*CANNON BEACH
(NORTH COAST)*

☷ **Cannon Beach Hotel.**
1116 S. Hemlock St.; (503) 436-1392
Erstwhile loggers' boardinghouse now a
cozy hotel. $$-$$$

☷ **Sea Sprite Motel.**
Nebesna and Oceanfront (Tolovana
Park); (503) 436-2266
South of town near Haystack Rock, this
has beachfront rooms with great views.
$$ (winter) and $$$ (summer)

*CHARLESTON
(SOUTH COAST)*

☷ **Captain John's Motel.**
Kingfisher and Boat Basin Drs.;
(541) 888-4041
Commercial and sport anglers stay here
(note the fish-cleaning tables), and it's
ideal for anybody who wants to brush
up against fishing culture. $-$$

X **Portside Inn.**
Kingfisher Rd. at the Boat Basin;
(541) 888-5544
Fish and chips with a view onto the har-
bor. Try the Friday night seafood buffet.
Charleston boat basin. $

*COOS BAY
(SOUTH COAST)*

X **Blue Heron Bistro.**
Commercial Ave. and S Broadway (US
101 S); (541) 267-3933
A comfortable spot with good seafood
and salads. $-$$

*DEPOE BAY
(NORTH COAST)*

☷ **Channel House.**
35 Ellington St.; (541) 765-2140
Good storm- and whale-watching from
very comfortable rooms perched right
on the ocean's edge. $$$

*FLORENCE
(SOUTH COAST)*

X **Alpha Bits Cafe.**
10780 Hwy. 126, 10 miles east of Flo-
rence in Mapleton; (541) 268-4311
Great veggie food. $

X **Bridgewater Seafood Restaurant.**
1297 Bay across from the wharf;
(541) 997-9405
Remarkably good clam chowder in old-
town Florence. $$

*GOLD BEACH
(SOUTH COAST)*

☷ **Rogue River wilderness lodges** following: They're all woodsy and remote,
with loyal clienteles. Reserve well in advance. (800) 525-2161

☷ **Half Moon Bar Lodge.**
(541) 247-6968
Jet boat, float, or hike in. It's 11 miles
upriver from Foster Bar. Cozy, with gen-
erator power supplementing the kero-
sene lamps. $$

🛏 **Illahe Lodge.**
(541) 247-6111
This small anglers' resort is seven miles up the Rogue from Agness, at the end of the Agness-Illahe Road. Jet boats stop here, too. **$$**

🛏 **Jot's Resort.**
(541) 247-6676
A nice riverside spot right by the north end of the US 101 bridge. Jet boats load up with passengers here. **$$**

🛏 **Paradise Bar Lodge.**
(541) 247-6022
Float, hike, or jet-boat in. Just above Half Moon. **$$**

🛏 **Tu Tu'Tun Lodge.**
96550 North Bank Rogue;
(541) 247-6664
Far enough from town yet with enough casual Northwest elegance to be a fine retreat. **$$$**

*LINCOLN CITY
(NORTH COAST)*

🛏 **Ester Lee Motel.**
3803 SW Hwy. 101; (541) 996-3606
High '50s style on the beach. **$$**

🛏 ✕ **Salishan Lodge.**
Gleneden Beach (between Lincoln City and Depoe Bay); (541) 764-3600 or (800) 452-2300
This sheltered resort has a golf course but no beach—it's a long walk through mud flats to the ocean. Come for golf, swimming in pool, tennis, or walks through landscaped wooded grounds. **$$$**
People will tell you Salishan Lodge has one of Oregon's best restaurants. **$$$**

Harbor seals lounging on the rocks near Strawberry Hill State Wayside.

✗ **Chez Jeanette.** ✶
Old US 101, just south of Salishan in
Gleneden Beach; (541) 764-3434
More intimate and less formal than its
neighbor. Good French food and
Northwest-style cuisine. **$$**

*MANZANITA
(NORTH COAST)*

☖ **Inn at Manzanita.**
67 Laneda Ave.; (503) 368-6754
Small inn with well-appointed rooms a
block from the beach. **$$$**

✗ **Blue Sky Cafe.**
154 Laneda Ave.; (503) 368-5712
Comfortable cafe where locals mingle
with visitors. It's worth waiting for the
innovative food. **$$**

✗ **Jarboe's.** ✶✶✶
137 Laneda Ave.; (503) 368-5113
A small (eight-table) restaurant in a con-
verted cottage with cooked meats and
seafoods sauced to flavorful perfection.
Well worth a special trip! **$$**

*NEWPORT
(NORTH COAST)*

☖ **Sylvia Beach Hotel.**
267 NW Cliff St.; (541) 265-5428.
At this "hotel for booklovers," theme
rooms are devoted to favorite authors,
and the library is the place to hang out.
Good management and interesting
guests keep it from feeling contrived.
Budget lodging in dorm rooms. Dinners
are family-style, with lots of good con-
versation between diners. **$-$$$**

✗ **Canyon Way Restaurant and
Bookstore.**
Near the intersection of Hwy. 101 and
Hurbert on Canyon Way;
(541) 265-8319
Book sales-reps like this one. **$**

✗ **Whale's Tale.**
452 SW Bay Blvd.;
(541) 265-8660
It's long been the best breakfast spot in
town, and a strong contender for the
best lunch burger or seafood dinner as
well. **$$**

*OCEANSIDE
(NORTH COAST)*

✗ **Roseanna's.** ✶
1490 Pacific (part of US 101);
(503) 842-7351
Good seafood, rich desserts, great view.
$-$$

*OTIS
(NORTH COAST)*

✗ **Otis Cafe.**
Hwy. 18 at Otis Junction;
(541) 994-2813
People say they're going to Lincoln City,
but they really spend the day eating
strawberry-rhubarb pie at the Otis. **$**

*YACHATS (NORTH
COAST)*

✗ **La Serre.** ✶✶
Second and Beach; (541) 547-3420
Great breakfasts. People have been
known to get up early in Portland, drive
four hours for a late breakfast here,
spend the afternoon at Cape Perpetua,
then drive home. **$$**

R E G I O N A L
T R A V E L   I N F O R M A T I O N

Note: Compass American Guides makes every effort to ensure the accuracy of its information; however, as conditions and prices change frequently, we recommend that readers also contact the general numbers listed below for up-to-date information.

■ ABOUT ACCOMMODATIONS

Smaller inns and lodgings are listed after chapters describing the area in which they can be found. A few general information numbers are as follows:

Washington Tourism. (800) 544-1800
Pacific Bed & Breakfast Agency. (206) 784-0539
Tourism B.C. (800) 663-6000
Oregon Tourism. (800) 543-8838 (in OR); (800) 547-7842 (out of state)

■ ROOM RATES AND RESTAURANT PRICES

Even though you are dealing with two currencies in the Pacific Northwest—U.S. and Canadian dollars—the dollar amounts charged per night are similar. If you're a U.S. citizen, just figure that every time you are quoted a rate in Canadian dollars, you get an automatic 25 to 30 percent discount (depending on the day's exchange rate); and if you're Canadian, unhappily, it's vice versa. Try to pay by credit card whenever possible. It gets you the best exchange rate.

Restaurant prices:
Per person, without drinks, tax, or tips:
$ = under $15; $$ = $15–30; $$$ = over $30

Room rates:
Per night, per room, double occupancy:
$ = under $70; $$ = $70–100; $$$ = over $100

Note: In B.C. these designations refer to Canadian dollars.

■ CHAIN HOTELS AND MOTELS

For chain lodging it's best to call the following toll free numbers to see what's available at what price.

Best Western. (800) 528-1234	**ITT Sheraton.** (800) 325-3535
Days Inn. (800) 325-2525	**Marriott Hotels.** (800) 228-9290
Doubletree. (800) 222-TREE	**Radisson.** (800) 333-3333.
Hilton Hotels. (800) HILTONS	**Ramada Inns.** (800) 2-RAMADA
Holiday Inn. (800) HOLIDAY	**Stouffers.** (800) HOTELS-1
Hyatt Hotels. (800) 233-1234	**Westin Hotels.** (800) 228-3000

■ CAMPING IN THE WET NORTHWEST

Don't rule out camping. It's one of the best ways to get a feel for some of the region's wilder areas. If it rains, be sure to pitch your tent under a spreading cedar, Douglas fir, or pine. And dig a shallow ditch to drain off surface water. Most state and provincial park campgrounds are fairly developed (read "showers") and on well-beaten paths. Many Pacific Northwest campgrounds have wooden picnic shelters adjacent to the campsites (some with electrical outlets and fireplaces), allowing you to stay dry even in the wettest night. The **Ministry of Parks in British**

Columbia will provide information on individual parks at (604) 387-5002; as will the **Washington Parks and Recreation Commission** at (206) 874-1283; the **National Parks and Forests Outdoor Recreation Information Center** at (206) 220-7450; and the **Oregon State Parks Information Center** at (800) 551-6949. Be advised that, due to budget cuts, several popular Oregon state parks have been closed in the off-season. National Forest and BLM sites are generally more primitive (pit toilets), more remote, and less expensive.

■ FOOD TOURS

Our four Food Tours and our essay on where to buy good seafood, will introduce you to the best the Northwest produces:

1 Okanagan Valley Winery Tour, page 78

2 Apple, Cheese and Oyster Tour, page 162

3 Buying Northwest Seafood, page 223

4 Yakima Valley Wine and Food Tour, page 248

5 Willamette Valley Hazelnut and Wine Tour, page 312

■ FOOD IN THE PACIFIC NORTHWEST

For restaurant price designations see the preceding page.
Individual restaurant listings follow each chapter.

The Northwest is truly a food paradise. Its waters produce some of America's best oysters, crabs, clams, shrimp, and prawns. Apples, pears, peaches, apricots, plums, raspberries, blueberries, strawberries, and cherries grow plump in orchards on both sides of the Cascade Mountains. Yakima Valley farmers grow succulent asparagus and hotly flavorful peppers. Willamette Valley farmers are known for vegetables, wine grapes and hazelnuts. This is dairy country and fine local cheeses are being made, including Oregon blue. Mountain and coastal forests provide chanterelle and morel mushrooms, and cooks are learning to create more and better mushroom recipes.

The cooking is evolving from an old-time American style of cuisine—steaks and potatoes (with a questionable salad bar)—to an original Northwestern style of light, delectable dishes containing the freshest local ingredients. The wine grapes and vineyards are coming into their own, as growers learn what this region can produce best (Oregon is growing and producing varietals such as pinot gris, chardonnay, and zinfandel, but pinot noir is the local favorite). Microbreweries create hand-crafted beers, ales, and stouts from locally grown barley and hops.

As the reputation of Northwest Cuisine has spread, many people now travel here just to eat. Vancouver, Seattle, and Portland all have great restaurants, as has the countryside—often in unexpected places. Vancouver, with its huge influx of residents from Hong Kong, now abounds in excellent Chinese restaurants. The orchards of the Columbia Gorge produce apples, pears, and peaches. As for coffee, a real Northwest coffee house will make some of the best to be found anywhere.

■ TRANSPORTATION IN BRITISH COLUMBIA

By Air. Most major airlines fly into Vancouver International Airport and Victoria International Airport. Smaller carriers such as Horizon Air (800) 547-9308, Air Canada (604) 688-5515 or (800) 776-3000 in the U.S., and Harbour Air (604) 688-1277 in Vancouver or (800) 665-0212, serve smaller cities throughout the province, using floatplanes to reach remote communities.

Harbour Air in B.C. has a marine terminal on the downtown waterfront. Seaplanes fly from here to Victoria, the Gulf Islands, and Vancouver International Airport; (604) 537-5525; (800) 665-0212. Helijet Airways helicopters fly from a pad near the SeaBus terminal to downtown Victoria; (604) 273-1414; (604) 382-6222.

By Car. Major roads and most secondary roads are paved; back country roads are gravel. The Trans-Canada Highway (THC, Route 1), runs from Victoria (via ferry) and Vancouver to eastern Canada.

By Train. Amtrak links Vancouver to Seattle. For schedules and information call (800) 872-9181. VIA Rail is the Canadian equivalent of Amtrack (800) 561-8630. B.C. Rail runs daily trains to Whistler from the B.C. train station, 1311 West First Street, North Vancouver; (604) 631-3500; SkyTrain runs from Vancouver south to New Westminster and Surrey between 5 A.M. and 1 A.M. For route assistance, call B.C. Transit, (604) 521-0400. All of these trains are wheelchair accessible.

By Bus. Greyhound Lines has scheduled runs between Vancouver and other British Columbia cities and Seattle. For more information call (800) 231-2222.

By Ferry. B.C. Ferries: (604) 277-0277 in Vancouver has year-round passenger service between Vancouver and Tsawwassen (south of Vancouver), and to Swartz Bay (30 minutes by car north of Victoria), with frequent sailings. Ferries also run between Tsawwassen and Nanaimo and between Nanaimo and Horseshoe Bay (north of Vancouver). B.C. ferries also provide service to the Gulf Islands— reserve ahead, to the Sunshine Coast north of Howe Sound, from Port Hardy through the Inside Passage to Prince Rupert, from Port Hardy to Ocean Falls, Bella Coola and other remote settlements on the central coast, and from Prince Rupert to the Queen Charlotte Islands.

■ TRANSPORTATION IN WASHINGTON

By Air. Most major airlines fly into Sea-Tac International (Seattle-Tacoma). Horizon Air (not always dependable) and San Juan Airlines serve the smaller cities throughout the state.

By Train. Amtrak links Seattle to most major American cities, and from Seattle, Amtrak's *Mount Rainier* has frequent service to Tacoma, Olympia, and Portland, Oregon. For schedules and information, call (800) USA-RAIL.

By Bus. Greyhound Lines has the greatest number of scheduled bus routes in the state but runs mainly along I-5 and I-90. For more information call (800) 231-2222. Call the local chamber of commerce for the telephone numbers of independent companies that service towns and cities not along these two highways.

By Ferry. Washington operates the largest ferry system in the United States. Most of the ferries carry cars, although some smaller boats that run between Seattle and Bremerton or Bainbridge and Vashon islands carry passengers only. All ferries carry bikes. At commuting hours and on summer weekends, cars line up well in advance of the scheduled departure time.

A daily Washington State ferry carries cars and passengers between Anacortes (west of Mount Vernon) and Sidney, British Columbia (north of Victoria). Be sure to call ahead as there's been talk of cancelling this run. Call Washington State Ferries at (206) 464-6400 or when in Washington State (800) 84-FERRY.

■ TRANSPORTATION IN OREGON

By Air. Oregon's major airport is Portland International Airport. From there service is available to the state's smaller cities. Horizon Air is the main carrier (and not always dependable) for these short hops. Other major airports are located in Eugene, Medford, Bend, Klamath Falls, Pendleton, and North Bend.

By Train. Amtrak's north-south route runs through Klamath Falls, Eugene, and Portland. The train from Salt Lake City comes in through Baker City, La Grande, Pendleton, The Dalles, and Hood River before it reaches Portland.

The Oregon Tourism Division can be reached at (800) 547-7842.

■ CANADIAN–U.S. BORDER

Crossing the border is easy (in either direction) if you follow common sense rules.:

Passports. Be sure to bring a passport. A law signed in 1996 replaced an older one that required U.S. citizens to carry only a driver's license and voter registration card. Chances are that the border guards will not ask to see any identification, but if they do, and you don't have any, you may not be able to reenter the country. Depending on the traffic, crossing the border may take as little as five minutes or as much as an hour or more. The best times are early on weekday mornings or in the late evening.

Smuggling. Don't even think about smuggling. If you're caught, you may not only have to pay a fine or go to jail, but your car may be confiscated. Declare all weapons. Handguns are not allowed in Canada. If you carry one in your car, check it at the border and pick it up on your return.

Fruits, vegetables, and alcoholic beverages. All three are subject to special laws. You're better off buying them where you consume them. Do not bring any into the U.S. (Or stop at the U.S. border station on your trip north and ask for a list of current exceptions.)

Gasoline. Gasoline is highly taxed and expensive in British Columbia (about 25 to 50 percent more than it is in the U.S.).

Money. U.S. money is accepted as legal tender in southern British Columbia, but at a discount charged by businesses to offset their cost of converting the money.

You get the best exchange rates if you pay with a credit card or take out money at a cash machine (Canadian banks give a better exchange rate than U.S. ones, making exchanging money before you leave home not so hot an idea). The money changer next to the visitor center just north of the border may seem convenient, but be prepared for the highest fees and the worst exchange rate.

Goods and Services Tax. Non-Canadian visitors can have Canada's 7 percent Goods and Services Tax (GST) refunded on goods they buy for use outside Canada and on short-term accommodation costs paid by visitors leaving Canada. Application forms are available at duty-free shops located at land crossings and airports. Claims must total $7 or more (the tax paid on goods worth $100 cdn or more). Visitors must show all receipts to prove they paid gst. No rebate for gifts left in Canada, meals, cleaning and repair bills, camping and trailer park fees, alcoholic beverages, and tobacco. For information call in Canada (800) 66-visit; from outside Canada, call (613) 991-3346.

■ METRIC CONVERSIONS

Canada now officially uses the metric system, although most people are still comfortable with the English system. Conversions follow:

1 foot = .305 meters
1 mile = 1.6 kilometers
Centigrade = Fahrenheit temperature minus 32, divided by 1.8
(Thus a warm day in Vancouver at 21 degrees, is a nice 70 in Seattle.)

■ CLIMATE

A brief description of the climate relevant to the area described in each chapter can be found in the chapter's "Travel and Climate."

Overview: It does rain a lot in the Pacific Northwest west of the Cascade and Coast ranges. But east of the Cascades, it rains very seldom. And even west of the Cascades, summers tend to be dry. (That summer dryness may in fact be the reason why western Washington is covered with conifers instead of deciduous trees; deciduous trees couldn't survive the summer droughts.) Even when it rains, however, it seldom rains hard. Seattle has many more cloudy and drizzly days than

New York, but it has less annual precipitation. Real downpours are rare. Locals rarely carry umbrellas.

Victoria, western and southern Vancouver Island, Vancouver, and the lower mainland have a maritime climate and rarely receive snow in winter. But when it snows, watch out! The first flakes often signal instant traffic gridlock. The rest of the province gets heavy snowfall each winter. Mountain roads and passes are very treacherous at such times.

A note of caution: According to the British Columbia Insurance Company, B.C. drivers are the worst in Canada. Drive extra cautiously and be sure to have sufficient insurance. Recently B.C. drivers have taken to running stop signs and red stoplights, resulting in a dramatic increase of collisions.

Location and season must both be considered when packing for a trip to Oregon and Washington. Generally speaking, the Cascades, which run north to south through the western part of the states, block moist Pacific air, leaving wet weather on the western side of the mountains, while the east side remains drier. The coast is the rainiest part of the state. It's typically stormy in the winter and foggy in the summer, though warm, sunny summer days are certainly not unheard of. It rarely gets below freezing here, but those who drive over the Coast Range passes or the I-5 pass near the California border in winter should check on snow and ice conditions. For road conditions throughout the state of Oregon call (541) 889-3999. Western Oregon valleys are slightly less rainy than the coast and typically enjoy dry summers. Snow falls occasionally.

The Cascades get cold weather and snow in the winter, with generally cool summer weather. Year round, there are distinct west slope and east slope climates; if it's cloudy west of a pass, the sun may be shining to the east.

Central and eastern Oregon and Washington get less rain and more extreme temperatures than the west. The mountainous areas do catch more moisture, especially as snow, and summer thunderstorms are no rarity here (as they are west of the Cascades).

Every year brings some unusual weather—sometimes it's a wet and cold summer, other years a sun-drenched Portland winter. It's never a mistake to pack a wool sweater and an umbrella, and it's also smart to include sunglasses.

TEMPS (F°) North to South	AVG. JAN. HIGH	LOW	AVG. APRIL HIGH	LOW	AVG. JULY HIGH	LOW	AVG. OCT. HIGH	LOW	RECORD HIGH	RECORD LOW
Vancouver	41	32	58	40	74	54	57	44	92	2
Victoria	43	35	55	43	68	52	56	46	95	4
Seattle	45	36	58	43	72	54	59	47	100	3
Olympic NP	46	34	55	37	68	49	59	41	97	5
Mt. Rainier	33	21	44	27	64	44	48	33	92	-20
Yakima	38	20	63	35	87	53	64	35	111	-25
Portland	44	34	61	43	77	56	62	47	107	-3
Astoria	49	38	56	40	68	53	60	44	101	6
Eugene	45	32	60	39	81	50	64	40	108	-12
Crater Lake	35	18	45	24	70	42	52	31	100	-21
Medford	45	30	65	39	90	54	70	40	115	-10

PRECIPITATION (INCHES)	AVG. JAN.	AVG. APRIL	AVG. JULY	AVG. OCT.	ANNUAL RAIN	SNOW
Vancouver	8.6"	3.3"	1.2"	5.8"	57"	21"
Victoria	4.3"	1.4"	0.5"	3.0"	26"	13"
Seattle	4.8"	2.3"	0.6"	2.9"	38"	7"
Olympic Coast	13.8"	7.4"	2.6"	10.4"	105"	15"
Mt. Rainier	14.5"	6.7"	1.7"	12.0"	114"	578"
Yakima	1.3"	0.5"	0.1"	0.5"	8"	24"
Portland	6.1"	2.8"	0.5"	3.3"	37"	7"
Astoria	10.3"	4.6"	1.1"	6.1"	68"	5"
Eugene	7.8"	2.8"	0.3"	3.7"	47"	7"
Crater Lake	10.9"	4.3"	0.6"	6.4"	67"	541"
Medford	3.0"	1.0"	0.3"	1.7"	19"	8"

■ BEST SKI AREAS OF THE NORTHWEST

Apex Alpine. Near Penticton, Okanagan Valley, B.C. Great powder snow. Full resort facilities; (800) 387-2739

Mount Bachelor. Near Bend, Oregon. Great powder snow and cross-country trails. No overnight lodging but close to Bend and its resorts. General information (800) 829-2442; ski report (541) 382-7888.

Mount Baker. East of Bellingham, WA. Most snow of any ski area in North America. Often the earliest to open and last to close (October to June). Basic facilities, no overnight lodging, but great ski runs. Cross-country skiing on lower slopes of mountain; (360) 734-6771.

Mission Ridge. Near Wenatchee, WA. Great powder snow; cross-country skiing; (509) 663-7631.

Mount Hood. Timberline Lodge. East of Portland, Oregon. Great snow, great setting, great lodge. Downhill and cross-country skiing. Timberline Lodge (503) 222-2211; Mt. Hood Meadows (503) 227-SNOW.

Whistler/Blackcomb. North of Vancouver, BC. Voted the continent's best for five years in a row. Great snow; other activities: heli-skiing, cross-country skiing, tobogganing, dog-sledding. Full service resort in inspiring, beautiful setting. Facilities range from the plain and affordable to the most luxurious. Uncommonly high quality of restaurants for a ski resort; (800) 944-7853 and in B.C. (604) 685-3650.

■ FESTIVALS AND EVENTS

■ JANUARY

Chelan, WA: Fire and Ice Winterfest. Chili cook-off, snow sculpting, snowmobiling, ice fishing, and cross-country skiing; (800) 4-CHELAN or (509) 682-2381.

San Juan Island, WA: Bald eagle count.

Seattle, WA: Chinese New Year celebration. Hosted by the International District. January or February; (206) 323-2700.

■ FEBRUARY

Ashland, OR: Shakespeare festival opens. Runs mid-February through October, three theaters with 11 plays in repertoire. PO Box 158, Ashland, OR 97520; (541) 482-4331.

Marblemount, WA: Upper Skagit Bald Eagle Festival. Celebration of eagle migration. Festivals are held in Concrete and Rockport; (360) 853-7009.

Seattle, WA: Fat Tuesday. Parade, pub run, Spam-carving contest; (206) 622-2563. **Northwest Flower and Garden Show.;** (206) 789-5333.

■ MARCH

Westport, WA: Gray whale migration.

■ APRIL

Hood River, OR: Cherry Blossom Festival.

Mount Vernon, WA: Skagit Valley Tulip Festival; (800) 4-TULIPS or (360) 428-8547.

Wenatchee, WA: Washington State Apple Blossom Festival. Parades, arts and crafts, musical performances, and carnival; (509) 662-3616.

Yakima County, WA: Yakima Valley Spring Barrel Tasting. Late April; (509) 829-6029.

■ MAY

Bellingham, WA: Ski-to-Sea Festival. Street fair and relay race from Mount Baker to salt water. Memorial Day weekend; (360) 671-3990.

Port Townsend, WA: Rhododendron Festival. The most popular event in Port Townsend; (360) 385-1456.

Seattle, WA: Northwest Folklife Festival. Immensely popular music festival. Crafts, clothing, and incense vendors. Memorial Day weekend; (206) 684-7300.

Tygh Valley, OR: All Indian Rodeo.

Yamhill County, OR: Match made in Heaven. Food and wine matching at local wineries. Yamhill County Wineries Association; Memorial Day weekend. (503) 434-5814.

■ MAY TO JUNE

Seattle, WA: Northwest Folklife Festival. Immensely popular music festival. Crafts, clothing, and incense vendors. Memorial Day weekend; (206) 684-7300.

Warm Springs, OR: Pi-Ume-Sha. Pow-wow and celebration of the heritage of three tribes sharing the Warm Springs Reservation; (541) 553-3468.

■ JUNE

Cannon Beach, OR. Sandcastle Contest.

Port Townsend, WA: Fiddle Tunes Festival. (800) 733-3608 or (360) 385-3102.

Portland, OR: Rose Festival. Two big parades, a waterfront carnival, and, the roses blooming up in Washington Park are the main attractions at the Rose Festival, which runs through the first half of June. For information, contact the Portland Visitors Association, (503) 222-2223.

■ JULY

Darrington, WA: Darrington Bluegrass Festival. Music festival celebrating the town's early settlers from North Carolina; (360) 436-1177.

Friday Harbor: San Juan Island, WA: Dixieland Jazz Festival; (360) 378-5509.

Seattle, WA: Seafair. Parades, hydro races, crowds; (206) 728-0123.

Vancouver, BC: Fort Vancouver Fourth of July Fireworks; (360) 693-5481.

Whidbey Island, WA: Loganberry Festival. Whidbey's Greenbank Berry Farm, Greenbank; (360) 678-3005.

■ JULY/AUGUST

Victoria, BC: Victoria International Festival. Classical music performances and recitals; ballet. Free concert by Victoria Symphony from a band-shell barge in the Inner Harbour. (604) 736-2119.

■ AUGUST

Long Beach, WA: Washington State International Kite Festival; (800) 451-2542.

Olympic Peninsula, Neah Bay, WA: Makah Days. Traditional dancing and singing, salmon bakes, and canoe races; (360) 645-2711.

Omak, WA: Omak Stampede and Suicide Run. The largest rodeo in northeastern Washington; (800) 933-6625 or (509) 826-1002.

■ SEPTEMBER

Port Townsend, WA: Wooden Boat Festival. Races, rides, craft shows; (360) 385-3628.

Puyallup, WA: Western Washington State Fair; (206) 845-1771.

Seattle, WA: Bumbershoot. Music and arts festival. Labor Day Weekend; (206) 684-7337.

■ OCTOBER

Ilwaco, WA: Cranberry Festival. Food booths, musical entertainment, and tours through the cranberry bogs; (800) 451-2542.

Shelton, WA. West Coast Oyster Shucking Championship and Seafood Fest; (360) 426-2021.

Okanagan Wine Festival, B.C. Call the B.C. Wine Institute for information at (604) 986-0440.

■ NOVEMBER

Yakima Valley, WA: Winery open houses. Over 20 wineries serve samplings of their wine, paired with the right food.

Yamhill, OR: Winery open houses. Thanksgiving Day Weekend. County Wineries Association; (503) 434-5814.

■ DECEMBER

Bellingham, WA: Lighted Boat Parade. Children's activities and music; (360) 671-3990.

Granger, WA: Berry Patch. A winter hayride—complete with hot cocoa and cookies—to chop down your own Christmas tree; (509) 854-1413.

Marblemount, WA: Eagles return to the Skagit River.

Sequim, WA: Victorian Tea and Home Tour. Self-guided tours of homes throughout the Sequim and Dungeness valleys. Begins at the Old Dungeness Schoolhouse; (360) 683-8110.

Vancouver. BC: Harbor Christmas Carol Ship Parade. Carolers cruise the waterfront on boats decorated with Christmas lights; (604) 682-2007.

White Swan, WA: New Year's Pow Wow. Traditional Indian food, dancing, and games beginning December 30 and lasting until New Year's Day; (509) 865-5121.

■ TOURS IN THE PACIFIC NORTHWEST

■ BRITISH COLUMBIA

Fraser River Canyon. Fraser River Raft Expeditions; (604) 863-2336.

Okanagan Valley, Kelowna. Okanagan Canoe Holidays; (604) 762-8156. Inland canoe trips on West Coast Trail–Pacific Rim NP: Hiking, kayaking information; (604) 726-7721

Vancouver Island, Nanaimo. Wild Heart Adventures; (604) 722-3683. Guided Kayak trips. **Tofino** (West Coast), Tofino Sea-Kayaking Company; (604) 928-3117. Sea kayak rentals.

■ WASHINGTON

Fidalgo and Whidbey islands. The Pedaler. 5603¹/₂ S. Bayview Rd., Langley; (360) 321-5040. Bike rentals. Enchanted Mountain Tours. 18555 Hazel Lane, Leavenworth; (509) 763-2975. Dog sled tours.

Long Beach Peninsula, Washington Coast: Pacific Salmon Charters. Ilwaco; (360) 642-3466. Year-round fishing charters.

Mount Rainier: Rainier Mountaineering, Inc. Tacoma; (206) 627-6242 or Paradise; (360) 569-2227. Leads expeditions up Mount Rainier and rents equipment.

Mount St. Helens. Mount St. Helens Adventure Tours. Castle Rock; (360) 274-6542. Offers van tours, shuttles to trailheads, and overnight camping trips in the blast zone.

North Cascades (Northwest Interior). American Alpine Institute. 1513 12th St., Bellingham; (360) 671-1505. Rents gear for rock-climbing, mountain climbing, and ice-climbing and leads expeditions in the North Cascades. Instruction also available.

San Juan Islands. San Juan Island Bicycles. 380 Argyle St., Friday Harbor; (360) 378-4941. San Juan Kayak Expeditions. Friday Harbor; (360) 378-4436. Rentals and expeditions.

Seattle. Northwest Outdoor Center. 2100 Westlake Ave. North; (206) 281-9694. Rents one-person and two-person kayaks for expeditions around Lake Union, Lake Washington, and Elliott Bay. Instruction provided. Emerald City Charters. Departs from Pier 56; (206) 624-3931. Sailboat excursions into Puget Sound.

Olympic Peninsula. Olympic Raft and Guide Service. Elwha Resort, eight miles west of Port Angeles; (360) 452-1443. Conducts two-hour trips down the Elwha River. Fairholm General Store. US 101, on the western end of Lake Crescent, 26 miles west of Port Angeles; (360) 928-3020. Boat launching, boat rentals, fishing tackle and supplies. Olympic Van Tours & Shuttles. Port Angeles; (360) 452-3858. Tours into Olympic National Park, trailhead shuttles, and transportation from Seattle.

Snoqualmie. Ski Acres Mountain Bike Center. Snoqualmie Pass; (206) 434-6646. Mountain bike rentals, shuttles, and instruction.Washington Outfitters and Guides Association. 3020 Issaquah Pine Lake Rd.; Issaquah; (206) 392-0111.

■ OREGON

Deschutes River. High Desert Drifter. Fishing Float trips on the Deschutes.;(541) 389-0607. Lacy's Whitewater and Wild Fish. Float and fish. Also trips to the Cascade Lakes; (541) 389-2434.

Columbia Gorge. Hood River, Port Marina Park. Rhonda Smith's Windsurfing Center. Sailboard rentals and lessons; (541)-836-9463. Friends of the Columbia Gorge. Guided hikes in the gorge; (503) 241-3762.

Mount Hood. Timberline Mountain Guides; (503) 636-7704 (Portland).

Oregon Coast, Cannon Beach. Cleanline Surf. Rents surfboards and wetsuits. 171 Sunset Blvd.; (503) 436-9726, and Seaside at 719 1st Ave.; (503) 368-6055.

North Umpqua, Southern Oregon. Cimarron Outfitters. Raft trips. Idleyld Park; (541) 498-2235. North Umpqua Outfitters. Rafting. Roseburg; (541) 673-4599. Umpqua Angler. Fly shop and guide service. 420 E Main, Roseburg; (541) 673-9809.

Rogue River. River Adventure Float Trips. A variety of trips, long and short. Grants Pass; (541) 476-6493. River Trips Unlimited. Variety of trips, some with stays at back country lodges. Medford; (541) 779-3798.

Willamette Valley. North Santiam Drift Fishing (steelhead, trout). Bill Sanderson, fishing guide; (503) 859-2105.

Comments, suggestions, or updated information?
Please write:
Compass American Guides
5332 College Ave., Suite #201
Oakland, CA 94618
http://www.fodors.com/

I N D E X

COMPASS
AMERICAN
GUIDES

Available at your local bookstore, or call (800) 733-3000 to order.

COMPASS AMERICAN GUIDES are available at special discounts for bulk purchases for sales promotions or premiums. Special editions, including personalized covers and corporate imprints, can be created in large quantities for special needs. For more information call Special Markets at Fodor's Travel Publications, (800) 800-3246.

Arizona (3rd Edition)
1-878-86772-5
$18.95 ($26.50 Can)

Chicago (2nd Edition)
1-878-86780-6
$18.95 ($26.50 Can)

Colorado (3rd Edition)
1-878-86781-4
$18.95 ($26.50 Can)

Hawaii (3rd Edition)
1-878-86791-1
$18.95 ($26.50 Can)

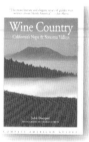

Wine Country (1st Edition)
1-878-86784-9
$18.95 ($26.50 Can)

Montana (3rd Edition)
1-878-86797-0
$18.95 ($26.50 Can)

Oregon (2nd Edition)
1-878-86788-1
$18.95 ($26.50 Can)

New Orleans (2nd Editio
1-878-86786-5
$18.95 ($26.50 Can)

South Dakota (1st Edition)
1-878-86726-1
$16.95 ($22.95 Can)

Southwest (1st Edition)
1-87866779-2
$18.95 ($26.50 Can)

Texas (1st Edition)
1-878-86764-4
$17.95 ($25.00 Can)

Utah (3rd Edition)
1-878-86773-3
$17.95 ($25.00 Can)

Boston (1st Edition)
1-878-867776-8
$18.95 ($26.50 Can)

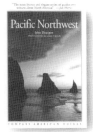

Pacific Northwest (1st Edition)
1-878-86785-7
$18.95 ($26.50 Can)

Alaska (1st Edition)
1-878-86777-6
$18.95 ($26.50 Can)

Minnesota (1st Edition)
1-878-86776-8
$18.95 ($26.50 Can)

Idaho (1st Edition)
1-878-86778-4
$18.95 ($26.50 Can)

New Mexico (2nd Edition)
1-878-86783-0
$18.95 ($26.50 Can)

Maine (2nd Edition)
1-878-86796-2
$18.95 ($26.50 Can)

Manhattan (2nd Edition)
1-878-86794-6
$18.95 ($26.50 Can)

Las Vegas (4th Edition)
-878-86782-2
18.95 ($26.50 Can)

San Francisco (4th Edition)
1-878-86792-X
$18.95 ($26.50 Can)

Santa Fe (1st Edition)
1-878-86775-X
$18.95 ($26.50 Can)

South Carolina (1st Edition)
1-878-86766-0
$18.95 ($26.50 Can)

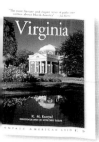

irginia (2nd Edition)
878-86795-4
8.95 ($26.50 Can)

Washington (1st Edition)
1-878-86758-X
$17.95 ($25.00 Can)

Wisconsin (2nd Edition)
1-878-86749-0
$18.95 ($26.50 Can)

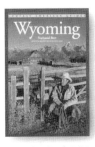

Wyoming (2nd Edition)
1-878-86750-4
$18.95 ($26.50 Can)

■ AUTHOR

John Doerper is the publisher and editor of *Pacific Epicure, A Quarterly Journal of Gastronomic Literature,* and has worked as a food and wine columnist and editor for numerous publications. His articles about food, wine, and travel have appeared in *Travel & Leisure* and *Pacific Northwest Magazine,* among others. He is also author of several books including *Shellfish Cookery: Absolutely Delicious Recipes from the West Coast* and Compass American Guides' *Wine Country.*

■ CONTRIBUTING AUTHOR

Judy Jewell, who wrote much of the Oregon section of this book, has traveled all over the state and has twice swum the Columbia River cross-channel swim. She has worked for many years as a book buyer for Powell's Travel Store in Portland.

PENELOPE JONES VAUGHN

■ PHOTOGRAPHER

Greg Vaughn is a freelance photographer specializing in travel, nature, and environmental concerns. His award-winning imagery has appeared in magazines such as *National Geographic, Outside, National Wildlife, Sierra, Natural History,* and *Travel & Leisure,* and he was the principal photographer for two books about Hawaii and Compass American Guides' *Oregon.* Other clients have included Hyatt Hotels & Resorts, Visa, United Airlines, The Nature Conservatory, the U.S. Fish & Wildlife Service, and the Hawaii Visitors Bureau. Greg lives in Eugene, Oregon with his wife and two sons.